大英图书馆
书籍史话

BOOKS

AS

HISTORY

大英图书馆书籍史话

| 超 越 文 本 的 书 |

[英国] 大卫·皮尔森 著

恺蒂 译

译林出版社

作者介绍

A B O U T — T H E — A U T H O R

大卫·皮尔森出生于1955年，毕业于剑桥大学，获博士学位。毕业后曾就职于大英图书馆、英国国立艺术图书馆，后任维康信托（Wellcome Trust）图书馆馆长（1996—2004）、伦敦大学研究图书馆馆长（2004—2009）、伦敦市法团（City of London Corporation）文化文物部部长（2009—2017）等职。皮尔森为国际著名的书史学家，研究书籍的收藏、使用和装帧，曾担任过英国目录学协会主席，著作包括《书籍历史中的来源研究指南》（*Provenance Research in Book History*）、《牛津书籍装帧：1500—1640》（*Oxford Bookbinding 1500—1640*）、《英国书籍装帧风格：1450—1800》（*English Bookbinding Styles 1450—1800*）、《大英图书馆书籍史话》（*Books as History: The importance of books beyond their texts*）等，他主编的有《装帧之爱》（*For the Love of the Binding*）、《伦敦千年史》（*London: 1000 Years*）等。

2017年，皮尔森从伦敦市法团退休，现定期在美国弗吉尼亚及伦敦的善本书学院任教，并任牛津大学书目学会研究院及伦敦大学研究院院士。

目 录

C — O — N — T — E — N — T — S

前言

P — R — E — F — A — C — E

《大英图书馆书籍史话》能在中国出版，我非常荣幸。它在英语世界中曾几次再版，受到欢迎的原因有二。一方面，这本书以大量的插图和简要的文字介绍了与书籍有关的许多基本概念，例如书籍的排版、印刷、装帧、收藏、批注、再利用等；另一方面，此书引发了有关书籍未来的讨论：在日益数字化的世界中，实体书的价值和前景究竟如何？我写这本书的一个目的是要让人们认识到书籍不仅是页面上的文字，它们还曾经被拥有、被阅读、被收藏、被代代相传，每一本书都有它独特的历史。一本书的实体形式、文字内容、个性历史等各方面，共同组成了这本书的整体。

在中国悠久的历史长河里，书籍也非常重要。造纸和印刷术都是中国发明的，中国的纸质印刷书籍，远远早于欧洲，中国书籍的制作、收藏及传播也有上千年的历史。但中国古典书籍的传统与西方相差很大，它们的刻版、印刷、装帧样式等都与西方不同，在这方面，我不是专家。但我希望知道我在这本书中提出的观点在中国书籍的研究中是否适用。例如通过对书籍被拥有的历史、对它们的批注及装帧的关注等，来更好地了解书籍的文化价值。如果这本书的中文版能促成这方面的讨论，我会很高兴。

这里，我要感谢恺蒂对这本书的介绍和翻译，我们曾一起在英国国立艺术图书馆共事。其实，这是她第二次用中文帮助了我。1996年，我们和英国国立艺术图书馆馆长一起参加在北京举行的第六十二届国际图联大会，会议结束后，她和另一位中国朋友带我们去了琉璃厂。在一家古董店中，她这位非常有技巧的谈判者，帮我购买了一只陶瓷罐，这只罐子至今还摆在我的书房中，得到许多朋友的欣赏，是我珍贵的藏品之一。更重要的是，那次大会还为我提供了了解北京的机会，让我看到那些伟大的历史文化景观，给我留下了深刻的印象。

感谢译林出版社。当然，更要感谢你们，我的中国读者，希望你们能接受并喜欢这本书。

大卫·皮尔森

2018 年 6 月于剑桥

IC
XC

CHAPTER ONE
BOOKS IN HISTORY

第一章 历史中的书籍

数百年来，书籍是人类文化的标志，是发达文明的特征。在众多宗教中，书籍有其象征意义，代表着博学多识与美德情操。书籍还是权力和魔法的证明甚至化身：在莎士比亚的戏剧《暴风雨》中，米兰公爵普洛斯帕罗说："书斋是我广大的公国"，占领并销毁他的书籍，也就是将他的权势推翻。与莎士比亚同时代的英国剧作家马洛（Christopher Marlowe）笔下的浮士德博士，为了逃避惩罚，破釜沉舟的最后一招是烧毁自己的藏书。书籍是交流及传播信息最重要的媒介，为了控制它们潜在的危险，多少政治强人机关算尽。后者会对雷·布拉德伯里（Ray Bradbury）在《华氏 451 度》（*Fahrenheit 451*）中描写的焚书手段举双手赞成，而焚烧书籍确实是令人动容的文化意象。书籍自出现以来，随着市场的普及，引发娱乐、教育和政治变革，为不计其数的人带来精神及智识上的成长。在英国，政府并不对书籍征收附加税，因为书籍如同食品和孩子们的衣服，乃是生活的必备，而非奢侈的选择。伊斯坦布尔圣索菲亚大教堂的墙壁上，一幅 11 世纪的马赛克图充分说明了，书籍及其蕴含的思想，千百年来被人尊重的崇高地位。在这幅画里，罗马皇帝君士坦丁九世和他的妻子侧坐拱卫着耶稣，皇帝手里捧着一袋钱，而耶稣则握着一本书。

书籍还是人们习以为常的物件，且容易得到。新书不停地出版，摆满了图书馆和书店，为人们提供知识信息，传承文化遗产。作为文

书籍一直是巫师和魔法师使用的重要器具，他们的形象经常是手握书本：普洛斯帕罗的书籍是他魔法的源泉，而浮士德博士也用手中之书召唤魔鬼

焚书是一种能够煽动情绪的文化意象（左图）。纳粹是臭名昭著的焚书者，20世纪30年代纳粹焚书的篝火（下页图）众所周知，但是焚书的历史还要更为久远。中国的第一个皇帝秦始皇，不仅以长城和兵马俑著名，也曾以“焚书坑儒”来控制人们的思想。美国作家雷·布拉德伯里的《华氏451度》之所以能成为现代经典，是因为书中描写了一个读书和拥有书籍都是犯罪的社会，书中消防员的职责之一就是焚书

Talks

Digitise or Die:
What Is the Future of the Book?

The roll-out of e-books could result in the availability of a plethora of material currently out of print, but will it also leave the book trade experiencing the same copyright problems as the movie and music industries? And whither the relationship between an author and a publisher when writers can publish their own work cheaply? These and other pertinent questions are pondered by a London Book Fair panel that includes Margaret Atwood (*below*), Andrew O'Hagan, Erica Wagner and Stephen Page, the chief executive of Faber & Faber. *QEH, London SE1 (08703 800 400) Tue* **Stuart Price**

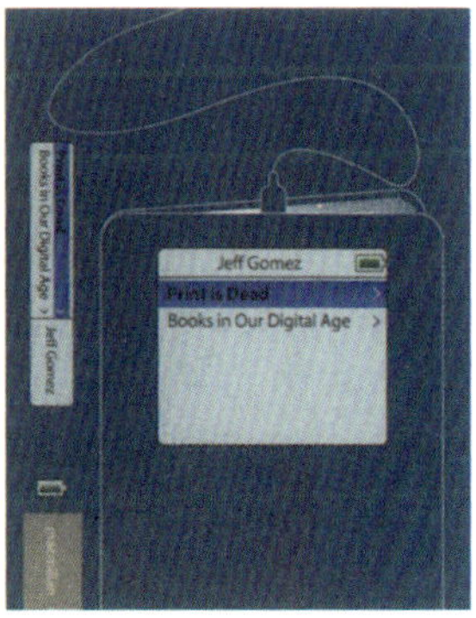

物收藏，书籍的价格并不昂贵，而且供应充足。一部品相上乘的 19 世纪甚或 17 世纪的书籍，它的价格与同时代的钟表、绘画或其他的家用品相比，简直微不足道。借助于研究型历史图书馆广布的网络，想要观赏、翻阅和研究各个时代的书籍也并非难事。

— 数字时代的挑战 —

无论过去如何，身处当下这样巨变的时代，书籍的地位和未来正愈发受到质疑。新技术带来通信革命，关于书籍是否濒临死亡的讨论已有一段时日。互联网的出现，正如当年印刷术的发明和工业的机械化，是影响人们思考和生活方式的重要分水岭，这点已然成为共识。因工作和娱乐的需要，人们互相传递信息，首选一直是通过纸质媒介。其他媒介相继出现，例如广播和电视，都一直能与书籍自在地共存。而新兴的互联网，可能就不仅仅是作为纸媒的补充，而更可能会取而代之。

书籍会死亡吗？众多预测都是在快速变化的背景下进行的。第一轮巨变才刚刚开始，我们还没有足够的历史纵深来准确估计它的后果，或是确认它的时间表。但我们可以做点预测，并试着分析某些对立的观点。对“书籍将死”的抗拒和否认，至少和赞成的观点一样强烈，部分是依据经验观察，部分是基于情感因素。人们喜欢书籍，众多爱书人认定书籍就是他们熟悉信赖的生活的一部分，本能地敌视所谓书籍不再必要的观点。事实上，每年出版和销售的书籍数量仍然在稳步增加，电子书还不是让人信服的替代品，电子媒介的长期稳定性尚未得到证实。就像有人曾错误地预测过“无纸的办公室”，“书籍的死亡”可能也同样会成为不会兑现的预言。

对于如上观点，我们应该有所警惕。数字技术才刚刚起步，况且进步神速。黑胶唱片被 CD 迅速取代便是明证（当然下载技术兴起之

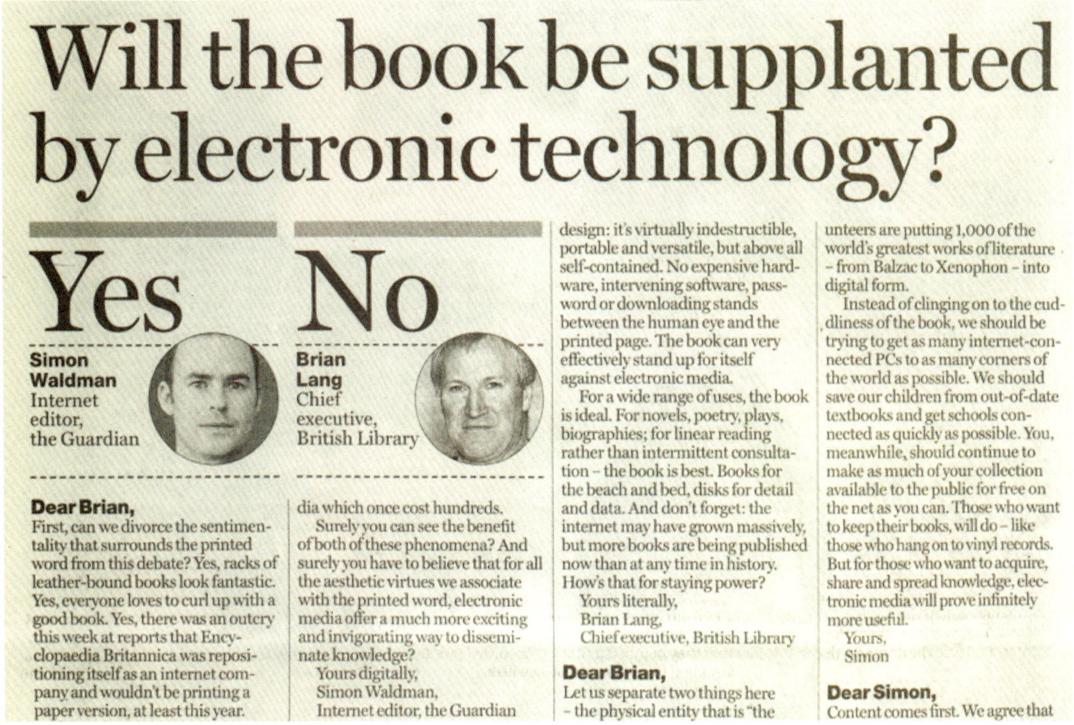

Will the book be supplanted by electronic technology?

Yes

Simon Waldman
Internet editor, the Guardian

No

Brian Lang
Chief executive, British Library

Dear Brian,
First, can we divorce the sentimentality that surrounds the printed word from this debate? Yes, racks of leather-bound books look fantastic. Yes, everyone loves to curl up with a good book. Yes, there was an outcry this week at reports that Encyclopaedia Britannica was repositioning itself as an internet company and wouldn't be printing a paper version, at least this year.

dia which once cost hundreds.
Surely you can see the benefit of both of these phenomena? And surely you have to believe that for all the aesthetic virtues we associate with the printed word, electronic media offer a much more exciting and invigorating way to disseminate knowledge?
Yours digitally,
Simon Waldman,
Internet editor, the Guardian

design: it's virtually indestructible, portable and versatile, but above all self-contained. No expensive hardware, intervening software, password or downloading stands between the human eye and the printed page. The book can very effectively stand up for itself against electronic media.
For a wide range of uses, the book is ideal. For novels, poetry, plays, biographies; for linear reading rather than intermittent consultation – the book is best. Books for the beach and bed, disks for detail and data. And don't forget: the internet may have grown massively, but more books are being published now than at any time in history. How's that for staying power?
Yours literally,
Brian Lang,
Chief executive, British Library

Dear Brian,
Let us separate two things here – the physical entity that is "the

unteers are putting 1,000 of the world's greatest works of literature – from Balzac to Xenophon – into digital form.
Instead of clinging on to the cuddliness of the book, we should be trying to get as many internet-connected PCs to as many corners of the world as possible. We should save our children from out-of-date textbooks and get schools connected as quickly as possible. You, meanwhile, should continue to make as much of your collection available to the public for free on the net as you can. Those who want to keep their books, will do – like those who hang on to vinyl records. But for those who want to acquire, share and spread knowledge, electronic media will prove infinitely more useful.
Yours,
Simon

Dear Simon,
Content comes first. We agree that

书籍的未来，它们是否能在数字时代生存，这个话题引起过许多讨论和争辩

后，CD 业已是明日黄花）。书籍出版的总量确实在持续增加，但其中包括许多电子出版物，还有近年按需印刷（print-on-demand）重版书的增长。大英图书馆 2010 年出版的《展望 2020 年》（*2020 Vision*）中预测，到了 2020 年，全世界 75% 的出版物会只出电子版，或同时以纸质和电子的形式出版。在某些领域，如科学期刊，电子版已经取代了传统的纸质版。科学家和生物医学家需要即时联通全球研究网络，于是主要依靠互联网的电子出版物来公布自身成果，获知同行的研究进展。人文学者也逐渐向科学家同行看齐，认识到互联网的潜力并不局限于文本资源的获取，可以通过建立互动的框架，用新的方式来研究课题和分享成果。脸书等社交网络更是影响了整整一代人（及

英国作家和印刷学家比阿特丽斯·沃德（Beatrice Warde）1932年编录了《印刷机功能之赞》。在数字时代，印刷所及其重要性已经成了过时的概念。下图为19世纪常见的手动印刷机，现在也已不再使用。文字和思想将持续出现，但其出版及存储方式将会截然不同

This is
a printing office

Crossroads of Civilization;
Refuge of all the Arts
against the ravages of time:
Armoury of fearless truth
against whispering rumour;
Incessant trumpet of trade!

From this place words may fly abroad—
not to perish on waves of sound,
not to vary with the writer's hand,
but fixed in time,
having been verified in proof.

Friend, you stand on sacred ground…
This is a printing office

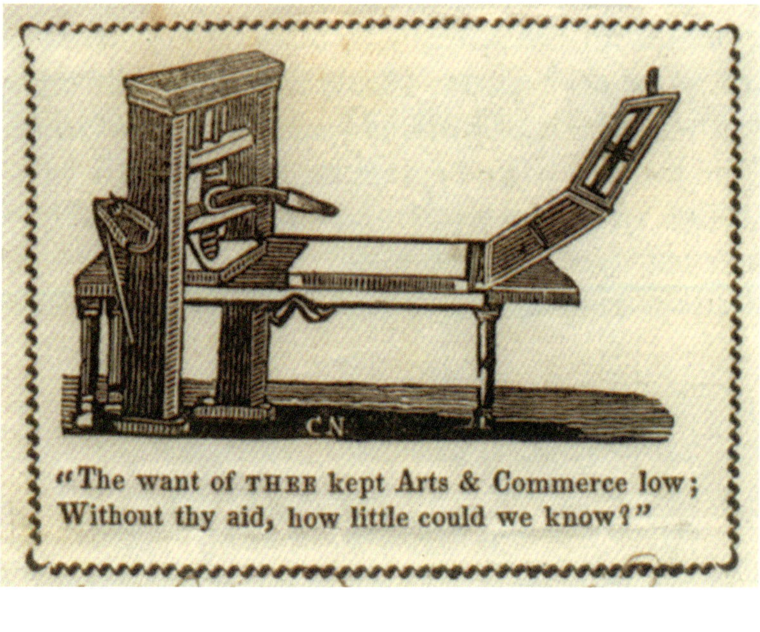

其后来者），网络空间成为他们获取和分享信息的主要阵地。

早在2004年，药企葛兰素史克（GlaxoSmithKline）就宣布会关闭公司的十四个图书馆，代之以完全的电子网络，来满足员工获取知识和信息的需求。2008年，英国思克莱德大学（Strathclyde University）宣布对图书馆新的投资将不再用于扩建，相反要减少纸质书的库藏空间，将更多资金投入积累电子资源上。2010年，利兹大学（Leeds University）给医学院的每位学生发放了一台iPhone，以便他们能实时查阅专业教材的电子版。大学正越发重视以教学资料中心和信息共享区来补充或替代传统图书馆（主要功能是书籍的储藏和阅览），学生可以在不失去图书馆公共空间的同时，享用电子媒介提供的信息。

书籍究竟会不会消失？人们质疑这一观点时，常用那些曾与书籍平行发展的媒介为论据。例如广播或电视刚出现时，都曾是书籍的竞争对手，但时过境迁，书籍依然蓬勃发展。在我看来，这个推论有误。 例如《傲慢与偏见》，它的改编电影与奥斯汀的文本并不是一回事，众所周知，人们希望两者都能体验，因为收获各不相同。所谓电子书的威胁，也可以说是对读者的承诺，是作为令人满意的改良替代品，在不明显改变阅读体验（而且电子书的出现，还可能催生全新的创作形式）的同时，完全取代纸质书。作家道格拉斯（J. Yellowlees Douglas）在2000年出版的《书籍末日》（*The End of Books*）中写道："在娱乐行业，杀手级的技术通常只会让设备过时，例如CD摧毁了唱盘和唱片的市场，但并没有改变任何一种音乐的流派。"当我们讨论书籍时，物质形态就是她所提到的"设备"。

电影《星球大战》中有一处图书馆的场景，欧比旺·克诺比（Obi-Wan Kenobi）去那里寻找一些过去采集和记录的信息。图书馆的空间与都柏林三一学院（Trinity College, Dublin）著名的长形阅读室（Long Room）非常相像，但里面的"书籍"都是存储电子信息的胶囊，要在电脑上读取。如果我们的书籍世界要彻底变成这样，有几

（下页图）
未来的图书馆会不会变得像《星球大战》中的绝地圣殿档案馆一样，书籍都是电子文档，阅读都在电脑上进行？

2004年底，谷歌宣布启动一项庞大的数字化项目，计划将一些大型图书馆的馆藏转换为数字形式。大多数人认为这是具有全球意义的里程碑项目，但也有人表示担忧，特别是在出版领域，谷歌的计划显然威胁到出版业的商业模式和版权利益

Google to put books from great libraries on internet

件事必须同时发生。首先当然是书籍的内容，也就是文本，这些必须以数字的方式提供，而不是纸上的文字。如今出版的书籍在付印之前肯定都以某种电子形式存在，向真正电子出版的过渡主要取决于商业的可行性和用户的接受度，电子期刊的现状也证明这种运作是可行的。

我们还传承了无数前辈留下的大量印刷和文字遗产。20 世纪 90 年代互联网刚出现时，许多专家预测，将如此庞大的文化遗产全面数字化处理，完全不可能实现。现在看来，言之过早。2004 年底，谷歌宣布了一项大型数字化工程，要与英国和美国多家大型图书馆合作，计划在互联网上免费提供数百万册书籍的全文内容。那之后，谷歌又将这一计划扩展到与欧洲大陆图书馆的合作，以及报纸的数字化上。近年来还有许多其他将书籍、手稿、图像和各种古籍文献转化为电子版的尝试，不久的将来，人们出于各种需要而阅读的大多数文本，都会有电子版这一选择。

数字化的内容最初要比数字阅读的硬件发展得更快。十多年前，许多人还在等待电子阅读设备能像平装本书那样方便，能捧在手上，带上火车甚至带进澡盆。如今，iPad、Kindle 以及其他类似设备已经非常好用，喜欢在电子屏幕上阅读文本的人越来越多，这项技术还在持续优化。而且现在许多孩子都是从电子屏幕上开始学习识读的，纸质书不再是他们阅读的入门工具，等到这些孩子长大成人，他们可能会自然而然地认为书籍就是种电子产品。这将是颠覆性的变化，可能很快就会到来。《星期日泰晤士报》报道，2012 年 1 月伦敦一所学校为那些不喜欢读书的孩子提供纸质书的电子替代品，成功让他们爱上了阅读。孩子们的老师说："我真的相信，如果每个孩子都有一个 iPad 或是 Kindle，他们的识读水平会突飞猛进。他们只是不喜欢纸质的课本，大部分人都更喜欢从屏幕上阅读。"

关于电子读物，还有其他一些重要因素我们需要考虑，特别是版权。这指的不仅是最新的出版物，也涉及将 20 世纪已经出版的书籍移到数字平台上。谷歌这方面的努力在美国和欧洲都遇到了法律问

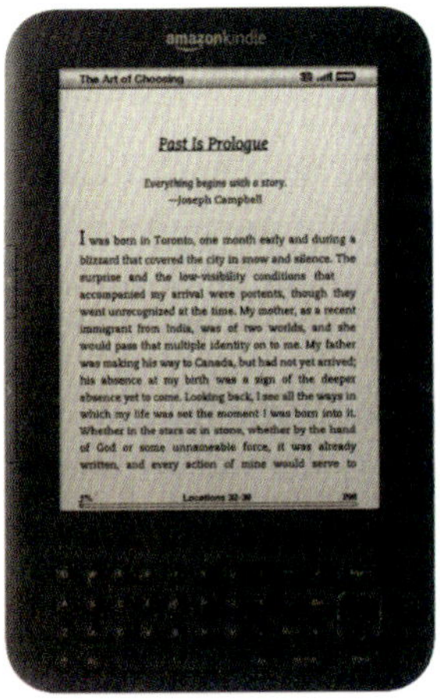

何时你可以手握此书的电子版本，就像阅读纸质版本一样满意？是否这个时代已经到来？到2010年底，互联网书商亚马逊的电子阅读器Kindle已经成为其最畅销商品，销售量甚至超过了“哈利·波特”系列书籍

题，而经济实力让它能够坚持下去。在数字版权上，音乐市场是先行者，实践已经证明了，前路虽会有波折，但冲突都是可以调和的。数字媒体是否能够长期保存也还存在着疑问。人们觉得，不管是纸质书还是黏土板，都比存在硬盘或光盘上的数字文件更稳定可靠。这么想也没错，前者可以存在数百年或数千年，而后者可能在十年内就会难以读取。电子媒体现在如此普遍且重要，它们的可持续性问题必须要得到解决。现在，人们投入许多精力试图解决数字文档的保存问题，相信在不久的将来，就会有解决方案。

很明显，各方面的准备很快就会完备，实现世界阅读习惯的全面转变，在不久的将来就会成为现实。文本将从纸质书的束缚中解脱出来，一首诗、一篇小说、一册烹饪书，会同时存在于网络空间和纸质印刷品上。在数字形式下，它的实际存在可能是一小段的电子代码，存储在计算机里，可以迅速地从一处传送到另一处，是一种无形的存在。莎士比亚在他的《十四行诗》第55首中写道：“世界上没有大理石的雕像或镏金的王公纪念碑，能够比得上诗篇的经久和权威”，现在，这种“经久和权威”已经不需要用实体书籍来保证了。

刻有文字的黏土板是人类最早的长期记录信息的手段之一，虽然一块黏土板上只能刻几句话，但它可以流传数千年，至今仍能被人阅读（只要你能读懂这种语言）。一张软盘可以容纳几十万字，但已经是过时的技术，因为计算机硬件的日新月异，现在这样的软盘已经基本上不可读取。技术的快速发展带来了挑战，为了保证电子媒体的长期性，目前在数字资料的保存方面已经做了大量的工作

这本书的主题并不是关于技术的变化，而是关于在巨大变化的背景下，我们对书籍的认识以及与书籍有关的重要事项。这些变化会影响到如何传播和阅读那些传统上由书籍承载的信息，还会影响到与之有关的人们的价值体系。技术的变化会影响到我们个体与书籍、我们群体与图书馆的关系。

— 一套新的价值观 —

写这本书主要是要挑战这样一种观点，即书籍只是文本的载体，其实书籍作为人类的文化历史工艺品还有很高的价值。如果书籍存在的理由纯粹是承载文本，那么它们的消亡指日可待。我们需要认识到书籍的意义远大于此，否则，我们就可能集体做出错误的决定，影响到后世的文化传承。这本书里希望能总结出书籍一些新的重要价值和特点，它们的重要性是建立在我们生活的当下，而非来自未经仔细反思过的传统。

“书籍”经常是指“具有教育和文化内容的文字”。此书出版于 1951 年，目的是为了支持书籍固定价格运动——也就是英国的“图书净价协议”（The Net Book Agreement）——保证公众能够最广泛地接触到“通过书籍这一媒体而自由表达的思想和想象”。“图书净价协议”于 1997 年被废除

把书籍和文本分开，在认识上会有些挑战，因为我们向来是把这两个概念混为一谈的。很久以来，书籍之所以受到尊重，往往不是作为实物，而是关乎它们蕴含的文本、思想及其传播。《失乐园》的作者、英国作家约翰·弥尔顿曾说，一本好书是“卓越思想者宝贵的生命之源，超越生命本身，值得永久保存并珍藏”，美国《独立宣言》的主要起草人托马斯·杰斐逊也曾说：“没有书，我就无法生存。”他们所赞美的是书籍的内容，由字词组成的文本能够传达信息、激发思想、教授知识、感动人心。书籍是载体，是硬件，也是管道，帮助作者把故事、思想分享给读者，并让文本流传到后代。

当然，书籍并不是被动的管道。书籍的三维实体和物理特征都影响到读者如何接受其承载的内容，书籍本身就有作为艺术品的潜力。20 世纪后期的新西兰书目学家唐·麦肯齐（Don McKenzie）提出过文本社会学的理论，也就是说承载文本的物质形式会影响到文本所要传达的意义，这一理论影响了许多当代学者，大家开始关注书籍整体的重要性，而不只是书页上的文字。作为文本的书籍可以有各种替代品，但作为实物的书籍则不可能被完全替代。人们可以对一本实体书籍涂鸦、书写、修改、销毁、美化和珍藏，这些举措会让每本书拥有它独特的历史，书籍作为艺术实物的特性，不仅是人类交流史的一部分，也是艺术设计史的一部分。

许多世纪以来，直到 19 世纪印刷和出版业的机械化，所有书籍都是独一无二的手工制品。书页上的文字都是手工排版而成，每一页都是印刷机上一次单独运转的过程，这些书页被单张印成后，经过手工的聚集、折叠、缝合、装订，然后才成册为书。所以，即使在它们出售之前，也没有任何两本书是完全相同的。这种手工印刷的过程让同本书的单册之间存在着细微的差异，这些书的装帧过程带来的差异就更大。我们现在所熟悉的书籍的统一装帧，是很现代的概念。如果你找到某种 18 世纪出版的书籍的其中二十本，你可能会发现这二十本的装帧完全不同。而且，装帧只是书籍个性化的开始，当一本书从

一位读者手中转入另一位读者手中，几代人下来，每位读者都会在书上留下他们的印记。这些印记可能来自铭文、注释、藏书票、重新装订、家族徽章、修改涂鸦等。到了 19 和 20 世纪，因为机械印刷技术的发展，每本新书本身几乎没有区别，但不同的读者或收藏家仍会在书上留下自己的印记。

我们很容易知道过去的那些世纪中，哪些书籍曾被出版，但是从这些书籍代代相传的拥有者们所留下的痕迹中，我们能更多地了解到这些书在历史上的影响以及公认的价值。书籍会渐渐拥有自己独特的历史，从而成为人类更广泛的历史遗产的一部分。我们头脑中已经有一套对历史上的作者们进行判断的价值观，这些价值观的决定因素不仅是我们自己所生活的时代，还有过去的那些时代给我们的历史积淀。如果我们想真正了解这些作家在他们自己时代的影响力和地位，我们应该着眼于其同代人对他们著作的拥有及处理方式上。例如，如今我们认为英国诗人约翰・多恩（John Donne）的主要成就是他的诗作，但是从 17 世纪的图书目录中，我们得知他的同时代人更重视他的布道辞，因为当时的图书馆对他的这类文字有更多的收藏。

将这种研究方法付诸实践的是哈佛大学的天文学和科技史教授欧文・金格里奇（Owen Gingerich）。他对哥白尼《天体运行论》第一、第二版的所有已知的流传下来的版本进行了详细的统计，在全球一共找到六百多本，通过研究这些书的拥有者、注释和其他实体特征，证明了在 16 世纪的欧洲，天文学家购买此书的速度非常快，原来当时的专家们就有一个分享交流信息的网络，他还从这些版本分析出第一代读者对哥白尼日心说的接受（或不接受）的程度。这种学术研究的方法正在不断发展，通过对版本证据的密切关注和分析，学者们能够更好地了解这些书籍对早期读者的影响。阅读、眉批和注释的历史，书籍的前任拥有者们在书上留下的其他痕迹，都越来越受到研究者的关注。书商、拍卖商、图书管理员等，也都开始在目录上详细记录书籍的这些信息，与过去相比，现在的目录会有更多的前人收藏以及书

对于哥白尼的《天体运行论》的所有已知的现存版本的调查。此书第一次提出日心说，这一调查从《天体运行论》的拥有者的身份以及书中的批注中可以看出哥白尼的思想如何被散布，同时代的科学家们对他的看法，还有当时的科学家们之间的交流网络

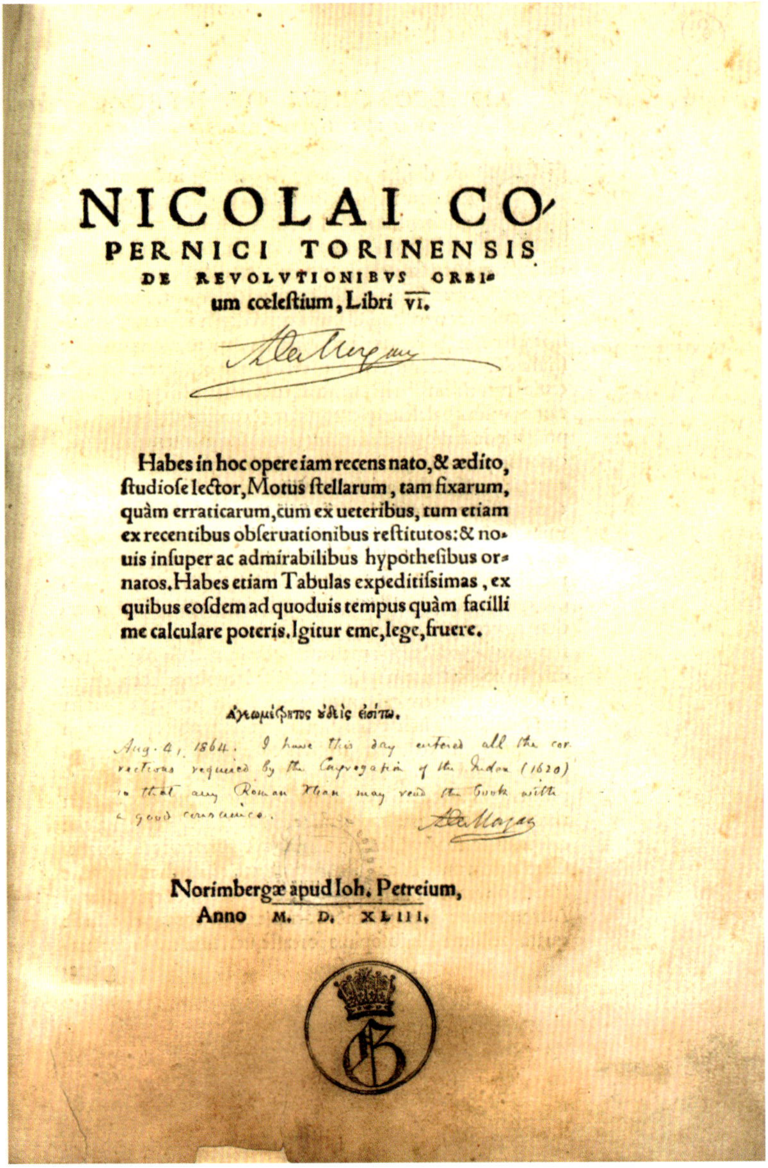
NICOLAI CO-
PERNICI TORINENSIS
DE REVOLVTIONIBVS ORBI-
um cœlestium, Libri VI.

Habes in hoc opere iam recens nato, & ædito, studiose lector, Motus stellarum, tam fixarum, quàm erraticarum, cum ex ueteribus, tum etiam ex recentibus obseruationibus restitutos: & nouis insuper ac admirabilibus hypothesibus ornatos. Habes etiam Tabulas expeditissimas, ex quibus eosdem ad quoduis tempus quàm facillime calculare poteris. Igitur eme, lege, fruere.

Ἀγεωμέτρητος οὐδεὶς εἰσίτω.

Aug. 4, 1864. I have this day entered all the corrections required by the Congregation of the Index (1620) so that any Roman may read the book with a good conscience.

Norimbergæ apud Ioh. Petreium,
Anno M. D. XLIII.

籍装帧的信息。这些都是书籍个性化的独特信息，藏品的管理人员也意识到准确记录这些信息的重要性。这些记录也是书籍安全的保障，一本被偷盗的书籍可能无法以它的排版或印刷来辨别，因为它们大同小异，但对每本书来说，拥有者的印记会让它独一无二。

当然，文本仍然处在书籍价值观的核心，也仍然是书籍的主要用途。过去如此，今后仍将如此。书中的文字是书籍的开始，也将是书籍的结束。但是在这一过程中，书籍承载文字的媒介作用可能会发生变化。本书将进一步探索并说明书籍作为历史艺术品本身的重要性，作为实物，书籍超越了其原有的承载并传送文本的目的。尽管书籍承载文本的功用可能会被其他媒体取代，但它们仍拥有自身的重要性，应该像其他文化遗产一样得到保护。此书中所举到的例子，展现了各类书籍所传递的不同历史意义，这些例子来自我们无数的图书馆、书店和私人收藏。“书籍成为历史”听上去似乎有些悲观，但是这里的“历史”的含义完全是积极的，让我们越来越认识到书籍是文化遗产结构中独特的文物，它们拥有值得保护和诠释的丰富意义。

A Puissant noble et excellent prince Jehan filz du Roy de France duc de berry et dauuergne. Conte de poitou. destampes. de boulongne et dauuergne. Jaurens de premier fait clerc et vostre moins digne secretaire et serf de bonne foy toute obeissance et subgection deue. comme a mon tresredoubte seigneur et bienfaitteur et aff

ytrablement receuoir le labeur de mon estude et benignement excuser la petitece de mon engin au regard de la grant besongne de vre commandement ia pieca entreprise et nouuellement finee. Cõbien que par vostre especial mandemẽt iaye soubz la confiance de vostre naturele benignite et en espoir de vostre gracieux ayde et confort. entrepris le dangereux et long traueil de la translation dun tresseus

2

CHAPTER TWO
BOOKS BEYOND TEXTS

第二章 超越文本的书籍

— 书的形象和作为形象的书 —

在西方文化中，书籍的形象非常普遍。书籍随处可见，实体书籍不仅存在于图书馆和书店中，书籍的图像也经常出现在绘画、建筑装饰、纪念雕塑以及各类标志和符号里。经常可见的还有作家、学者向统治者和圣者奉献他们的书籍，这些形象表示一项有价值工作的完成，也象征着智慧的传授。这些形象，从中世纪一直持续到早期现代社会（如左页图例）。无数的圣者、政治家、神职人员和作家的肖像，也都或是手持书本，或是以书房做背景。许多大学在它们的校徽上使用书籍的图像，律师行的办公室也总是书籍满架，不仅因为书籍是律师们的常用工具，更因为书籍能创造一个理想的氛围。政客们接受电视采访时，也经常选择以满架书籍为背景。人们喜欢把自己的形象与书籍相联系，因为书籍让他们看上去谨严而博学。

（左页图）
15世纪手抄书插图：法国贝利公爵（Duc de Berry）接受译者劳伦斯·杜普米非（Laurens du Premierfait）递交的刚刚完成的作品

当然，以上各种图像中展示的书籍的重要性，主要还是因为书籍是文本的载体，书籍包含着知识、艺术、救赎的内容。这些图像的创作者，希望以书籍唤起观众对其内容的共识。书籍作为一个物品，作为三维的实体，它们的功能难道仅仅是承载文本让人们阅读？它们的存在是否还有其他的价值？它们的实体表征究竟有多重要？除了文字，书籍还能给我们带来什么？它们的实体及设计的特征会如何影响

自古以来，在圣者、政治家、国王、学者、医生、神职人员等许多人的肖像画中，都会描画他们手持书本或以书籍为背景。此处列举：圣杰罗姆（St Jerome）；亨利八世；17世纪的东方学者埃德蒙·卡斯特尔（Edmund Castell）；17世纪查尔柯特庄园（Charlecote Park）的主人理查德·卢西（Richard Lucy）；18世纪的莫尔加尼医生（Giovanni Morgagni）

It was the worst year of her life when Trisha Goddard, queen of daytime TV, lost her mother and her close friend. Now she's through it, and ready to tackle other people's problems once again

BY RACHEL COOKE

IN A Soho hotel, Trisha Goddard, doyenne of the television bear pit that is daytime chat, sips peppermint tea. Staying healthy — which includes avoiding caffeine — is one way she "manages" her mental health. "I'm not taking any risks with it again," she says, as if it were a recalcitrant child.

In 2004, Goddard lost both her mother, Agnes (to cancer of the brain) and her personal trainer, Darryl, a close friend (he died after a run-of-the-mill bang to his head led to severe complications).

Thanks to the beady eye she keeps on both her stress levels and the alcohol she consumes, Trisha survived. "I know shit happens, but I've got enough in my arsenal to be able to get through. Last year was crap.

政治家（如此处的尼克松总统）和其他名人，在公众面前都喜欢以书籍和书架来作为背景，因为书籍帮他们塑造形象

"Isn't this a bit excessive, Dad? We're not even sure if I failed yet."

（漫画插图）书籍也可以让一个好笑的场面严肃起来

大学校徽上常常会有书籍的图像，因为高等学府是传授知识的地方（此处是英国利兹大学和美国哈佛大学的校徽）；书籍也代表知识和学问，例如“泰晤士报高等教育奖”的标志（居中图）

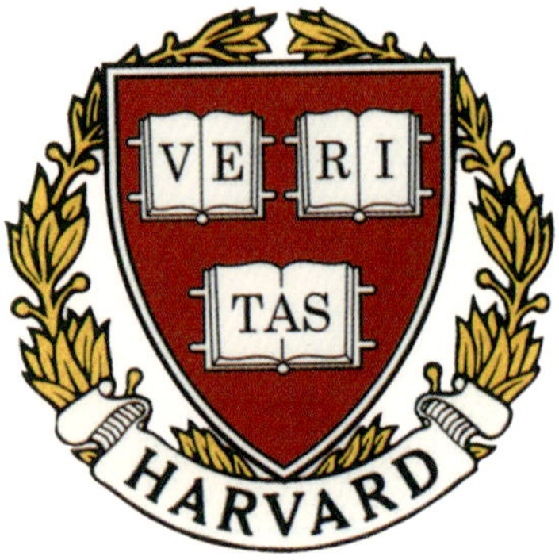

THE TIMES
HIGHER
Awards 2007

众所周知，书籍象征着智慧、有价值的追求、永恒的成就。此图为伊丽莎白一世时代的印刷师约翰·怀特（John Wight），他手持《知识之书》（*Scientia*），敦促读者对书籍的创造者们表示支持

牛津大学博德利图书馆的创始人，托马斯·博德利（Thomas Bodley）在牛津大学默顿学院教堂中的纪念碑，以另一种方式展现了书籍的重要性，博德利在此被书籍环绕

（下页图）

德国当代艺术家安塞尔姆·基弗（Anselm Kiefer）的雕塑《高级女祭司》（*The High Priestess*），铅制的书架及书本，意味着其神秘或高深莫测的内容

到它们总体的功用？作为艺术实体的书籍和作为文本承载物的书籍之间是否存在界限？书籍的内容虽然可以由其他媒体承载，但书籍的另一些特质却无法被完全复制，这些特质是什么？本章试图考察作为艺术实体的书籍所具有的一些特质，这些特质让书籍独一无二，让它们的存在超越于其所承载的文本内容之上。

— 媒体和信息：设计对交流的影响 —

书籍具有丰富的表达和交流的潜力。许多人能够背诵莎士比亚的《十四行诗》，你能记住这些词句，在脑海中重复这些诗篇，你可以不借助任何印刷形式或媒介，欣赏到《十四行诗》的艺术。《伊利亚特》和《奥德赛》等诗篇，也都曾是口头传诵的，在它们被书面记录下来之前的几个世纪，都是通过朗诵让人们体验欣赏、铭记在心并代代相传。许多人会同意，通过聆听朗诵得到的体验，与通过阅读书页得到的体验是不一样的，从整体体验来说，眼睛阅读印刷页面也是一个重要的部分。你可以阅读四个世纪以来各种不同的莎士比亚戏剧和诗歌的印刷版本，它们可能是经济实用的精简版，也可能是私人印书馆用精心挑选的字体和手工纸印制出来的豪华收藏版。你可以阅读单纯的只有文字没有插图的版本，也能读到文字与精美的插图及装饰相得益彰的版本。这些不同的版本的阅读体验完全一样吗？不同的读者会喜欢不同的版本，但大多数人会同意，不同版本给读者的观感及手感是不同的，阅读的体验也就有着细微的区别。文本的表现形式究竟会给读者的感知和阅读体验带来怎样的影响，这是让现代文本学者越来越感兴趣的课题。文本的意义和对文本的解释不是绝对的，而是通过历代读者的不同体验在不断地更新，文本的字体、版式、实体特征以及其他与文字有关的任何因素，都会影响到文本意义的框架建构。

人们对书籍的实体样式非常熟悉，这种设计实用性强，赏心悦目。

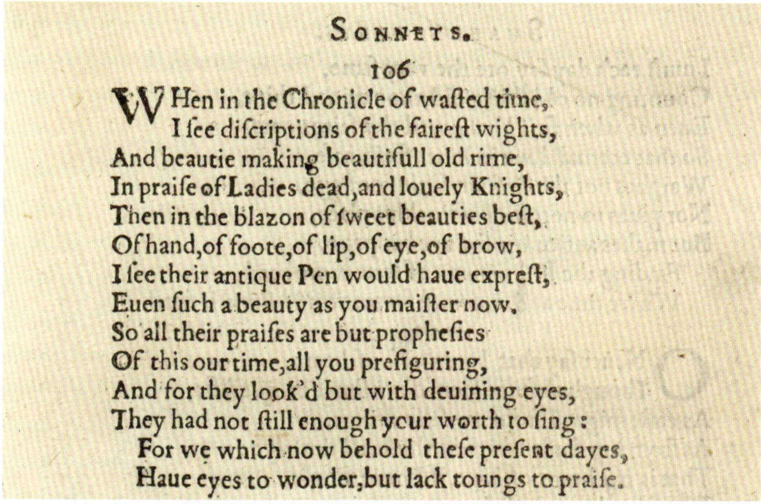
SONNETS.

106

WHen in the Chronicle of waſted time,
I ſee diſcriptions of the faireſt wights,
And beautie making beautifull old rime,
In praiſe of Ladies dead, and louely Knights,
Then in the blazon of ſweet beauties beſt,
Of hand, of foote, of lip, of eye, of brow,
I ſee their antique Pen would haue expreſt,
Euen ſuch a beauty as you maiſter now.
So all their praiſes are but propheſies
Of this our time, all you prefiguring,
And for they look'd but with deuining eyes,
They had not ſtill enough your worth to ſing:
For we which now behold theſe preſent dayes,
Haue eyes to wonder, but lack toungs to praiſe.

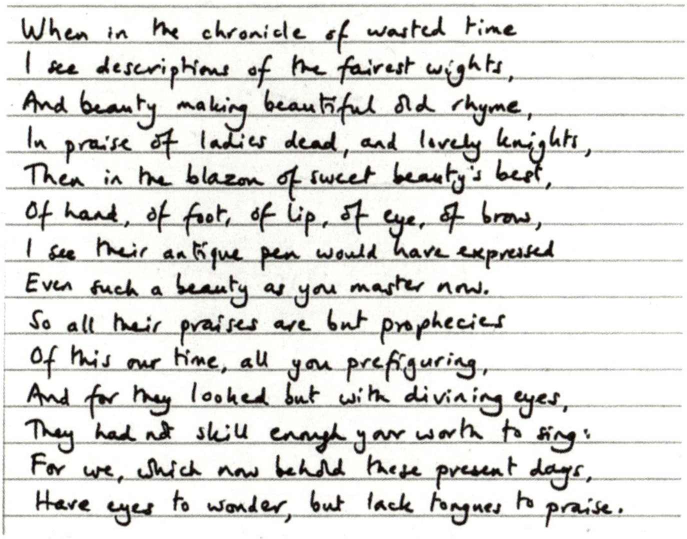
When in the chronicle of wasted time
I see descriptions of the fairest wights,
And beauty making beautiful old rhyme,
In praise of ladies dead, and lovely knights,
Then in the blazon of sweet beauty's best,
Of hand, of foot, of lip, of eye, of brow,
I see their antique pen would have expressed
Even such a beauty as you master now.
So all their praises are but prophecies
Of this our time, all you prefiguring,
And for they looked but with divining eyes,
They had not skill enough your worth to sing:
For we, which now behold these present days,
Have eyes to wonder, but lack tongues to praise.

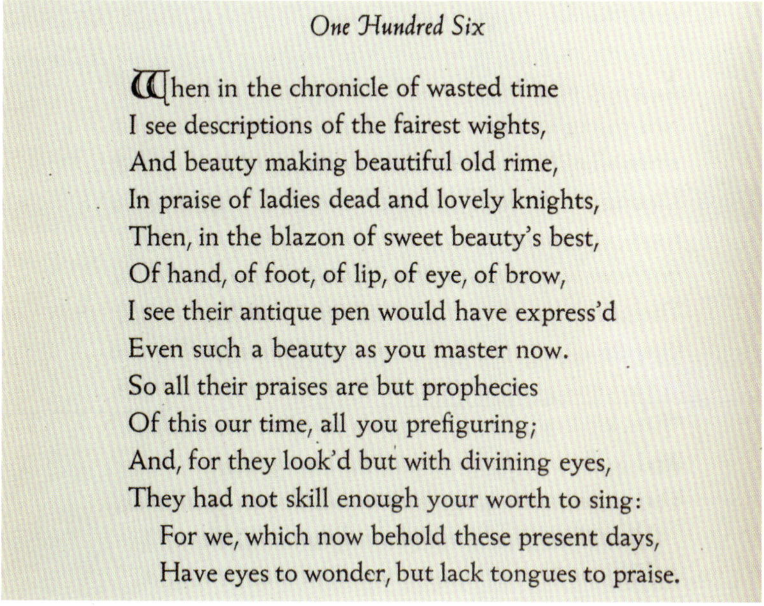
One Hundred Six

When in the chronicle of wasted time
I see descriptions of the fairest wights,
And beauty making beautiful old rime,
In praise of ladies dead and lovely knights,
Then, in the blazon of sweet beauty's best,
Of hand, of foot, of lip, of eye, of brow,
I see their antique pen would have express'd
Even such a beauty as you master now.
So all their praises are but prophecies
Of this our time, all you prefiguring;
And, for they look'd but with divining eyes,
They had not skill enough your worth to sing:
For we, which now behold these present days,
Have eyes to wonder, but lack tongues to praise.

莎士比亚的《十四行诗》第106首，分别取自1609年版、手书文本、20世纪版，这三种版本是否会给读者提供相同的阅读经验？三者不同的单词拼写方式、字体、段落设计以及其他因素对读者有着怎样的影响？

THE VALLEY OF UNREST

Once it smiled a silent dell
Where the people did not dwell;
They had gone unto the wars,
Trusting to the mild-eyed stars,
Nightly, from their azure towers,
To keep watch above the flowers,
In the midst of which all day
The red sun-light lazily lay.
Now each visitor shall confess
The sad valley's restlessness.
Nothing there is motionless—
Nothing save the airs that brood
Over the magic solitude.
Ah, by no wind are stirred those trees
That palpitate like the chill seas
Around the misty Hebrides!
Ah, by no wind those clouds are driven
That rustle through the unquiet Heaven
Uneasily, from morn till even,
Over the violets there that lie
In Myriad types of the human eye
Over the lilies there that wave
And weep above a nameless grave!
They wave:—from out their fragrant tops
Eternal dews come down in drops.
They weep:—from off their delicate stems
Perennial tears descend in gems.

BRIDAL BALLAD

The ring is on my hand,
  And the wreath is on my brow;
Satins and jewels grand
Are all at my command,
  And I am happy now.

And my lord he loves me well;
  But, when first he breathed his vow,
I felt my bosom swell—
For the words rang as a knell,
And the voice seemed *his* who fell

443

The Valley of Unrest

ONCE it smiled a silent dell
Where the people did not dwell;
They had gone unto the wars,
Trusting to the mild-eyed stars,
Nightly from their azure towers,
To keep watch above the flowers,
In the midst of which all day
The red sunlight lazily lay.
Now each visitor shall confess
The sad valley's restlessness.
Nothing there is motionless,
Nothing save the airs that brood
Over the magic solitude.
Ah, by no wind are stirred those trees
That palpitate like the chill seas

58

THE VALLEY OF UNREST.

ONCE it smiled a silent dell
Where the people did not dwell:
They had gone unto the wars,
Trusting to the mild-eyed stars,
Nightly from their azure towers
To keep watch above the flowers,
In the midst of which all day
The red sunlight lazily lay.

美国作家埃德加·艾伦·坡（Edgar Allen Poe）的诗作《动荡谷》（*The Valley of Unrest*）的三个版本：1870、1908 和 1952 年，不同的版式设计，一本无插图，两本有插图。三本不同的表现形式对读者的影响是什么？插图是提升还是干扰了读者的想象力？哪种页面能让读者对诗歌有最佳的欣赏？

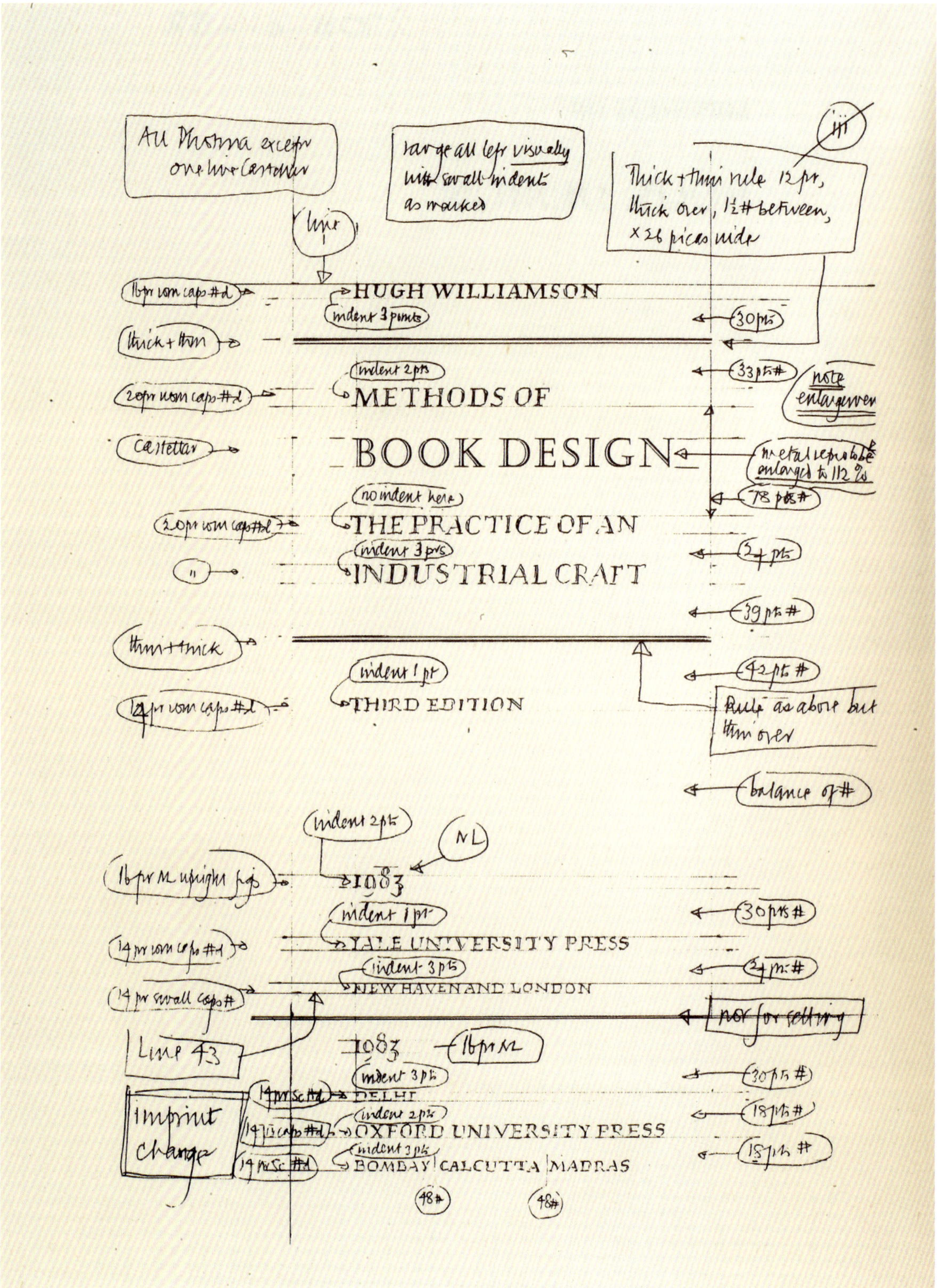
All Photina except one line Castellar
Range all left visually with small indents as marked
Thick + thin rule 12 pt, thick over, 1½# between, x 26 picas wide
line 1
16 pt rom caps #d
HUGH WILLIAMSON
indent 3 points
30 pts
thick + thin
indent 2 pts
33 pts #
20 pt rom caps #d
METHODS OF
note enlargement
Castellar
BOOK DESIGN
metal repro to be enlarged to 112%
no indent here
78 pts #
20 pt rom caps #d
THE PRACTICE OF AN
indent 3 pts
2 pts
INDUSTRIAL CRAFT
39 pts #
thin + thick
indent 1 pt
42 pts #
14 pt rom caps #d
THIRD EDITION
Rule as above but thin over
balance of #
indent 2 pts
NL
16 pt upright figs
1983
indent 1 pt
30 pts #
14 pt rom caps #d
YALE UNIVERSITY PRESS
indent 3 pts
2 pts #
14 pt small caps #
NEW HAVEN AND LONDON
not for setting
Line 43
1983
16 pt
indent 3 pts
30 pts #
Imprint change
14 pt sc #d
DELHI
indent 2 pts
18 pts #
14 pt caps #d
OXFORD UNIVERSITY PRESS
indent 3 pts
18 pts #
14 pt sc #d
BOMBAY CALCUTTA MADRAS
48#
48#

你可以将一册书拿在手中，很容易地一页页翻阅。将文本印在书页的两面上，并将这些书页缝订在一起，这种册子本（codex format）是我们所熟悉的书本形态，公元前几世纪首先出现在近东地区。历史证明了这种设计的长久魅力，它易带易用，非常成功，至今没有其他样式能取代它。所以，书籍是一种用起来方便又舒服的物品。

自古以来对书籍的外观和手感的关注，源自历史悠久的商业追求，因为书籍的出品方总是希望他们的产品有人购买。一本成功的书籍必须是各种设计因素的成功组合。它的字体必须清晰可辨，页面的布局和各部分文字的排版必须让人看着舒服，最终产品的大小和形状必须容易打开和翻阅。了解书籍的历史，了解人们如何通过书籍来交流思想，必须考虑到书籍的实体样式如何影响读者的感受和预期。

书籍的形态和格式可能会以某种方式微妙地影响到读者如何阅读，因此读者对文本的阅读不可能完全客观。例如围绕着学术研究成果的讨论，有时候人们对研究成果质量的评估是依据其发表成果的期刊而不是其研究结果的实际内容，这是不公平的。一篇精彩的论文如果是发表在某本名不见经传的刊物上，它的影响可能比不上一篇发表在更有声望的期刊上的差劲的论文，这不仅因为前一本刊物的读者群比较小，更因为读者对它的期望值很低。以什么方式将文本呈现给读者，会让读者在阅读之前已经有了某种先入之见。读者打开一本制作精美的书，此书的样式和设计就会对他产生影响，让读者对此书的内容有一种先入为主的期待，这种感觉是不同于打开一本制作简陋便宜的书的。在历史长河中，任何特定时期，人们如何对文本进行包装，这是书籍历史也是人类历史的一部分。

书籍设计是种微妙的技巧，正如理查德·亨德尔（Richard Hendel）1998年出版的《书籍设计》（*On Book Design*）一书中所写的："如果印刷是黑色的艺术，书籍设计就是无形的艺术"，最有效最成功的设计恰恰是那种不被读者注意到的设计。许多世纪以来，为了吸引鉴赏家和收藏家，人们制作了无数伟大的书籍，它们美轮美奂，依

（左页图）

成功的书籍设计需要关注页面每个细节，页面的总体布局和视觉效果。左页为设计师休·威廉姆森（Hugh Williamson）的经典著作《关于书籍设计》标题页的设计图，此图让我们看到这位设计大师一丝不苟、精益求精的态度

（下页图）

"人人系列"效果极佳的设计，20世纪的许多出版社试图面对广大普通读者，"人人系列"之所以成功，很大程度上要归功于它们的设计

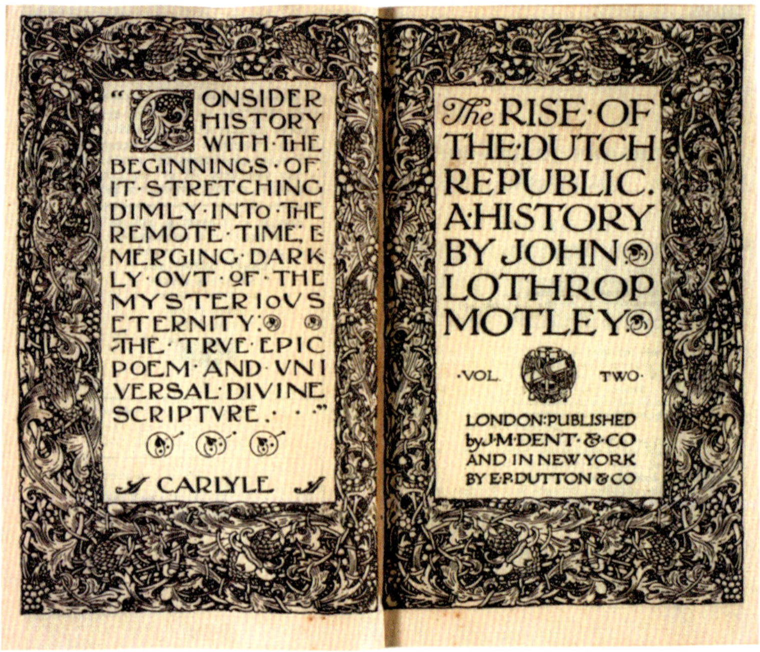

然被图书馆视为珍品，但这些善本珍本不一定像普通书籍那样被广泛阅读。与这些宏大壮观的书籍相比，廉价的其貌不扬的书籍，在交流和传播信息上可能会更有效果，也会对更多的受众产生更大的影响。众所周知，15 世纪末，阿尔杜斯·马努提乌斯（Aldus Manutius）在威尼斯创立了阿尔丁出版社，以一种新型小巧的形式出版古典文本，这一举动不仅具有精明的商业意识，也是印刷文化在欧洲传播和影响的里程碑。

20 世纪初开始出版的“人人系列”（Everyman series），将各类文学作品带给广大的普通读者，取得了巨大成功。不仅因为这一系列的书籍价格便宜，而且因为它们的设计异常漂亮。早期“人人系列”书籍的扉页充满了 19 世纪末美术工艺运动的风格，成功地将英国工艺大师威廉·莫里斯（William Morris）的美学理念带给千百万的读者。

2004 年，箭书出版社（Arrow Books）以全新的封面重新出版英国浪漫小说家乔伊特·海耶尔（Georgette Heyer）的作品，她的小说通常被认为是中产趣味的历史浪漫故事，新封面让这些作品拥有了一种简·奥斯汀般的风味，销售量显著上升

这样在公众层面上的极大成功，是莫里斯的私人印书坊凯尔姆斯科特（Kelmscott Press）出版的那些精美昂贵珍稀书籍不可能取得的。1935 年企鹅出版社成立，随后不久平装本被读者广泛接受，这些成功不仅因为书籍的出版成本大大降低，也因为这些书的设计都相当精美。

书籍是某个时代的美学和价值的组成部分，也是其表征。这一点，在 19 世纪中叶以后出版的书籍中特别明显，因为出版社的组织架构和书籍印刷方式的变化，封面设计变得特别重要，封面也开始体现图书的内容，和销售也大有关系。在 19 世纪末 20 世纪初出现书籍护

WON
AT LAST

THE ENGLISH
COTTAGE
BRIAN COOK

Wives
who
went
to
College
by
JUDITH
HUBBACK

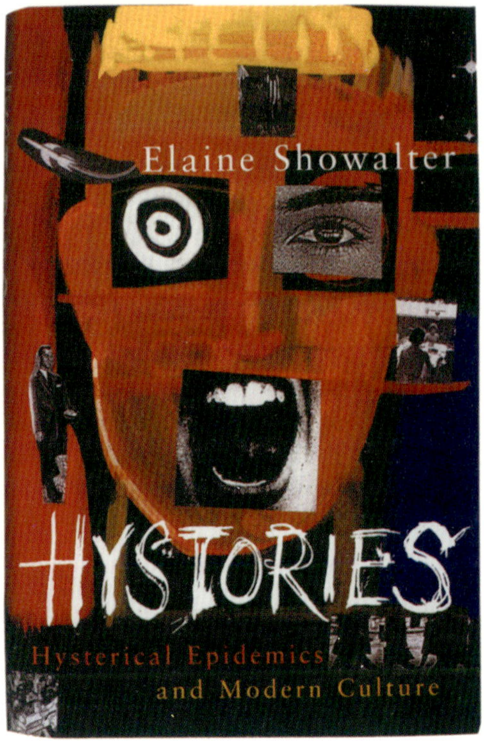
Elaine Showalter
HYSTORIES
Hysterical Epidemics
and Modern Culture

封之前，出版商就开始使用带有装饰的布面装帧，这是我们如今所知的各种封面图形设计的缘起。人们对护封的历史重要性的认识非常缓慢。过去，护封一直被视为琐碎的不值得保存的东西，所以，在一般的公共图书馆中，很难看到保留了护封的书籍。一张维多利亚时代的带着装饰的护封，或是 20 世纪两次大战之间书籍的护封，就像当时其他的任何艺术品一样，能够充分表达那个时代的精神。同一个文本在不同年代出版的不同版本，如果按照时间顺序将它们的封面进行排列，我们能看到公众对文本及作者不断变化着的文化取向和态度。如今出版商们大量投资于封面设计，他们充分认识到引人注目、充满趣味、奇妙无比的封面设计在销售上的重要性，他们用封面设计来强化他们的品牌和身份认同。出版社也常常以不同的封面设计来出版经典文本，其目的是要用新奇的图像来吸引新一代读者。“不要以貌取书”，这句话说起来容易做起来难。

（左页图）
书的封面不仅可以表达文本的内容，也代表着那个时代的审美和文化取向。此处四张封面分别出自 1892、1938、1957 和 1997 年，我们能看到它们明显的时代特征，换句话说，这些封面也是不同时代的艺术史记录

— 字体和排版 —

在一本书中，字体和排版这种不显眼的设计技巧也非常重要，它们会影响到最后的书籍成品，形成书籍的性格，但它们却往往会被我们忽略。字体设计是一种微妙的艺术，它涉及字母线条的粗细、曲线的比例和平衡，这些因素决定着字母设计是否成功。最早的字体有罗马时代的大写字体（Roman capitals）和后罗马时代的安色尔字体（uncial book hands）。我们如今常用的字母形状和字体，说到底都是从这两种字体中发展出来的。15 世纪后期，这些字体第一次在印刷上得到使用和完善，最著名的是威尼斯印刷商尼古拉斯·简森（Nicolaus Jenson）和阿尔杜斯·马努提乌斯。最早的印刷书籍所使用的字体，是对同时代的哥特式用于抄写书籍的黑色手书字体的有意识复制。早期的“罗马”印刷字体是受到文艺复兴时期书法的启发而

Alice's Adventures
In Wonderland

ALICE IN WONDERLAND

PENGUIN CLASSICS
LEWIS CARROLL
ALICE'S ADVENTURES IN WONDERLAND AND THROUGH THE LOOKING-GLASS
CENTENARY EDITION

LEWIS CARROLL
ALICE'S adventures in WONDERLAND
LYNX
ILLUSTRATED BY JUSTIN TODD

《爱丽丝漫游奇境》在不同年代的封面设计，这些封面一方面反映了设计的历史，另一方面也反映出不同时期读者们对此书的看法和期望

读者头脑中的爱丽丝究竟是怎样的形象？这些封面上的图像会不会给读者一种先入之见？爱丽丝的性格是温柔还是脆弱？是单纯无邪还是调皮捣蛋？

这些版本出版于1888—1999年间

尼古拉斯·简森发明的罗马字体，首次用在1470年出版的《优西比乌斯》(*Eusebius*)中，长久以来被誉为西文字体设计的里程碑，被后人广泛使用。它字体清晰、比例恰到好处、线条简洁，让整个文本页面优雅易读

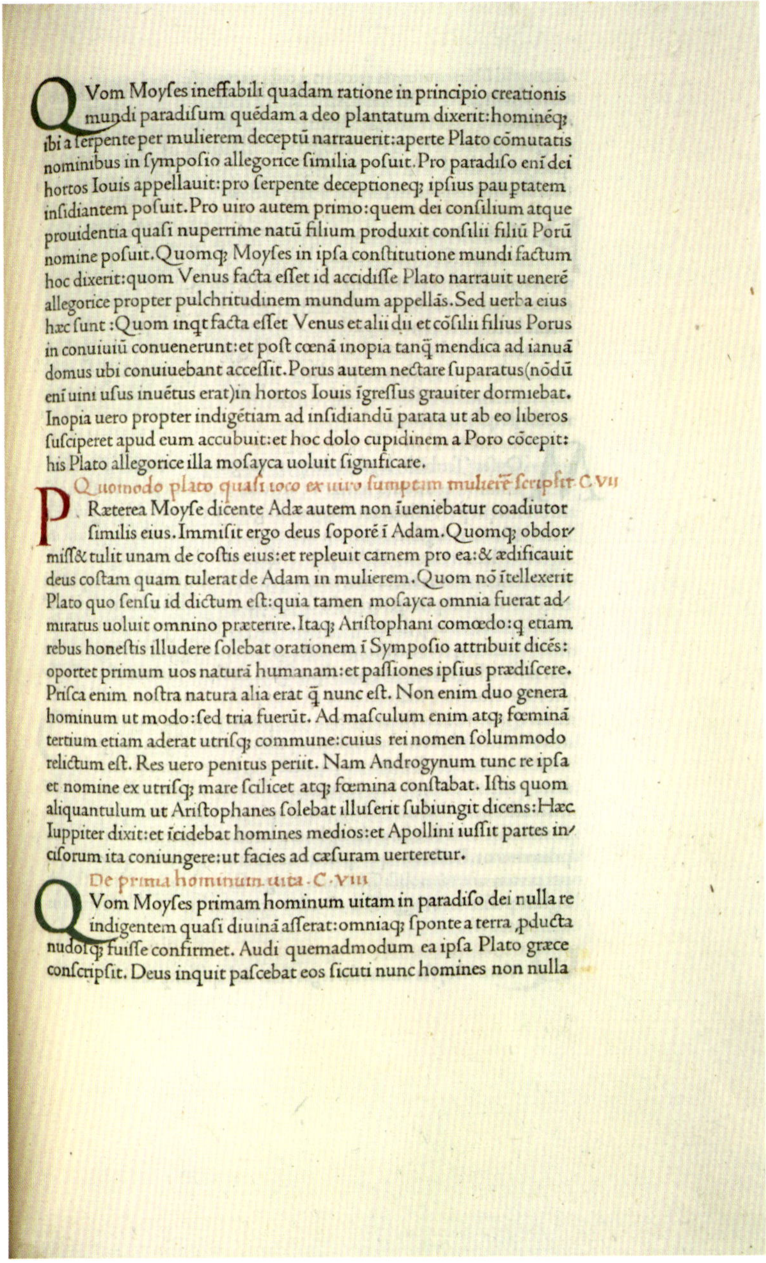
QVom Moyſes ineffabili quadam ratione in principio creationis mundi paradiſum quédam a deo plantatum dixerit: hominéq; ibi a ſerpente per mulierem deceptũ narrauerit: aperte Plato cõmutatis nominibus in ſymposio allegorice ſimilia poſuit. Pro paradiſo enĩ dei hortos Iouis appellauit: pro ſerpente deceptioneq; ipſius pau ptatem inſidiantem poſuit. Pro uiro autem primo: quem dei conſilium atque prouidentia quaſi nuperrime natũ filium produxit conſilii filiũ Porũ nomine poſuit. Quomq; Moyſes in ipſa conſtitutione mundi factum hoc dixerit: quom Venus facta eſſet id accidiſſe Plato narrauit uenerẽ allegorice propter pulchritudinem mundum appellãs. Sed uerba eius hæc ſunt: Quom inqt facta eſſet Venus et alii dii et cõſilii filius Porus in conuiuiũ conuenerunt: et poſt cœnã inopia tanq̃ mendica ad ianuã domus ubi conuiuebant acceſſit. Porus autem nectare ſuparatus (nõdũ enĩ uini uſus inuẽtus erat) in hortos Iouis ĩgreſſus grauiter dormiebat. Inopia uero propter indigẽtiam ad inſidiandũ parata ut ab eo liberos ſuſciperet apud eum accubuit: et hoc dolo cupidinem a Poro cõcepit: his Plato allegorice illa moſayca uoluit ſignificare.

Quomodo plato quaſi ioco ex uiro ſumptam mulierẽ ſcripſit. C. VII

PRæterea Moyſe dicente Adæ autem non ĩueniebatur coadiutor ſimilis eius. Immiſit ergo deus ſoporẽ ĩ Adam. Quomq; obdormiſſ& tulit unam de coſtis eius: et repleuit carnem pro ea: & ædificauit deus coſtam quam tulerat de Adam in mulierem. Quom nõ ĩtellexerit Plato quo ſenſu id dictum eſt: quia tamen moſayca omnia fuerat admiratus uoluit omnino præterire. Itaq; Ariſtophani comœdo: q etiam rebus honeſtis illudere ſolebat orationem ĩ Sympoſio attribuit dicẽs: oportet primum uos naturã humanam: et paſſiones ipſius prædiſcere. Priſca enim noſtra natura alia erat q̃ nunc eſt. Non enim duo genera hominum ut modo: ſed tria fuerũt. Ad maſculum enim atq; fœminã tertium etiam aderat utriſq; commune: cuius rei nomen ſolummodo relictum eſt. Res uero penitus periit. Nam Androgynum tunc re ipſa et nomine ex utriſq; mare ſcilicet atq; fœmina conſtabat. Iſtis quom aliquantulum ut Ariſtophanes ſolebat illuſerit ſubiungit dicens: Hæc Iuppiter dixit: et ĩcidebat homines medios: et Apollini iuſſit partes inciſorum ita coniungere: ut facies ad cæſuram uerteretur.

De prima hominum uita. C. VIII

QVom Moyſes primam hominum uitam in paradiſo dei nulla re indigentem quaſi diuinã aſſerat: omniaq; ſponte a terra ꝑducta nudoſq; fuiſſe confirmet. Audi quemadmodum ea ipſa Plato græce conſcripſit. Deus inquit paſcebat eos ſicuti nunc homines non nulla

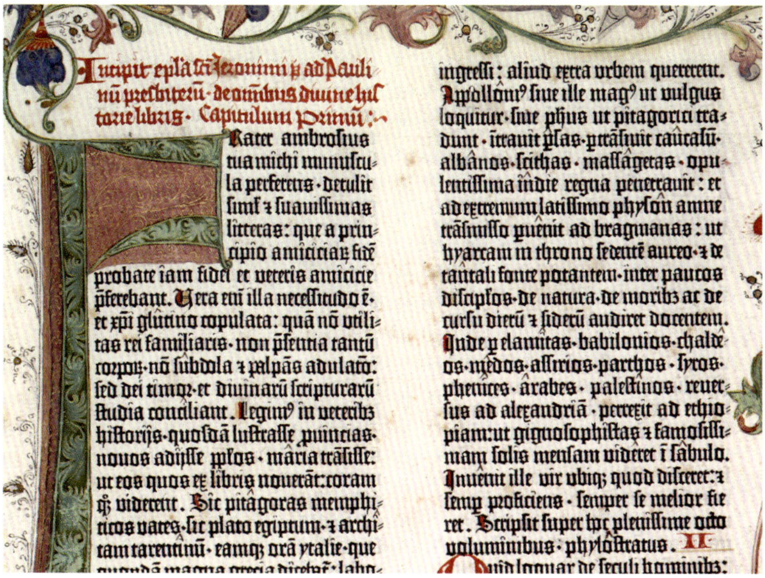

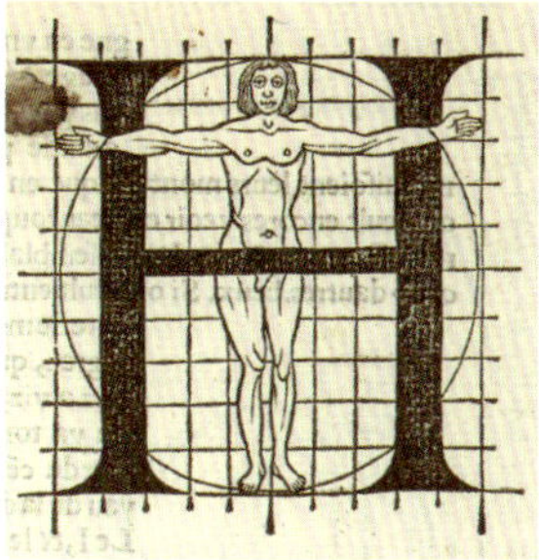

（左图）
西方最早的印刷书籍，例如古腾堡《圣经》，大多使用手抄经书所钟爱的哥特式手书字体，这是新的印刷技术对手书体的刻意模仿

（右图）
法国学者杰弗里·托里（Geofrey Tory）1529 年的著作《天堂》（*Champ Fleury*），以网格来反映罗马字母与人体比例之间的关系，提出依据古罗马风格能设计出最佳字体样式

形成的，这种字体是对古典的字母形式的重新发现，这一运动开始于 15 世纪初的佛罗伦萨。简森字体（Jenson's type）是在 1470 年首次使用的罗马字体，它并不是罗马字体的第一种，却是最被广泛推崇并在后来的几个世纪中最受尊崇，也是使用最多的字体。

印刷字体和书籍封面一样，能够代表它所处的时代。因为印刷字体的变化，书籍能够具有某个时期的独特性。在过去五百年中，新的工艺师、设计师不断创新，提高印刷标准，树立了新型印刷字体设计史上的一座座里程碑。手工印刷的年代就诞生了多位巨匠，例如：16 世纪的法国的字体设计师加拉蒙（Claude Garamond）和格拉荣（Robert Granjon），17 世纪的荷兰的印刷师埃尔萨瓦（Lodewijk Elzevir）和法国印刷师克罗姆西（Sebastien Cramoisy），18 世纪的英国字体设计师巴斯克维尔（John Baskerville）和意大利设计师、印刷师波蒂尼（Giambattista Bodoni），等等。到了机械化印刷的时代，字体上的创新更是层出不穷。19 世纪无数华丽无比、充满实验性的字体，其视多年来字体的演变，不仅表现出字体与信息传递的微妙关系，也能在我们的头脑中建立起各个历史时代的形象。例如我们看到哥特式黑色手书体，就会想到“中世纪”；而右边这一张传单，让我们联想到“19世纪”，因为它的设计充满活力，来自工业革命时代的企业家精神

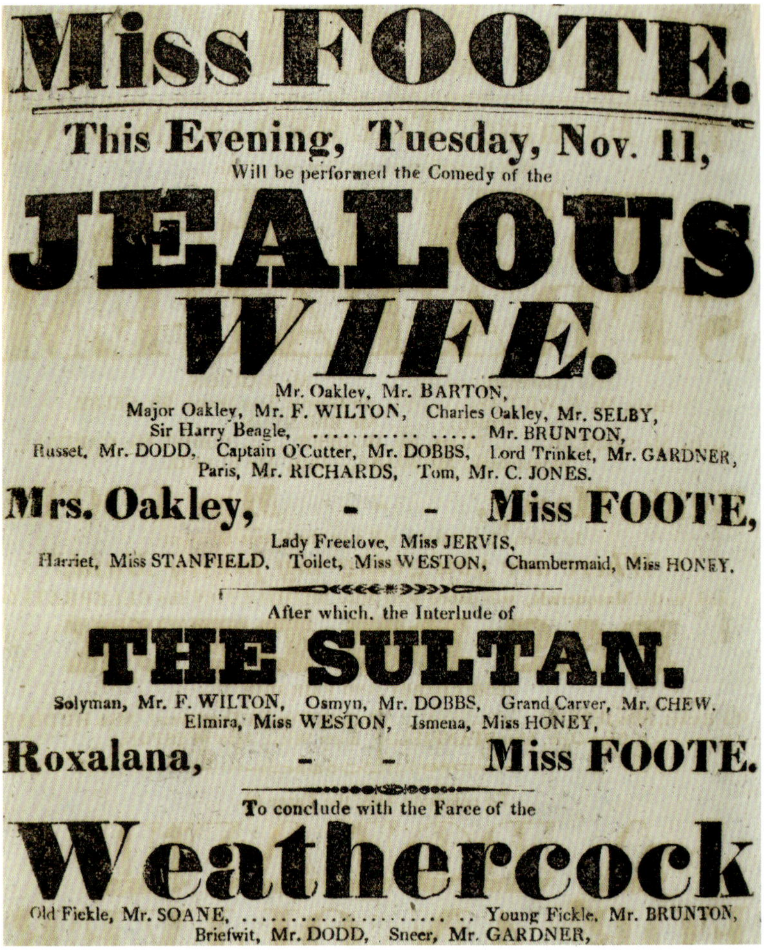

斯坦利·莫里森的“泰晤士新罗马字体”是他在1932年专为《泰晤士报》设计的。 整个20世纪后半叶，这种字体不仅对报纸，而且对书籍和文献的风格都有巨大的影响

觉效果直接影响着我们对维多利亚时代的印象，也对当时的文本多有影响。如今英语世界广泛使用的字体都受到英国字体设计师、印刷史学家斯坦利·莫里森（Stanley Morison，1889 — 1967）的很大影响，他在 1932 年为《泰晤士报》设计了“泰晤士新罗马字体”（Times New Roman），并在 20 世纪的二三十年代设计了一系列其他新字体，它们至今仍然主导着我们在书页和屏幕上所看到的那些字体。

— 文字之外：插图和装饰 —

书籍诞生以来，它们的文字内容就一直有各种各样的视觉辅助。图像能以各种方式对文本进行补充，让书籍的内容更明确、清晰、鲜活。早在公元前 12 世纪，古埃及的纸莎草卷上就有插图，可以说它们是世界上现存最古老的插画书。亚里士多德在他的文字中提到相关的图画，可惜没有实例流传下来。这本书延续着将图像与文本相结合的悠久传统，文本和插图，缺少其一，图书的效果就会大大减弱。

梵蒂冈图书馆保存了两本 5 世纪的“维吉尔诗集”手抄书，都配有图画。它们是西方最早的插图书之一，插图描绘的都是文本中所提到的场景或活动，其目的是为了帮助读者将文本内容视觉化。从那时起，直到现在，插图书籍数不胜数，书中配有插图，我们早就习以为常。这些插图可能是描绘事实的，可能是概念性的，也可能是图表。它们可大可小，可繁复可简约，插图本身就是一种艺术形式。

到了书籍印刷的年代，插图几乎是与印刷术同步出现，最早带有插图的印刷书籍出现在 1461 年，比西方第一本印刷书籍古腾堡《圣经》只晚几年。 从那以后，人们使用种种新技术，让在书页的有限空间之内大批量印刷图像成为可能。15 世纪书籍插图的主要技术是木刻版画，到了 16 世纪，这种技术被铜版画代替，与木刻版画相比，铜版画更为复杂和细腻。

wie der man· Reit vnd lest den iungē gan· Liesz er
den knabē reitē· Vnd lief dem knaben pei der seiten

Daran thet er vil pasz· Do der alt erhoret das· Vō
dem esel sasz er do· Der iung sasz auff vnd was fro
Der ein zu dem andern sprach· Do er den knaben
reitē sach· wart getreuer geselle meȳ· Der alt mag
wol ein narre sein· Das er lest reiten den knaben·
Der solt laufen vnd trabē· Vnd solt der alt reiten·
Vil kaum mocht er gepeiten· Das der alt auff den
esel kam· zu dem knaben vnd reiten hin dan·

（左页图）
瑞士作家乌尔里希·博纳（Ulrich Boner）的德文寓言集《宝石》出版于 1461 年（仅晚于古腾堡《圣经》几年），这是第一本带有插图的印刷书籍

（左图）
现藏于梵蒂冈图书馆的 5 世纪手抄书，维吉尔的《埃涅阿斯纪》（*Aeneid*），是我们所知的现存最早的插图本书籍之一

中世纪的手抄书都是单本制作的，其中的插图大多是彩色。到了手动操作印刷的年代，大规模的印刷过程中，印制彩色插图几乎不可能。在 19 世纪之前印刷的书籍中，有时我们能看到彩色插图，但这些都是在黑白插图上手绘的［附图所示的《宝石》（*Edelstein*）就是其中一例］。到了 19 世纪，随着一系列新技术的发明，印刷也有了革命性的变化，全彩插图的印刷成为可能，大批量生产的成本也在下降。同一时间，摄影的发明带来了以照片为插图的书籍。从那时起，书籍制作的技术不断发展，书籍插图也变得越发简单、便宜和精致。到现在，我们早已对图文并茂的书籍习以为常。

增强书籍的视觉效果并不一定都需要写实的插图。在 1066 年诺曼底公爵征服英国之前，有许多不列颠岛国手抄书，例如著名的《林迪斯法恩福音书》（*Lindisfarne Gospels*）和《凯尔斯之书》（*Book of Kells*），这些手抄书的传统证明了抽象的装饰也同样能在书页上起到强有力的惊人效果。此外，中世纪的手抄书也证明，加强书页的视觉效果，不只是单靠插图，精心装饰的边框和首字到15世纪末，印刷书籍中使用木刻版画插图已经很成熟，此为1494年出版的德国作家塞巴斯蒂安·勃朗特（Sebastian Brandt）的《愚人船》（*Narrenschiff*）中的一页

Von achtung des geſtirns

Der iſt ein narr der me verheißt
Dann er in ſeym vermögen weiſſzt
Oder dann er zu thun het mut
Verheyſſen iſt den ertzten gut
Aber eyn narr verheiſſzt ein tag
Me dann all welt geleyſten mag.
Auff kunfftig ding man yetz vaſt lendt
Was das geſtyrn vnd firmament
Vnd der planeten lauff vns ſag

从16世纪开始，和木刻版画相比，金属版画让书籍插图更为精妙细腻，17世纪中期，丹尼尔·金（Daniel King）等艺术家创作了一批英格兰和威尔士的大教堂铜版画，此为一例

在16和17世纪，附有格言或寓言诗的寓意画非常流行，它们图文并茂，图像让文字的道德教育意义大大增强

（下页图）

19世纪40年代，彩色石印术的发明，让彩色插图的印刷成为可能，维多利亚时代的出版商和插画家大量使用了这一技术，此例为1848年英国插画家诺埃尔·汉弗莱斯（H.Noel Humphreys）的《主的奇迹》（*The Miracles of our Lord*）

still, and commanded him to be called. And they called the blind man saying unto him, Be of good comfort, arise; he calleth thee. And he, casting away his garment, rose, and came to Jesus. And Jesus answered and said unto him, what wilt thou that I should do unto thee? The blind man said unto him, Lord, that I might receive my sight. And Jesus said unto him, Go thy way; thy faith hath made thee whole. And immediately he received his sight, and followed Jesus in the way.

Luke xiii. 11 17.

A Woman of eighteen years Infirmity cured.

And behold there was a woman which had a spirit of infirmity eighteen years, and was bowed together, and could in no wise lift up herself. And when Jesus saw her, he called her to him, and said unto her, Woman, thou art loosed from thine infirmity. And he laid his hands on her; and immediately she was made straight, & glorified God. And the ruler of the synagogue answered with indignation, because that Jesus had healed

英国科学家威廉·福克斯·塔尔博特（William Fox Talbot）的《自然画笔》（*Pencil of Nature*）出版于1844年，这是第一批用照片来做插图的书籍之一

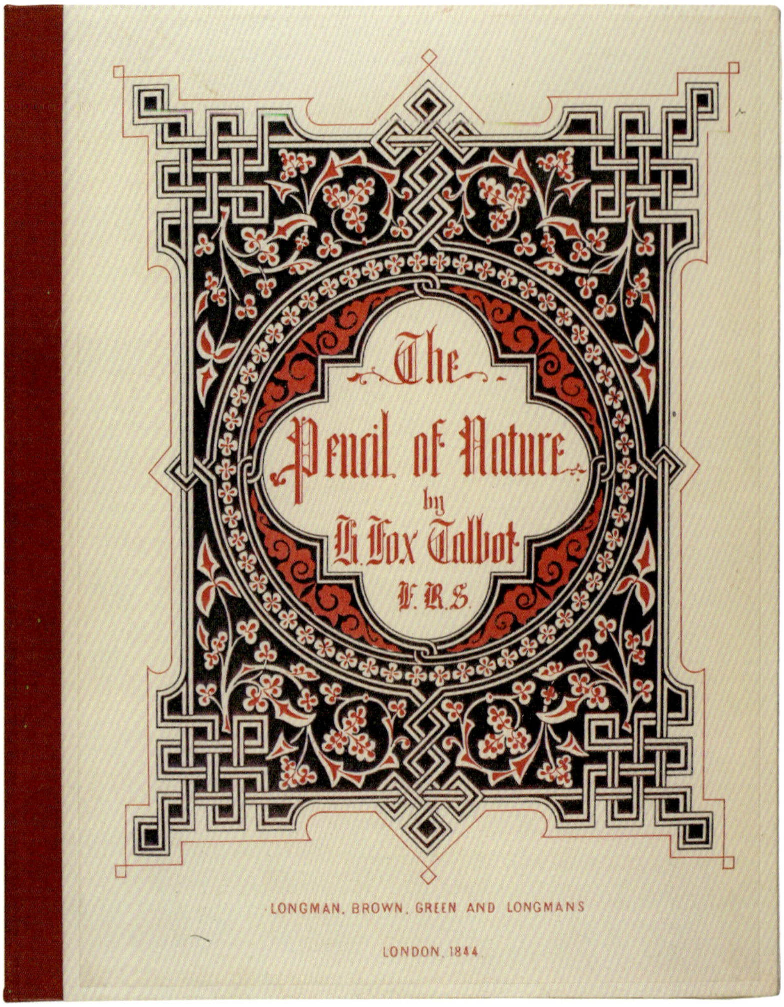

用装饰来增强页面及文本的效果，这一传统可追溯到数百年前，许多中世纪的手抄书都装饰有页面边框和首字母

COnuerte nos deus ſa-
lutaris noſter.
Et auerte iram tuam
à nobis.
Deus in adiutorium
meum intende.
Domine ad adiuuandum me feſtina.
Gloria patri,& filio,& ſpiritui ſancto.
Sicut erat in principio,& nunc,& ſem
per:& in ſecula ſeculorum. Amen.
Hallelu ia. Pſalmus.
SAEpe expugnauerũt me à iuuen-
tute mea,dicat nunc Iſrael,
Sæpe expugnauerunt me à iuuentute
mea,etenim non potuerunt mihi.
Supra dorſum meum fabricauerunt
peccatores,prolongauerunt iniquita-
tem ſuam.
Dominus iuſtus cõcidet ceruices pec-
catorum: confundantur, & conuertã-

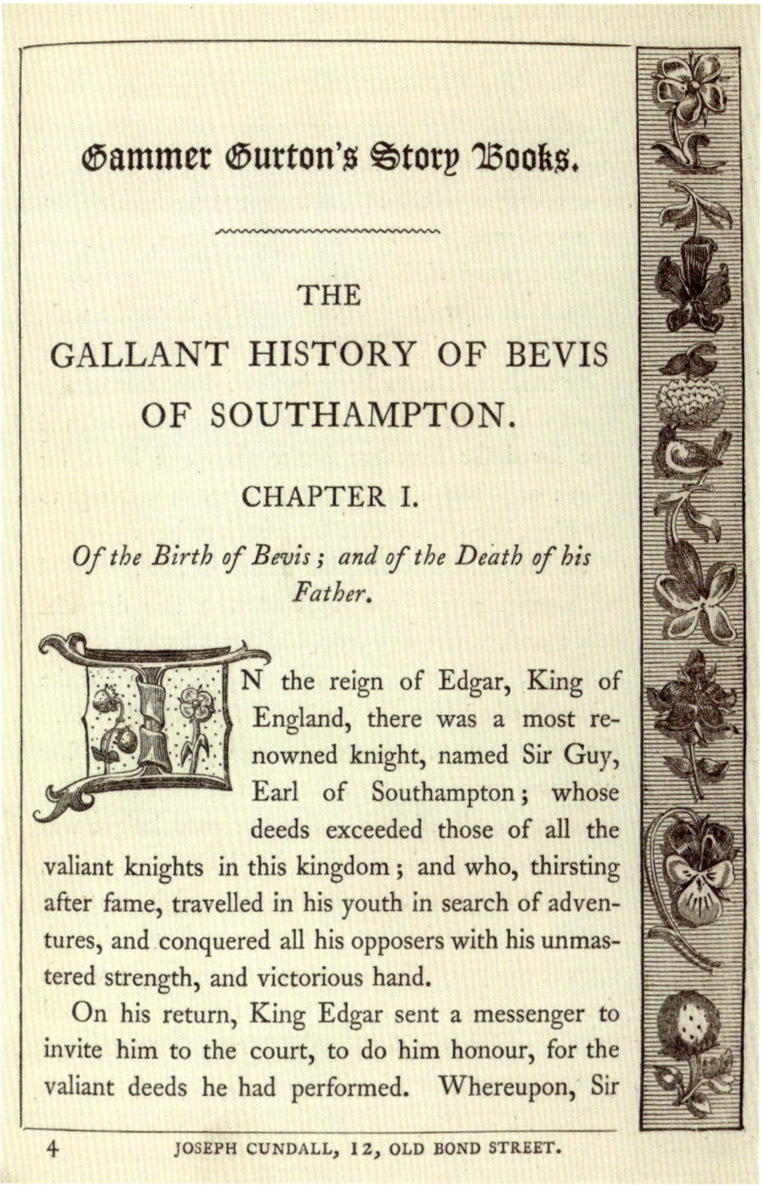
Gammer Gurton's Story Books.

THE

GALLANT HISTORY OF BEVIS OF SOUTHAMPTON.

CHAPTER I.

Of the Birth of Bevis; and of the Death of his Father.

IN the reign of Edgar, King of England, there was a most renowned knight, named Sir Guy, Earl of Southampton; whose deeds exceeded those of all the valiant knights in this kingdom; and who, thirsting after fame, travelled in his youth in search of adventures, and conquered all his opposers with his unmastered strength, and victorious hand.

On his return, King Edgar sent a messenger to invite him to the court, to do him honour, for the valiant deeds he had performed. Whereupon, Sir

4 JOSEPH CUNDALL, 12, OLD BOND STREET.

使用页面边框、首字母以及类似的装饰来增强页面的视觉效果，这种方式在手工印刷的阶段仍很流行，一直延续到19世纪。如今，类似的装饰方法已经不再常用，现在，书籍设计师更多地使用插图而不是装饰来达到视觉效果。此处为16世纪中期（左页图）和19世纪中期（左图）仍以这种方式进行装饰的两本书籍

英国外交家威廉·汉密尔顿（William Hamilton）关于维苏威火山爆发的书，其中的插图是彩色手绘版画，画面壮观，此书本身就是一件艺术品

母也非常有效，这些方式在中世纪手抄书中被广泛使用，后来的印刷书籍也继承了这些传统。在整个手工印刷书籍的时代，各种花饰、页面边框和装饰字母的使用也很常见，它们的效果可醒目也可微妙。现代书籍中这种装饰方式的使用虽然减少，但直到 19 世纪，它们依然流行。

（下页图）
整个 20 世纪，许多私人书坊依然保留着制作至美书籍的理念，它们手工印出的书籍在设计、纸张和印刷上都精益求精，追求最高的工艺水平。此图为塞缪尔·约翰逊博士的诗作《人类愿望之虚荣》（*The Vanity of Human Wishes*），1984 年由狂狮出版社（Rampant Lions Press）出版

— 作为艺术品的书籍 —

一本制作精美的书，或是拥有精美插图的书籍，往往会被视为独立的艺术品。例如 1779 年出版的威廉·汉密尔顿的《燃烧的土地》（*Campi Phlegraei*），汉密尔顿是英国派驻意大利那不勒斯的外交家，他每天记录维苏威火山喷发的情况，书中有艺术家彼得·法布里斯

LET Observation with extensive View,
Survey Mankind, from *China* to *Peru*;
Remark each anxious Toil, each eager Strife,
And watch the busy Scenes of crouded Life;
Then say how Hope and Fear, Desire and Hate,
O'erspread with Snares the clouded Maze of Fate,
Where wav'ring Man, betray'd by vent'rous Pride,
To tread the dreary Paths without a Guide,
As treach'rous Phantoms in the Mist delude,
Shuns fancied Ills, or chases airy Good;
How rarely Reason guides the stubborn Choice,
Rules the bold Hand, or prompts the suppliant Voice;
How Nations sink, by darling Schemes oppress'd,
When Vengeance listens to the Fool's Request.
Fate wings with ev'ry Wish th'afflictive Dart,
Each Gift of Nature, and each Grace of Art,
With fatal Heat impetuous Courage glows,
With fatal Sweetness Elocution flows,
Impeachment stops the Speaker's pow'rful Breath,
And restless Fire precipitates on Death.

But scarce observ'd, the Knowing and the Bold
Fall in the gen'ral Massacre of Gold;
Wide-wasting pest! that rages unconfin'd,
And crouds with Crimes the Records of Mankind;
For Gold his Sword the Hireling Ruffian draws,
For Gold the hireling Judge distorts the Laws;
Wealth heap'd on Wealth, nor Truth nor Safety buys,
The Dangers gather as the Treasures rise.

Let Hist'ry tell where rival Kings command,
And dubious Title shakes the madded Land,
When Statutes glean the Refuse of the Sword,
How much more safe the Vassal than the Lord;
Low skulks the Hind beneath the Rage of Pow'r,
And leaves the *wealthy Traytor* in the *Tow'r*,
Untouch'd his Cottage, and his Slumbers sound,
Tho' Confiscation's Vulturs hover round.

The needy Traveller, secure and gay,
Walks the wild Heath, and sings his Toil away,
Does Envy seize thee? crush th'upbraiding Joy,

of Jesus, which said unto him, Before the cock crow, thou shalt deny me thrice. And he went out, and wept bitterly.

WHEN THE MORNING WAS COME, ALL THE CHIEF PRIESTS and elders of the people took counsel against Jesus to put him to death: And when they had bound him, they led him away, and delivered him to Pontius Pilate the governor.

Then Judas, which had betrayed him, when he saw that he was condemned, repented himself, and brought again the thirty pieces of silver to the chief priests and elders, Saying, I have sinned in that I have betrayed the innocent blood. And they said, What is that to us? see thou to that. And he cast down the pieces of silver in the temple, and departed, and went and hanged himself. And the chief priests took the silver pieces, and said, It is not lawful for to put them into the treasury, because it is the price of blood. And they took counsel, and bought with them the potter's field, to bury strangers in. Wherefore that field was called, The field of blood, unto this day. Then was fulfilled that which was spoken by Jeremy the prophet, saying, And they took the thirty pieces of silver, the price of him that was valued, whom they of the children of Israel did value; And gave them for the potter's field, as the Lord appointed me.

（Peter Fabris）手绘的五十四幅不同尺寸彩色插图。19 世纪后期出现的私家印书坊运动（the private press movement），是对大规模的书籍机械化印刷出版的反动，一时非常盛行。这些私家印书坊制作了许多书籍，工艺精湛，整体美感高，备受赞赏。

书籍要成为独立艺术品，不能只因为图文并茂，或因为有赏心悦目的字体和排版，制书人需要将创造力用于构成一本书的所有元素上，运用书籍功能性的实体形式，做到文字、图像、排版、设计等各方面的真正融合。英国艺术与工艺运动的领导人威廉·莫里斯和艺术家爱德华·伯恩－琼斯（Edward Burne-Jones）合作的凯尔姆斯科特印书坊的《乔叟寓言》（*Kelmscott Chaucer*）就是书籍所有方面的最完美组合。翻阅这本至美的书，你会觉得书籍的所有组成部分都为此书之美做出了贡献。另一个例子是英国艺术家埃里克·吉尔（Eric Gill）为金鸡印书坊（Golden Cockerel Press）制作的《四福音书》（*Four Gospels*），此书的图像、字体和排版都由吉尔设计，也构成完美的整体组合。

关于书籍的版面和排字，历史上曾有过许多充满想象力的实验。1633 年，威尔士诗人乔治·赫伯特（George Herbert）关于天使之翼的诗歌，排版展现的是翅膀的形状。这种“有形诗篇”的观念很早就出现，我们所知的最早的例子是公元前 300 年古希腊罗德岛诗人西米亚斯（Simmias of Rhodes）的作品。中世纪早期也有一些“有形文本”的例子存在，如载有古罗马的西塞罗（Cicero）翻译的古希腊诗人阿拉托斯（Aratus）的诗作的一本 9 世纪的手抄书中，有的诗句就是被排版成星座的形状。在对孩子的教育和交流上，文字和图像交互使用，也具有悠久的历史，18 世纪晚期的《象形文字圣经》（*Hieroglyphick Bible*）就是很好的例子。到了 20 世纪，在排版上进行尝试的嬉戏之作更为激进，例如比利时诗人保罗·范·奥斯泰琴（Paul van Ostaijen）的诗作《沦陷之城》（*Bezette Stad*），视觉上错乱和割裂的文本，反映了第一次世界大战中德国对安特卫普的占领。这

埃里克·吉尔为金鸡印书坊 1931 年制作的《四福音书》（左页图），和凯尔姆斯科特印书坊 1896 年出版的《乔叟寓言》（下页图）都是将文本、字体、排版、插图融为一体的最佳典范

Feithful, and ful of stabilite.
Good-Hope alwey kepe by thy syde,
And Swete-Thought make eek abyde,
Swete-Loking and Swete-Speche;
Of alle thyn harmes they shal be leche.
Of every thou shalt have greet plesaunce;
If thou canst byde in sufferaunce,
And serve wel without feyntyse,
Thou shalt be quit of thyn empryse,
With more guerdoun, if that thou live;
But al this tyme this I thee yive.

THE God of Love whan al the day
Had taught me, as ye have herd say,
And enfourmed compendiously,
He vanished awey al sodeynly,
And I alone lefte, al sole,
So ful of compleynt and of dole,
For I saw no man ther me by.
My woundes me greved wondirly;
Me for to curen nothing I knew,
Save the botoun bright of hew,
Wheron was set hoolly my thought;
Of other comfort knew I nought,
But it were through the God of Love;
I knew nat elles to my bihove
That might me ese or comfort gete,
But if he wolde him entermete.

THE roser was, withoute doute,
Closed with an hegge withoute,
As ye toforn have herd me seyn;
And fast I bisied, and wolde fayn
Have passed the haye, if I might
Have geten in by any slight
Unto the botoun so fair to see.
But ever I dradde blamed to be,
If men wolde have suspeccioun
That I wolde of entencioun
Have stole the roses that ther were;
Therfore to entre I was in fere.
But at the last, as I bithought
Whether I sholde passe or nought,
I saw come with a gladde chere
To me, a lusty bachelere,
Of good stature, and of good hight,
And Bialacoil forsothe he hight. Bialacoil
Sone he was to Curtesy,
And he me graunted ful gladly
The passage of the outer hay,
And seide: Sir, how that ye may
Passe, if it your wille be,
The fresshe roser for to see,
And ye the swete savour fele.
Your warrant may I be right wele;

So thou thee kepe fro folye,
Shal no man do thee vilanye.
If I may helpe you in ought,
I shal not feyne, dredeth nought;
For I am bounde to your servyse,
Fully devoide of feyntyse.
THAN unto Bialacoil saide I:
I thank you, sir, ful hertely,
And your biheest I take at gree,
That ye so goodly profer me;
To you it cometh of greet fraunchyse,
That ye me profer your servyse.
Than aftir, ful deliverly,
Through the breres anoon wente I,
Wherof encombred was the hay.
I was wel plesed, the soth to say,
To see the botoun fair and swote,
So fresshe spronge out of the rote.
And Bialacoil me served wel,
Whan I so nygh me mighte fele
Of the botoun the swete odour,
And so lusty hewed of colour.
BUT than a cherl, foule him bitydel
Bisyde the roses gan him hyde,
To kepe the roses of that roser,
Of whom the name was Daunger. Daunger
This cherl was hid there in the greves,
Covered with grasse and with leves,
To spye and take whom that he fond
Unto that roser putte an hond.
He was not sole, for ther was mo;
For with him were other two
Of wikkid maners, and yvel fame. Wikked/
That oon was clepid, by his name, Tonge
Wikked/Tonge, God yeve him sorwe!
For neither at eve, ne at morwe,
He can of no man no good speke;
On many a just man doth he wreke.
Ther was a womman eek, that hight
Shame, that, who can reken right, Shame
Trespas was hir fadir name,
Hir moder Resoun; and thus was Shame
On lyve brought of these ilk two.
And yit had Trespas never ado
With Resoun, ne never ley hir by,
He was so hidous and ugly,
I mene, this that Trespas hight;
But Resoun conceyveth, of a sight,
Shame, of that I spak aforn. Chastitee
AND whan that Shame was thus born,
It was ordeyned, that Chastitee
Shulde of the roser lady be,
Which, of the botouns more and las,
With sondry folk assailed was,
That she ne wiste what to do.
For Venus hir assailith so,

乔治·赫伯特是较早的版式布局的实验者，他试图以文字在页面上的排列来反映文本的内容，右图是他的诗作《复活节翅膀》（*Easter Wings*）。之后有更为极端的例子：保罗·范·奥斯泰琴的诗歌（下图）

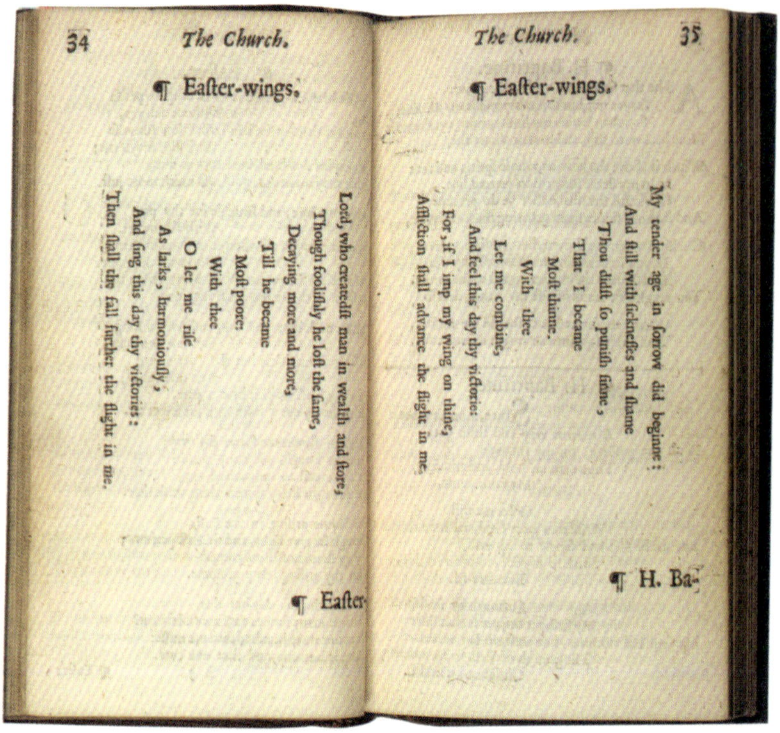

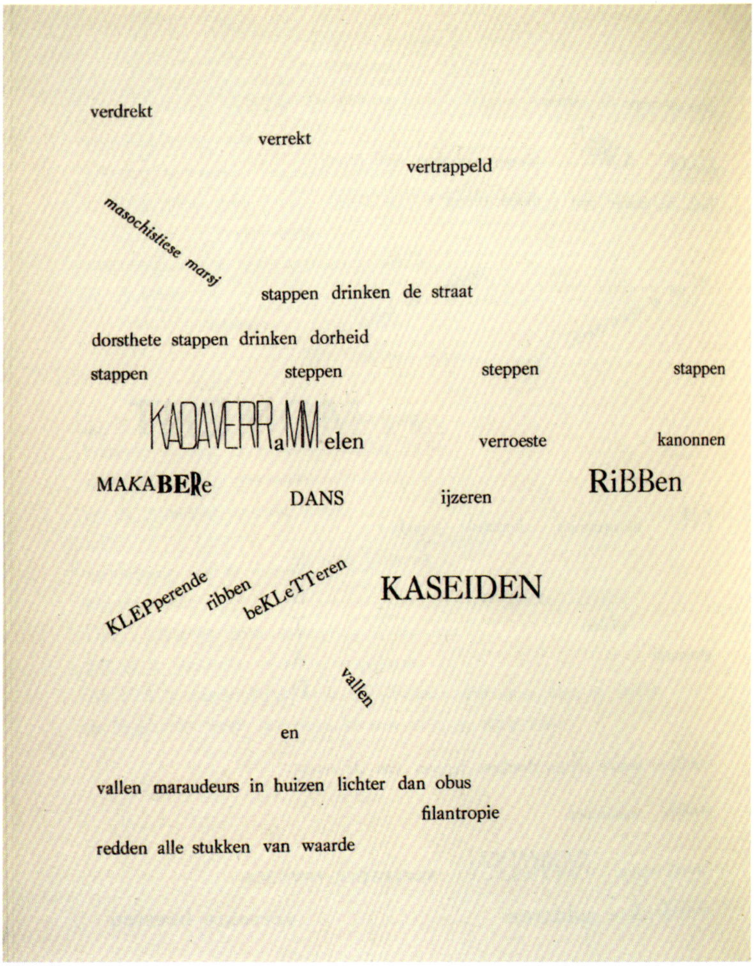
verdrekt
verrekt
vertrappeld
masochistiese marsj
stappen drinken de straat
dorsthete stappen drinken dorheid
stappen steppen steppen stappen
KADAVERRaMMelen verroeste kanonnen
MAKABERe DANS ijzeren RiBBen
KLEPperende ribben beKLeTTeren KASEIDEN
vallen
en
vallen maraudeurs in huizen lichter dan obus
filantropie
redden alle stukken van waarde

《狗》（下页右下图）取自9世纪古希腊诗人阿拉托斯的手抄书，展示早期的将文字进行游戏般排列所产生的视觉效果。下页右上图为18世纪晚期的《象形文字圣经》，此书图文并茂，让孩子们在学习时更有趣味

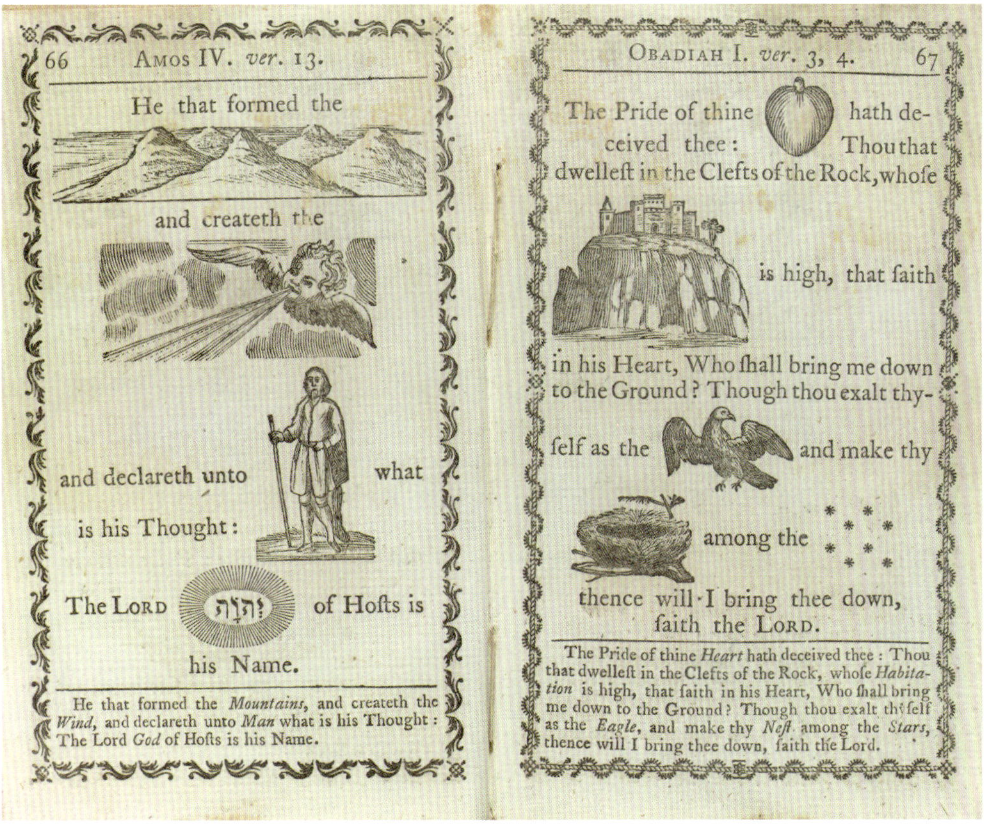
66 AMOS IV. ver. 13.
He that formed the
and createth the
and declareth unto
what
is his Thought:
The LORD
יְהוָה
of Hosts is
his Name.
He that formed the *Mountains*, and createth the *Wind*, and declareth unto *Man* what is his Thought: The Lord *God* of Hosts is his Name.
OBADIAH I. ver. 3, 4. 67
The Pride of thine
hath deceived thee: Thou that dwellest in the Clefts of the Rock, whose
is high, that saith
in his Heart, Who shall bring me down to the Ground? Though thou exalt thyself as the
and make thy
among the
thence will I bring thee down, saith the LORD.
The Pride of thine *Heart* hath deceived thee: Thou that dwellest in the Clefts of the Rock, whose *Habitation* is high, that saith in his Heart, Who shall bring me down to the Ground? Though thou exalt thyself as the *Eagle*, and make thy *Nest* among the *Stars*, thence will I bring thee down, saith the Lord.

Namquepedes subter rutilo cumlumine clare
Feruidusillecanis stellarum lucere fulgens
Hunctegit obscurus subter praecordia uesper
Etuero toto spirans decorpore flammam
Aestiferos ualidis erumpit flatibus ignes
Totus ab ore micans iacitur mortalibus ardor
Hic ubi se pariter cum sole inlumina caeli
Extulit haud patitur foliorumtegminefrustra
Suspensos animos arbusta ornata tenere

NICANOR PARRA
ANTIPOEMS
THE ANTI - LAZARUS
WHATEVER YOU DO DON'T RISE UP FROM THE GRAVE
WHY SHOULD YOU BE NERVOUS
LIKE THE POET ONCE SAID
YOU HAVE YOUR WHOLE DEATH IN FRONT OF YOU.
PIANO SOLO
I WANT MY SOUL TO FIND ITS PROPER BODY
I WISH TO MAKE A NOISE WITH MY FEET
PUSSYKATTEN
WHITE WITH ASHES HIS SPINE
SHOWS HE'S A CAT
WHOSE PLACE IS BEYOND GOOD OR EVIL

些诗歌往往被称为“具象诗歌”，有时也被称为“图画诗”或“立体诗”，西文为calligrams，来自法国诗人纪尧姆·阿波利奈尔（Guillaume Apollinaire）的组诗*Calligrammes*，此组诗于1918年在诗人去世后不久出版，这类诗歌以此得名。

艺术家手制书（Livre d'artiste或Artist's Book）的概念在20世纪初期于法国出现。法国画商安博罗斯·沃拉尔（Ambroise Vollard）出版的魏尔伦（Paul Verlaine）的《平行》（*Parallelement*，1900年，见下页图），将平面艺术家和诗人结合起来，试图创造一本超越插图本的书籍。到了20世纪后期，更富有想象力的艺术家手制书真正蓬勃发展起来，艺术家们的出发点不再只是文字和图像，而是书籍这种物质实体，在他们的作品中，书籍的实体和书内的文本是同等重要的概念。例如美国艺术家玛格丽特·考夫曼（Margaret Kaufman）的《莎莉姑妈的哀歌》（*Aunt Sallie's Lament*），从表面上来看，这是一首缝制被子的诗篇，它被印制在多种形状的纸页上，仿佛拼凑被面所用的不同布料；同时，这本书能以不同的顺序打开，字词的组合会随之改变，如果没有这种实体形式，字词本身就不会有什么意义。智利诗人尼可那·派拉（Nicanor Parra）的《反传统书》（*Antibook*）由一系列短诗组成，如果将此书按照传统习惯从左往右翻阅，读者看到的只是一些不规则、不连贯的字句，但如果你将页面拆开，重新折叠成一个三维多面体，你就能看到完整流畅的诗句。按照这种思路进行创作，走得比较极端的可能要算是美国艺术家基思·史密斯（Keith Smith）的《线书》（*String Book*），这本艺术家手制书的内容是一些根本没有文字的空白页面，每页上有不同数量的小孔，白线从这些小孔中穿过。翻阅这些页面时，能给读者带来视觉、触觉和听觉的体验，这是一件艺术品，它依靠书本的实体形式来达到效果，让读者将注意力完全集中在作为物体的书上。一本没有文字的书，是否还能被称为书呢？

（左页图）

尼可那·派拉的《反传统书》，只有在从传统书本形式转换为三维立体后，其内容才得以显现

（下页图）

安博罗斯·沃拉尔出版的魏尔伦的诗集《平行》，邀请艺术家博纳尔（Paul Bonnard）创作石版画插图，图文并茂，让诗作内容更生动，此书被视为第一本真正的“艺术家手制书”

«Elle a, ta chair, le charme sombre
Des maturités estivales,
Elle en a l'ambre, elle en a l'ombre;

«Ta voix tonne dans les rafales,
Et ta chevelure sanglante
Fuit brusquement dans la nuit lente.»

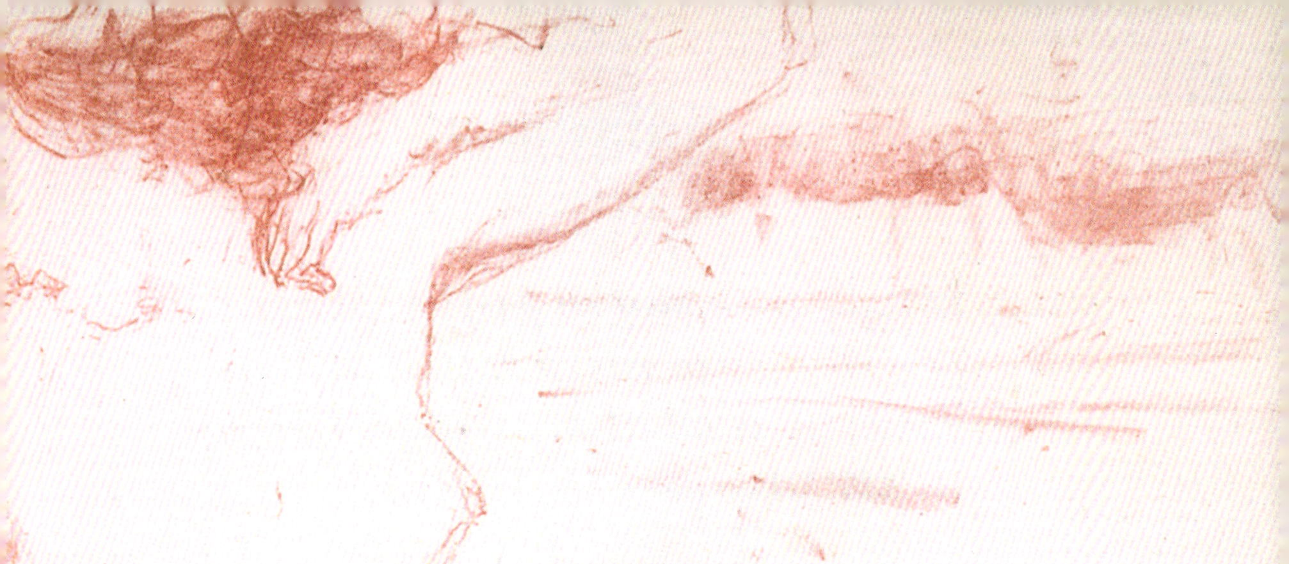

SAPPHO.

Furieuse, les yeux caves & les seins roides,
Sappho, que la langueur de son désir irrite,
Comme une louve court le long des grèves froides;

Elle songe à Phaon, oublieuse du Rite,
Et, voyant à ce point ses larmes dédaignées,
Arrache ses cheveux immenses par poignées;

Puis elle évoque, en des remords sans accalmies,
Ces temps où rayonnait, pure, la jeune gloire
De ses amours chantés en vers que la mémoire
De l'âme va redire aux vierges endormies :

《莎莉姑妈的哀歌》，此书是文本和实体形式的实验，两者共同反映书之主题

基思·史密斯的《线书》，此书舍弃了文字内容，读者的感官体验完全来自它的实体形式

当代艺术家们对书籍的形式和内容进行了各种尝试，有些尝试被推到极致。他们有的用镜子或草制成书，上面没有任何文字；有的制作了有文字的书形雕塑。大家会争论一本“艺术家手制书”究竟是书，还是艺术品，或两者都不是。无论如何，这些作品可以引发人们对书籍的样式及概念的进一步思考

牛津
OXFORD
高阶英汉双解词典
ADVANCED LEARNER'S
English-Chinese Dictionary
第6版

3

CHAPTER THREE

INDIVIDUALITY WITHIN MASS PRODUCTION

第三章
同一性中的个性

（左页图）
中国的大型印刷厂为中国及海外的许多出版社印刷书籍，工人正在生产《英汉词典》

印刷的书籍——我们手中持有的实体物品——是工厂的批量产品。从最广义、最简单的理论层面来说，从原材料开始，到最终一大批出厂，它们是生产线上的产物。在这里，可复制性和统一性是很重要的概念，它们是印刷发明带来的结果，文本用金属活字排版后可被印刷，被大批量复制，让无数读者同时拥有。这是印刷书和手抄书之间的重要区别。手抄书独一无二，即使出自同一位抄书人，两次抄写出的同一个文本，也会有差异。如果出自两位抄书人之手，并在不同的地方抄写而成，那么它们会拥有更明显的个体特征。

— 印刷中的多样性 —

事实上，说某种书印刷出的所有印本都完全相同，这个泛泛的声明可能过分简单。因为在印刷厂的生产过程中，有意或无意之间，可能会有意外发生。从理论上讲，出版社让印刷厂印制一定数量的某一书籍，那么每本在离开生产线时，应该都是完全一样的，当读者在书店要购买此书时，这一本和那一本应该没有区别。但如果其中某一本在印刷时出了点小差错，例如某页上的油墨没有处理好，或书页剪裁时不准确，那么，这本和那本就会有明显的差异。

印刷的程序：

在19世纪印刷机械化之前，书籍印刷和其他环节一样，也是全手工的过程。印刷作坊的工匠们接受过培训，他们尽量争取同一本书的不同印本之间没有区别。但与现在的大规模机械化生产相比，手工印制的过程中，印本之间不可避免地会容易出现差别

印刷的第一步是排版，排版师挑选铅字字母，将它们按照文本的正确顺序排好，排完一个完整的页面后，这些铅字会被锁定在一个框架之内，以供印刷

印刷机上放置排好的铅字版面，印刷师正在手工用墨垫为版面上墨。印刷所用的纸张会被放入特制的框架中（压纸格和夹纸框），框架被折回到涂过油墨的版面上进行印刷。每张纸都将被正反印刷两次，纸上可能有书中的多个页面

印刷的最后一个步骤，将涂过油墨并覆盖好纸张的版面放在印刷机的正中，用有螺旋构造的压力机将纸张压在排字版上。印好后的纸张被悬挂晾干，然后被折叠并按照一定顺序排列。每本书的每一页都是以这种方法印成的，手动印刷的基本技术和设备，几个世纪以来一直没有改变

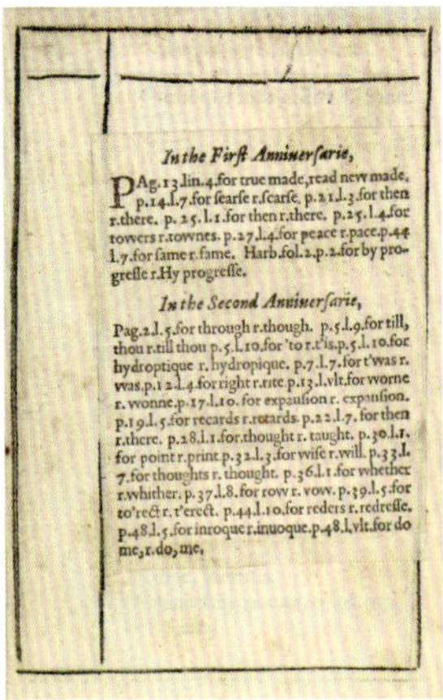
In the First Anniversarie,

PAg.13.lin.4.for true made,read new made. p.14.l.7.for fearse r.scarse. p.21.l.3.for then r.there. p.25.l.1.for then r.there. p.25.l.4.for towers r.townes. p.27.l.4.for peace r.pace.p.44 l.7.for same r.fame. Harb.fol.2.p.2.for by progresse r.Hy progresse.

In the Second Anniversarie,

Pag.2.l.5.for through r.though. p.5.l.9.for till, thou r.till thou p.5.l.10.for 'to r.t'is.p.5.l.10.for hydroptique r.hydropique. p.7.l.7.for t'was r. was.p.12.l.4.for right r.rite p.13.l.vlt.for worne r. wonne.p.17.l.10. for expausion r. expansion. p.19.l.5.for recards r.retards. p.22.l.7. for then r.there. p.28.l.1.for thought r. taught. p.30.l.1. for point r.print p.32.l.3.for wise r.will. p.33.l. 7.for thoughts r. thought. p.36.l.1.for whether r.whither. p.37.l.8.for row r. vow. p.39.l.5.for to'rect r. t'erect. p.44.l.10.for reders r.redresse. p.48.l.5.for inroque r.inuoque.p.48.l.vlt.for do me,r.do,me,

1612年出版的约翰·多恩的《周年纪念》(*Anniversaries*)的勘误表，现存书中，只发现一本内有此勘误表

在现代书籍的制作过程中，因为技术的进步，类似的错误已经基本上被消除。当然，任何参与过现代出版商有损版销售的人都知道，错误依然可能发生。在过去的几个世纪中，书籍制作的每个环节都是手工完成，因此印刷过程中的差别也就层出不穷。前两页的插图显示了印刷的几个步骤，文本中的每个字母都是独立的铅字，这些铅字被排好后锁定在一个框架中，形成版面，印刷时先要为版面上墨，然后将纸张按压在版面上得到书页的印痕，这些都是手工完成的，每个环节上都可能出错。字母上的油墨可能涂得不均匀，铅字可能会掉落或损坏，在印刷过程中，如果发现有差错，印工会做些刻意的纠正。印刷书籍是一个耗时的过程，可能需要几周甚至更长的时间才能完成，所以，从开始到结束，印张之间出现不同的机会非常多。在印刷的同时，校对人员也会检查文本，如有错误，印刷会暂停，对单词或拼写进行修正。

那些无法在文本上直接修正的错误，可以通过印刷勘误页来处理。勘误的一种方式是将重新印出的正确字句粘贴在错处上，还有一种方式就是整张重印，在装订时将新印的页面插入书中代替错误页面，因为它们是单页，所以能看出它们不是原来的印刷页面。书籍印刷时出的差错以及对之的修正，都能带来同一版书的多样性，在一批同时出版的书中，可能有几本没有插入勘误的页面，书中的错误没有修正；也可能有的错误页没被取出，勘误页和原页被装订到一起。

这些都是印刷过程中产生的多样性，有些是微不足道的，有些则比较重要。可能有人会争辩说，某一字母的油墨不匀或印刷机的压力不均，这些因素所造成的印本之间的不同，只有目录学迷才会感兴趣，这类似于只有集邮迷才会注意到某张邮票上四周的齿孔是否太多。相比之下，被取消或勘正的书页可能更为重要，因为从勘正的原因或可以看出作者意图的改变，或可以看出当时政治的敏感性。例如1667年首次出版的英国作家约翰·德莱顿(John Dryden)的诗歌《奇迹年》(*Annus Mirabilis*)，此诗庆祝英国海军打败荷兰海军，初版本

中的一句诗对某位英国海军上将有比较严厉的批评，后来重印了一张新的修改过的书页，替代了大多数印本中的那页。1775年，塞缪尔·约翰逊博士（Dr Samuel Johnson）的《西部岛屿之旅》（*Journey to the Western Isles*）的初版本第一次印刷时，有一段文字批评利奇菲尔德大教堂的教长和全体教士，指责他们试图出售大教堂屋顶上的铅块，这段言论很快被修改，取而代之的是一段口气温和的文字，新印的修订页也取代了原页，除了一本外，所有的印本都得到修正。此类勘正不仅出现在古籍中，现代书籍中也常有发生。有时因为法律上的原因，书籍可能会在发行前的最后一刻还要修改。格雷厄姆·格林（Graham Greene）出版于1932年的《斯坦布尔列车》（*Stamboul Train*）就是一个例子。

1932年，格雷厄姆·格林的小说《斯坦布尔列车》由海涅曼出版社（Heinemann）出版，它在预发行时，引起另一位英国作家普莱斯列（J. B. Priestley）的注意，因为格林借书中某个角色讽刺后者，普莱斯列威胁要提起诉讼。当时，他们两位都是海涅曼出版社的作者，但普莱斯列比格林名气更响更重要，所以，格林不得不做了修改，出版社重新印刷发行。此书的第一次印刷本基本都被销毁，只有少量幸存，在市场上可以卖到很高的价格

书目学家们曾提出过“最佳版本”的概念，试图对书籍印刷过程中产生的多样性进行理性的分析。它的基本思想是，印刷厂印制的每本书中，总会有一本是最完美的印本，能够最好反映作者和出版社意图。“同一版本的书”，指的是同一套排字版式所印刷出的所有书籍，在印刷过程中，这个版式没有被拆散或重新拼合，也没有其他明显改变。一本书的不同版本之间有变化和发展，这是很自然的，作者的意图可能会有改变，也有其他原因会造成版本之间的变化。研究并记录不同版本的差异，这是文本目录学的重要部分。近年来，“最佳版本”的合理性越来越受到质疑，因为人们认识到，文本以及早期读者对此文本的认知是不确定的，远远不像“最佳版本”理论中所说的那样死板。同一版本根据印刷数量，在装订前可能有数百甚至数千个印张，它们可能包含我们上面所提到的错误或修正，与“最佳版本”相去甚远。同一个版本中，还可能有各别的子版本，被单独出版和发售。如果几百套书由几家不同的书商销售，那么标题页可能会被单独印刷，以适应不同书商的销售网络。有时候，没被售出的书页可能在多年后会被配上新印刷的标题页重新装订发行，新标题页上会有新的日期，或有新的措辞，让读者觉得这是个全新的版本，其实除了标题页外，

（右图）

在1775年出版的约翰逊博士的《西部岛屿之旅》的原文中，作者写道："利奇菲尔德大教堂的神职人员应该把熔铅喝下"，后来作者觉得此话不妥，进行了修改。书中的原印刷页几乎全被销毁，取代它们的是文字温和的新书页

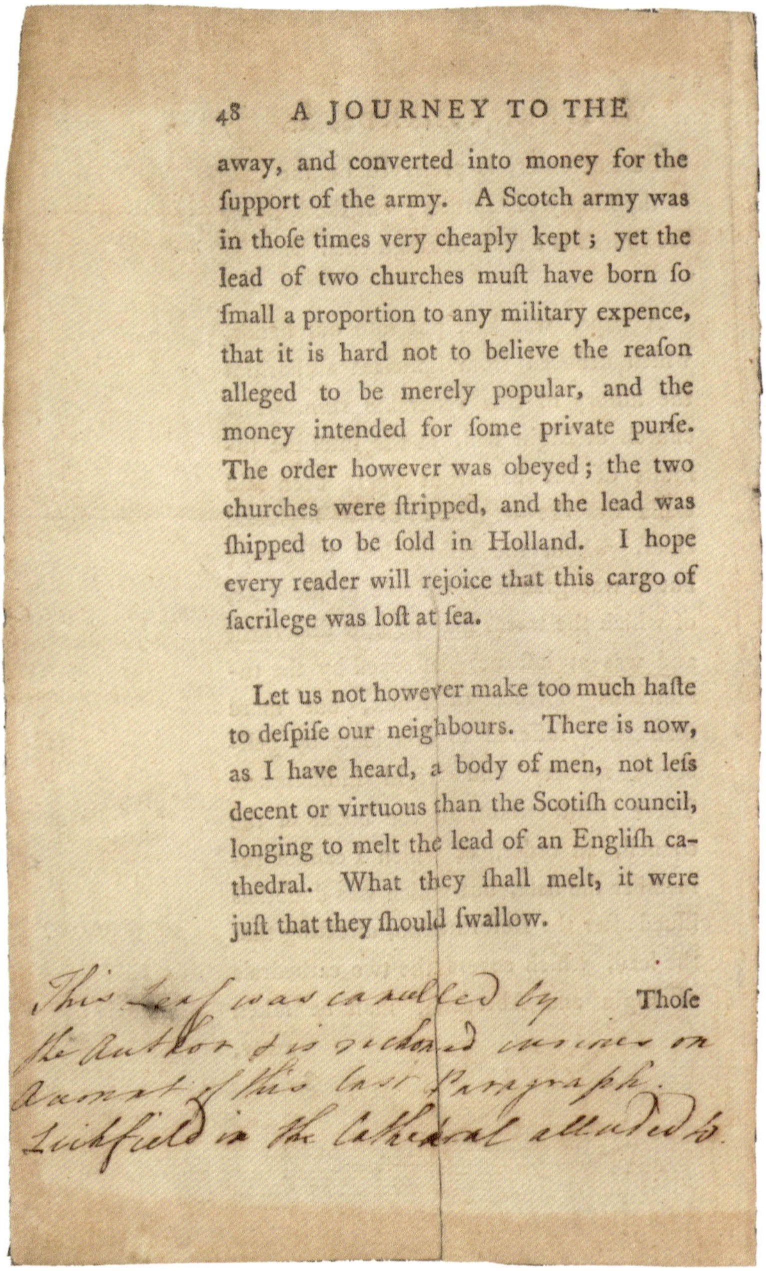

48 A JOURNEY TO THE

away, and converted into money for the ſupport of the army. A Scotch army was in thoſe times very cheaply kept; yet the lead of two churches muſt have born ſo ſmall a proportion to any military expence, that it is hard not to believe the reaſon alleged to be merely popular, and the money intended for ſome private purſe. The order however was obeyed; the two churches were ſtripped, and the lead was ſhipped to be ſold in Holland. I hope every reader will rejoice that this cargo of ſacrilege was loſt at ſea.

Let us not however make too much haſte to deſpiſe our neighbours. There is now, as I have heard, a body of men, not leſs decent or virtuous than the Scotiſh council, longing to melt the lead of an Engliſh cathedral. What they ſhall melt, it were juſt that they ſhould ſwallow.

Thoſe

This Leaf was cancelled by the Author & is reckoned curious on account of this last Paragraph. Litchfield is the Cathedral alluded to.

（右页图）

英国作家约翰·兰德尔（John Randall）的《艺术与科学导论》（*Introduction to ... arts and sciences*）于1765年在伦敦首次出版（标题页没有标注年份），二十多年后还有许多未售出的书页，于是出版商就印刷了新的标题页，用了完全不同的书名，省去了作者的名字，重新发行。两个版本除了标题页不同外，其他都完全一样，使用的都是初版印刷的那些书页

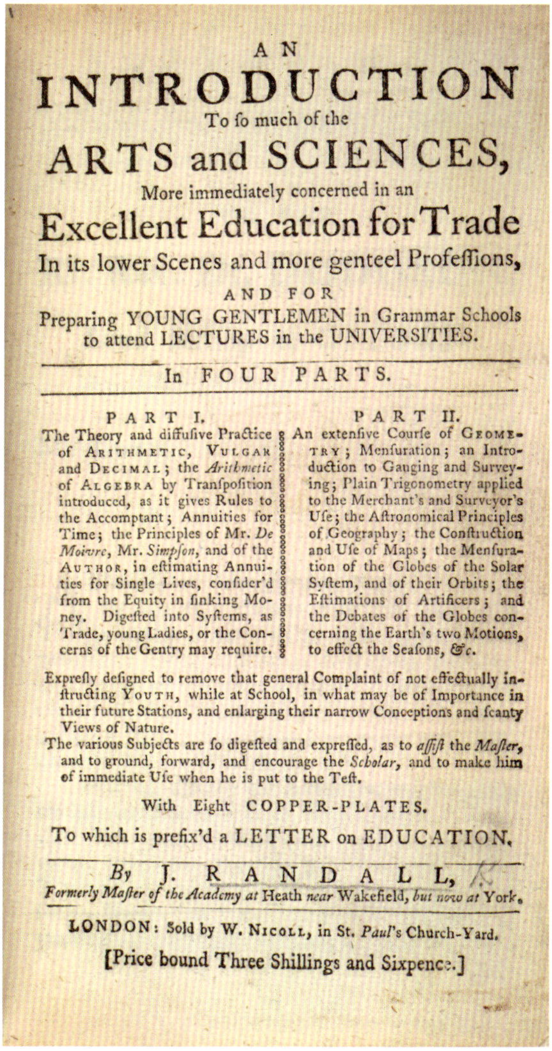

AN

INTRODUCTION

To ſo much of the

ARTS and SCIENCES,

More immediately concerned in an

Excellent Education for Trade

In its lower Scenes and more genteel Profeſſions,

AND FOR

Preparing YOUNG GENTLEMEN in Grammar Schools to attend LECTURES in the UNIVERSITIES.

In FOUR PARTS.

PART I.

The Theory and diffuſive Practice of ARITHMETIC, VULGAR and DECIMAL; the *Arithmetic* of ALGEBRA by Tranſpoſition introduced, as it gives Rules to the Accomptant; Annuities for Time; the Principles of Mr. *De Moivre*, Mr. *Simpſon*, and of the AUTHOR, in eſtimating Annuities for Single Lives, conſider'd from the Equity in ſinking Money. Digeſted into Syſtems, as Trade, young Ladies, or the Concerns of the Gentry may require.

PART II.

An extenſive Courſe of GEOMETRY; Menſuration; an Introduction to Gauging and Surveying; Plain Trigonometry applied to the Merchant's and Surveyor's Uſe; the Aſtronomical Principles of Geography; the Conſtruction and Uſe of Maps; the Menſuration of the Globes of the Solar Syſtem, and of their Orbits; the Eſtimations of Artificers; and the Debates of the Globes concerning the Earth's two Motions, to effect the Seaſons, *&c.*

Expreſly deſigned to remove that general Complaint of not effectually inſtructing YOUTH, while at School, in what may be of Importance in their future Stations, and enlarging their narrow Conceptions and ſcanty Views of Nature.

The various Subjects are ſo digeſted and expreſſed, as to *aſſiſt* the *Maſter*, and to ground, forward, and encourage the *Scholar*, and to make him of immediate Uſe when he is put to the Teſt.

With Eight COPPER-PLATES.

To which is prefix'd a LETTER on EDUCATION.

By J. RANDALL,

Formerly Maſter of the Academy at Heath *near* Wakefield, *but now at* York.

LONDON: Sold by W. NICOLL, in St. *Paul's* Church-Yard.

[Price bound Three Shillings and Sixpence.]

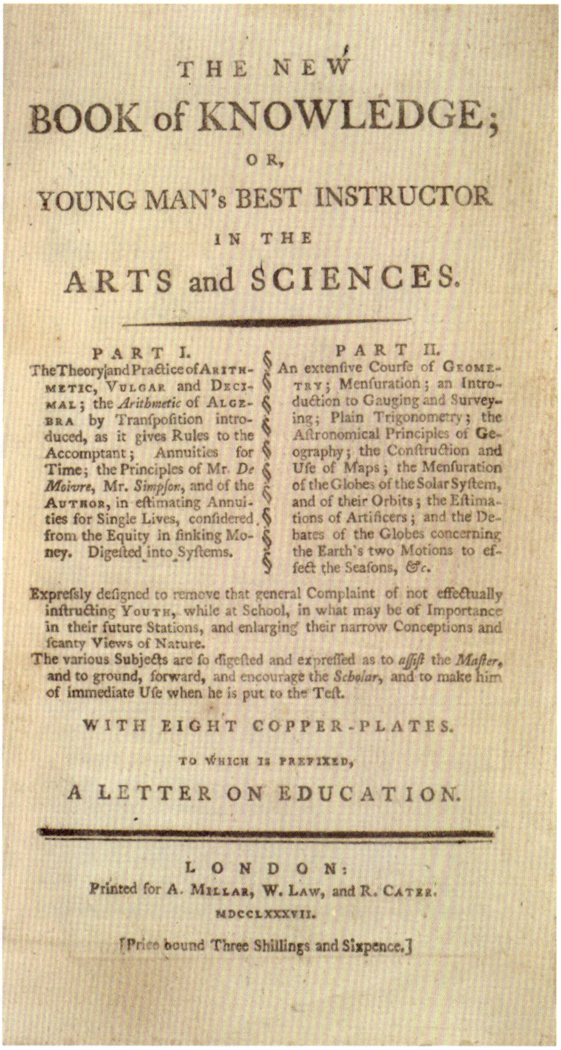

THE NEW

BOOK of KNOWLEDGE;

OR,

YOUNG MAN's BEST INSTRUCTOR

IN THE

ARTS and SCIENCES.

PART I.

The Theory and Practice of ARITHMETIC, VULGAR and DECIMAL; the *Arithmetic* of ALGEBRA by Tranſpoſition introduced, as it gives Rules to the Accomptant; Annuities for Time; the Principles of Mr. *De Moivre*, Mr. *Simpſon*, and of the AUTHOR, in eſtimating Annuities for Single Lives, conſidered from the Equity in ſinking Money. Digeſted into Syſtems.

PART II.

An extenſive Courſe of GEOMETRY; Menſuration; an Introduction to Gauging and Surveying; Plain Trigonometry; the Aſtronomical Principles of Geography; the Conſtruction and Uſe of Maps; the Menſuration of the Globes of the Solar Syſtem, and of their Orbits; the Eſtimations of Artificers; and the Debates of the Globes concerning the Earth's two Motions to effect the Seaſons, *&c.*

Expreſly deſigned to remove that general Complaint of not effectually inſtructing YOUTH, while at School, in what may be of Importance in their future Stations, and enlarging their narrow Conceptions and ſcanty Views of Nature.

The various Subjects are ſo digeſted and expreſſed as to *aſſiſt* the *Maſter*, and to ground, forward, and encourage the *Scholar*, and to make him of immediate Uſe when he is put to the Teſt.

WITH EIGHT COPPER-PLATES.

TO WHICH IS PREFIXED,

A LETTER ON EDUCATION.

LONDON:

Printed for A. MILLAR, W. LAW, and R. CATER.

MDCCLXXXVII.

[Price bound Three Shillings and Sixpence.]

¶ The third Sunday in Advent.

The Collect.

LORD, we beseech thee give eare to our prayers, and by thy gracious visitation lighten the darknesse of our hearts, by our Lord Jesus Christ. Amen.

The Epistle.

Let a man ſo account of us, as of the Miniſters of Chriſt, and ſtewards of the myſteries of God. Moreover it is required in ſtewards, that a man bee found faithfull. But with mee it is a very ſmall thing that I ſhould bee judged of you, or of mans judgement: yea, I judge not mine own ſelf. For I know nothing by my ſelf, yet am I not hereby juſtified: but he that judgeth me is the Lord. Therefore judge nothing before the time, untill the Lord come, who both will bring to light the hidden things of darkneſſe, and will make manifeſt the counſels of the 1 Cor.4.1.

¶ The third Sunday in Advent.

The Collect.

LORD, we beseech thee give eare to our prayers, and by thy gracious visitation lighten the darknesse of our hearts, by our Lord Jesus Christ. Amen.

The Epistle.

Let a man ſo account of us, as of the Miniſters of Chriſt, and ſtewards of the myſteries of God. Moreover it is required in ſtewards, that a man bee found faithfull. But with me it is a very ſmall thing that I ſhould be judged of you, or of mans judgement: yea, I judge not mine own ſelf. For I know nothing by my ſelf, yet am I not hereby juſtified: but he that judgeth me is the Lord. Therefore judge nothing before the time, untill the Lord come, who both will bring to light the hidden things of darkneſſe, and will make manifeſt the counſels of the 1 Cor.4.1.

书中的其他页面全部是几年前印刷的。

畅销书籍可以在短时间内被重印很多次（《圣经》就是最明显的例子），这对试图了解它们的出版历史的人来说，情况可能非常复杂。因为相隔数月甚至数年的印刷书页，可能会被混在一起，装订成最后的书籍。所以，我们经常发现，有一批书籍可能有相同的标题页，但内容可能来自不同时期的印刷页组合。即使是同一个版次的书籍也可能有多样性。例如1637年在苏格兰出版的一本祈祷书，此书的出版是为了将《公祷书》（*Book of Common Prayer*）强加给苏格兰人，结果导致了民众的起义，这本书的目录学历史就反映了当时因它引起的争议。此书的整个印刷过程大约持续了一年半的时间，在这段时间里，书中的部分内容不止一次地被重新排版，页面进行了大量的更正和修改。有一些印张虽然内容和版式都一样，但使用的铅字完全不同，而且，在某些印本中，个别字句被删除或更改。所以，最后的成书虽然乍看起来没有区别，但实际上没有两本是完全相同的。如果你把现存的任何两本并排放置，你就会发现它们有这样或那样的如内容、版式、字体、装饰等不同。

由于以上种种原因，书籍在印刷过程中会出现多样性，因此我们所期望的同一版本的书籍一致性也就不完全是现实。这些在印刷或装订时因为偶然因素造成的多样性，往往不被购买者察觉。这种多样性和我们下文要讲到的在印刷过程中故意为之的同一版本的多样性有所区别，下文所述，是出版商特地给购买者提供的不同选择。

15世纪印刷发明之时，纸张早已是手抄书或文件最常见的载体。纸张当然也是大规模印刷书籍的自然选择，但如果要出品质量更高更具永久性的文本，牛皮（特别是小牛皮）仍然是制书人的首选。所以，早期出版印刷商们在生产纸质书的同时，通常也会印一些牛皮版本，为买家提供一种更为奢侈的选择。这两种书从同一块版上印出，纸质书的数量一般占大多数。这个传统可以追溯到书籍印刷的最早阶段，第一本印刷书籍古腾堡《圣经》就同时有牛皮纸和纸质印本。整

（左页图）

此处为两本1637年出版的《苏格兰祈祷书》（*Scottish Prayer Book*），这两页有所不同，最明显的是页面上大写字母“L”周围的装饰。两页上的文字和排版乍看都一样，但仔细观察就能看出它们的细微区别，这两页显然是从不同的铅字版上印刷而成

（下页图）

这本17世纪出版的《圣经》是由两版不同的印刷书页混合装订而成。左手书页所用的是罗马字体，右手书页是黑体字。这样的混合装订可能发生在此书历史的任何阶段，可能在初印发行时，也可能在后来，如果某一本的书页被损坏或遗失，书主或书商可能从另一本中抽出书页来进行弥补，重新装订出“最佳”版本

19 A e seruant will not bee chastised with
words: though hee vnderstand, yet hee will
not || answere.
20 Seest thou a man hastie in his mat-
ters? there is more hope of a foole, then of
him.
21 He that delicately bringeth vp his ser-
uant from youth, at length he will be euen as
his sonne.
22 * An angry man stirreth vp strife, and
a furious man aboundeth in transgression.
23 * The pride of a man shall bring him
low: but the humble in spirit shall enioy
glory.
24 Hee that is partner with a thiefe, ha-
teth his owne soule: he heareth cursing and
declareth it not.
25 The feare of man bringeth a f snare:
but he that trusteth in the Lord shall bee ex-
alted.
26 Many doe seeke the face of the ruler:
but euery mans g iudgement commeth from
the Lord.
27 A wicked man is abomination to the
iust, and he that is vpright in his waye, is a-
bomination to the wicked.

e He that is of a seruile and rebellious nature.
|| Or, regard.
Chap. 15. 18.
Iob 22. 29.
f He that feareth man more then God, falleth into a snare, and is destroyed.
g Hee needeth not to flatter the ruler: for what God hath appointed, that shall come to him.

CHAP. XXX.

2 To humble our selues in consideration of Gods works 5 The word of God is perfit. 11 Of the wicked and hypocrites. 15 Of things that are neuer saciate. 18 Of others that wonderfull.

¶ The words of a AGVR the sonne
of IAKEH.

The prophesie which the man spake vnto
Ithiel, euen to b Ithiel and Ucal.
2 Surely I am more c foolish then any
man, and haue not the vnderstanding of a
man in me.
3 For I haue not learned wisedome, nor
attained to the knowledge of holy things.
4 Who hath ascended vp to d heauen, and
descended? Who hath gathered the winde in
his fist? Who hath bound the waters in a
garment? Who hath established all the ends
of the world? What is his name, and what
is his sonnes name, if thou canst tell?
5 * Euery word of God is pure: he is a
shield to those that trust in him.
6 * Put nothing vnto his words, lest hee
reproue thee, and thou be found a liar.
7 Two e things haue I required of thee:
denie me them not before I die.
8 Remoue farre from mee vanitie and
lies: giue me not pouertie, nor riches: feede
me with food conuenient for me,
9 Lest I bee full and denie thee, and say,
f Who is the Lord? or lest I bee poore, and
steale and take the Name of my God in vaine.
10 Accuse not a seruant vnto his master,
lest hee curse thee g when thou hast offen-
ded.
11 There is a generation that curseth their
father, and doeth not blesse their mother.
12 There is a generation that are pure in
their owne conceit, and yet are not washed
from their filthinesse.
13 There is a generation, whose eyes are
haughty, and their eye lids are lifted vp.

a Who was an excellent man in vertue & knowledge in the time of Salomon.
b Which were Agurs schollers or friends.
c Herein hee declareth his great humilitie, who would not attribute any wisedome to himselfe, but all vnto God.
d Meaning, to know the secrets of God, as though he would say, None.
Psal. 19. 8.
Deut. 4. 2. and 12. 32.
e He maketh this request to God.
f Meaning, that they that put their trust in their riches, forget God, & that by too much wealth men haue an occasion to the same.
g In accusing him without

vp the afflicted out of the earth, & the poore
from among men.
15 The horseleach hath two h daughters,
which cry, Giue, giue. There be three things
that will not be satisfied: yea, foure that say
not, It is enough.
16 The graue, and the barren wombe: the
earth that cannot bee satisfied with water,
and the fire that saith not it is enough.
17 The eye that mocketh his father, and
despiseth the instruction of his mother, let
the rauens i of the valley picke it out, and the
yong eagles eate it.
18 There bee three things hid from mee;
yea, foure that I know not,
19 The way of an eagle in the ayre, the
way of a serpent vpon a stone, the way of a
ship in the mids of the sea, and the way of a
man with a maide.
20 Such is the way also of an adulte-
rous woman: she eateth, and k wipeth her
mouth, and saith, I haue not committed ini-
quitie.
21 For three things the earth is moued:
yea, for foure it cannot susteine it selfe:
22 For a l seruant when he reigneth, and
a foole when he is filled with meate,
23 For the hatefull woman when she is
married, and for a handmaid that is m heire
to her mistresse.
24 These bee foure small things in the
earth, yet they are n wise, and full of wise-
dome:
25 The pismires a people not strong, yet
prepare they their meate in summer:
26 The conies a people not mightie, yet
make they their houses in the rocke,
27 The grashopper hath no king, yet goe
they forth all by bands.
28 The spider taketh holde o with her
hands, and is in kings palaces.
29 There be three things that order well
their going: yea, foure are comely in going.
30 A lion which is strong among beasts,
and turneth not at the sight of any:
31 A lusty grayhound, and a goate, and a
king against whom there is no rising vp.
32 If thou hast beene foolish in lifting thy
selfe vp, and if thou hast thought wickedly,
lay thine hand p vpon thy mouth.
33 When one churneth milke, he bringeth
foorth butter: and he that wringeth his nose,
causeth blood to come out: so he that forceth
wrath, bring foorth strife.

h The le[…] two for[…] tongue[…] here he[…] her two[…] ters, wh[…] she suc[…] blood, […] uer sat[…] so are[…] tous e[…] ners in[…]
i Whi[…] in the[…] carion[…]
k She[…] desire[…] count[…] as tho[…] were[…] wom[…]
l The[…] monk[…] state[…] they[…]
m W[…] ried t[…] fter, a[…] death[…] mist[…]
n T[…] grea[…] and[…]
o If[…] able[…] these[…] thin[…] wife[…] can[…] wise[…] man[…]
p M[…] and[…] ind[…]

CHAP. XXXI.

2 He exhorteth to chastitie and iustice, 10 And sheweth the conditions of a wise and worthy woman.

¶ 1 THE WORDS OF KING a LE-
MVEL: The b prophesie which his
mother taught him.

What my sonne! and what the sonne
of c my wombe! and what O sonne
of my desires!
3 Giue not thy strength vnto women, d nor

a T[…] lom[…] call[…] that[…] bec[…] ord[…] be l[…] Isra[…]
b The doctrine which his mother Bath-sheba taught this often repetition of one thing, she declareth her […]

him.
21 He that delicately bringeth up his servant
from a childe, shall have him become *his* son at the
length.
22 * An angry man stirreth up strife, and a
furious man aboundeth in transgression.
23 * A mans pride shall bring him low: but
honour shall uphold the humble in spirit.
24 Whoso is partner with a thief, hateth
his own soul: he heareth cursing, and bewrayeth
it not.
25 The fear of man bringeth [f] a snare: but
whoso putteth his trust in the LORD, † shall
be safe.
26 * Many seek † the rulers favour, but every
mans [g] judgement *cometh* from the LORD.
27 An unjust man *is* an abomination to the
just: and he that *is* upright in the way, *is* abomi-
nation to the wicked.

CHAP. XXX.

1 *Agurs confession of his faith.* 7 *The two points of
his prayer.* 10 *The meanest are not to be wronged.*
11 *Four wicked generations.* 15 *Four things
insatiable.* 17 *Parents are not to be despised.*
18 *Four things hard to be known.* 21 *Four
things untolerable.* 24 *Four things exceeding
wise.* 29 *Four things stately.* 32 *Wrath is to be
prevented.*

THe words of [a] Agur the son of Iakeh, *even*
the prophecie: the man spake unto Ithiel,
even unto [b] Ithiel and Ucal.
2 Surely I *am* more [c] brutish then *any* man,
and have not the understanding of a man.
3 I neither learned wisdom, nor † have the
knowledge of the holy.
4 * Who hath ascended up into [d] heaven, or
descended? * who hath gathered the winde in
his fists? who hath bound the waters in a gar-
ment? who hath established all the ends of the
earth? what *is* his name, and what *is* his sons
name, if thou canst tell?
5 * Every word of God *is* † pure: he *is* a
shield unto them that put their trust in him.
6 * Adde thou not unto his words, lest he
reprove thee, and thou be found a liar.
7 [e] Two things have I required of thee, † de-
nie me *them* not before I die.
8 Remove farre from me vanitie and lies; give
me neither poverty, nor riches, * feed me with
food † convenient for me:
9 * Lest I be full, and † deny *thee*, and say,
Who *is* the LORD? or lest I be poor, and steal,
and take the name of my God *in vain*.
10 † Accuse not a servant unto his master, lest
he curse thee, and thou be found [g] guilty.
11 *There is* a generation *that* curseth their fa-
ther, and doth not blesse their mother.
12 *There is* a generation *that are* pure in
their own eyes, and yet is not washed from their
filthinesse.
13 *There is* a generation, O how * lofty are
their eyes! and their eye-lids are lifted up.
14 * *There is* a generation, whose teeth *are as*
swords, and their jaw-teeth *as* knives, to devour
the poor from off the earth, and the needy from
among men.
15 The horsleach hath [h] two daughters,
crying, Give, give. There are three things *that*
enough:
16 The grave, and the barren womb, the earth
that is not filled with water, and the fire *that*
saith not, *It is* enough.
17 The eye *that* mocketh at *his* father, and
despiseth to obey his mother, the ravens of ‖ the
[i] valley shall pick it out, and the young eagles
shall eat it.
18 There be three things *which* are too wonder-
full for me; yea, four which I know not:
19 The way of an eagle in the air, the way of
a serpent upon a rock, the way of a ship in the
† midst of the sea, and the way of a man with a
maid.
20 Such *is* the way of an adulterous woman;
she eateth, and [k] wipeth her mouth and saith, I
have done no wickednesse.
21 For three things the earth is disquieted, and
for four *which* it cannot bear:
22 * For [l] a servant when he reigneth, and a
fool when he is filled with meat,
23 For an odious *woman* when she is married,
and an handmaid that is [m] heir to her mistresse.
24 There be four things which are little upon
the earth, but they *are* † [n] exceeding wise:
25 * The ants *are* a people not strong, yet they
prepare their meat in the summer;
26 The conies *are but* a feeble folk, yet make
they their houses in the rocks;
27 The locusts have no king, yet go they forth
all of them † by bands;
28 The spider taketh hold with her [o] hands,
and is in kings palaces.
29 There be three things which go well, yea
four are comely in going:
30 A lion *which is* strongest among beasts, and
turneth not away for any,
31 A ‖ † grey-hound, an he-goat also, and a
king against whom *there is* no rising up.
32 If thou hast done foolishly in lifting up thy
self, or if thou hast thought evil, * [p] *lay* thine hand
upon thy mouth.
33 Surely the churning of milk bringeth forth
butter, and the wringing of the nose bringeth
forth blood: so the forcing of wrath bringeth
forth strife.

‖ Or, *the brook*.
i Which haunt in the valley for carrions.
† Heb. *heart*.
k She hath her desires, and after counterfeiteth as though she were an honest woman.
* Chap. 19. 10.
l These commonly abuse the state whereunto they are called.
m Which is married to her master after the death of her mistresse.
† Heb. *wise, made wise*.
n They contain great doctrine and wisdom.
* Chap. 6. 6, &c.
† Heb. *gathered together*.
o If man be not able to compasse these common things by his wisdom, we cannot attribute wisdom to man but folly.
‖ Or, *horse*.
† Heb. *girt in the loins*.
* Job 21. 5. and 40. 4.
p Make a stay, and continue not in doing evil.

CHAP. XXXI.

1 *Lemuels lesson of chastity and temperance.* 6 *The
afflicted are to be comforted and defended.* 10 *The
praise and properties of a good wife.*

THe words of king [a] Lemuel, the prophecie that
his [b] mother taught him.
2 What, my son? and what, the [c] son of my
womb? and what, the son of my vows?
3 Give not thy strength unto women, nor thy
wayes to that which [d] destroyeth kings.
4 *It is* not for kings, O Lemuel, *it is* not for
kings to drink wine, nor for princes, [e] strong
drink:
5 Lest they drink, and forget the law, and † per-
vert the judgement † of any of the afflicted.
6 * Give strong drink unto him that is ready
to perish, and wine to those that be † of heavy
hearts.
7 Let him drink and forget his poverty, and
remember his misery [f] no more.
8 Open thy mouth for the [g] dumb in the
cause of all † such as are appointed to destru-
ction.

a That is, of Solomon, who was called Lemuel, that is, of God, because God had ordained him to be king over Israel.
b The doctrine which his mother Bath-sheba taught him.
c By this often repetition of one thing she declareth her motherly affection.
d Meaning, that women are the destruction of kings, if they haunt them.
e That is, the king must not give himself to wantonnesse, and neglect

e same.
* Chap. 6. ... † Heb. *hurt not with thy tongue*. g In accusing him

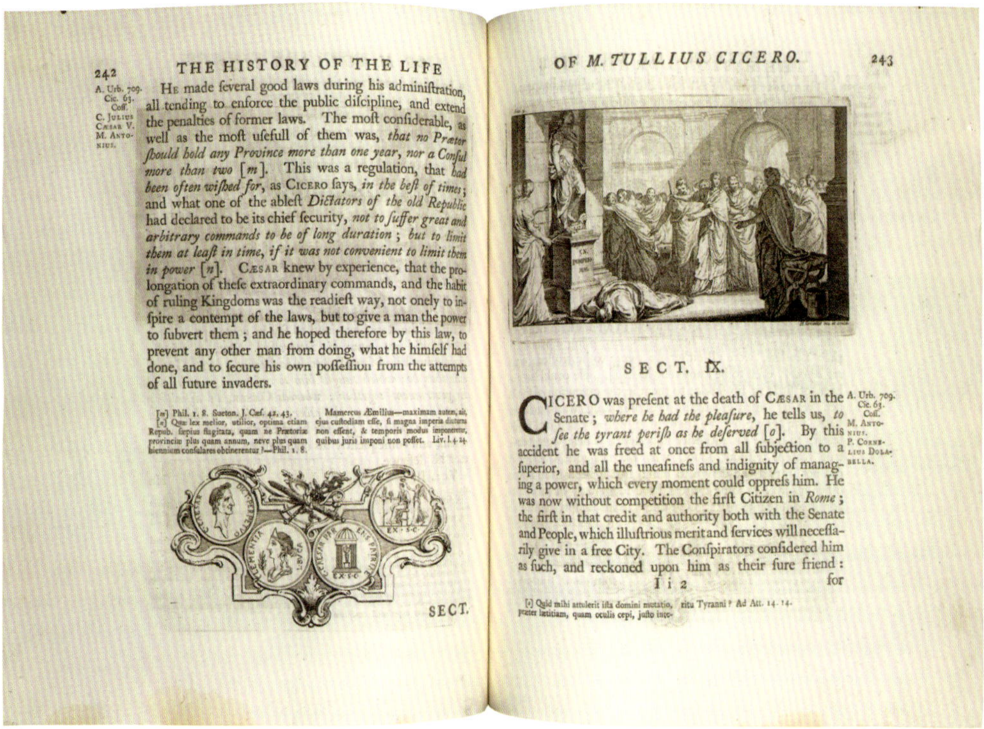
242 THE HISTORY OF THE LIFE

A. Urb. 709. Cic. 63. Coss. C. Julius Cæsar V. M. Antonius.

He made ſeveral good laws during his adminiſtration, all tending to enforce the public diſcipline, and extend the penalties of former laws. The moſt conſiderable, as well as the moſt uſefull of them was, *that no Prætor ſhould hold any Province more than one year, nor a Conſul more than two* [m]. This was a regulation, that *had been often wiſhed for*, as Cicero ſays, *in the beſt of times*; and what one of the ableſt *Dictators of the old Republic* had declared to be its chief ſecurity, *not to ſuffer great and arbitrary commands to be of long duration; but to limit them at leaſt in time, if it was not convenient to limit them in power* [n]. Cæsar knew by experience, that the prolongation of theſe extraordinary commands, and the habit of ruling Kingdoms was the readieſt way, not onely to inſpire a contempt of the laws, but to give a man the power to ſubvert them; and he hoped therefore by this law, to prevent any other man from doing, what he himſelf had done, and to ſecure his own poſſeſſion from the attempts of all future invaders.

[m] Phil. 1. 8. Sueton. J. Cæſ. 42, 43.
[n] Quæ lex melior, utilior, optima etiam Repub. ſæpius flagitata, quam ne Prætoriæ provinciæ plus quam annum, neve plus quam biennium conſulares obtinerentur?—Phil. 1. 8. Mamercus Æmilius—maximam autem, ait, ejus cuſtodiam eſſe, ſi magna imperia diuturna non eſſent, & temporis modus imponeretur, quibus juris imponi non poſſet. Liv. l. 4. 24.

SECT.

OF M. TULLIUS CICERO. 243

SECT. IX.

A. Urb. 709. Cic. 63. Coss. M. Antonius. P. Cornelius Dolabella.

Cicero was preſent at the death of Cæsar in the Senate; *where he had the pleaſure*, he tells us, *to ſee the tyrant periſh as he deſerved* [o]. By this accident he was freed at once from all ſubjection to a ſuperior, and all the uneaſineſs and indignity of managing a power, which every moment could oppreſs him. He was now without competition the firſt Citizen in *Rome*; the firſt in that credit and authority both with the Senate and People, which illuſtrious merit and ſervices will neceſſarily give in a free City. The Conſpirators conſidered him as ſuch, and reckoned upon him as their ſure friend:

I i 2 for

[o] Quid mihi attulerit iſta domini mutatio, præter lætitiam, quam oculis cepi, juſto interitu Tyranni? Ad Att. 14. 14.

个手工印刷的年代，也一直保留着这一传统。到了16世纪早期以后，印书时使用牛皮这种奢侈材料不太常见了，但并没完全消失。18和19世纪也有一些用牛皮印刷发行的书籍。更为常见的是印刷所提供不同纸张的选择，出版商用不同厚度或色度的纸张来印刷某书的同一版本。从1569年到1572年，安特卫普的出版商克里斯托弗·普朗丁（Christopher Plantin）印刷的大型多卷本《圣经》，就是用四种不同的纸张和牛皮印刷的，价格依据纸张质量而定。除了使用不同的普通白纸外，出版商为追求新奇，有时也会用彩色纸印刷一部分。

书籍出版的另外一种能在印刷过程中使用的技巧是出版某本书的

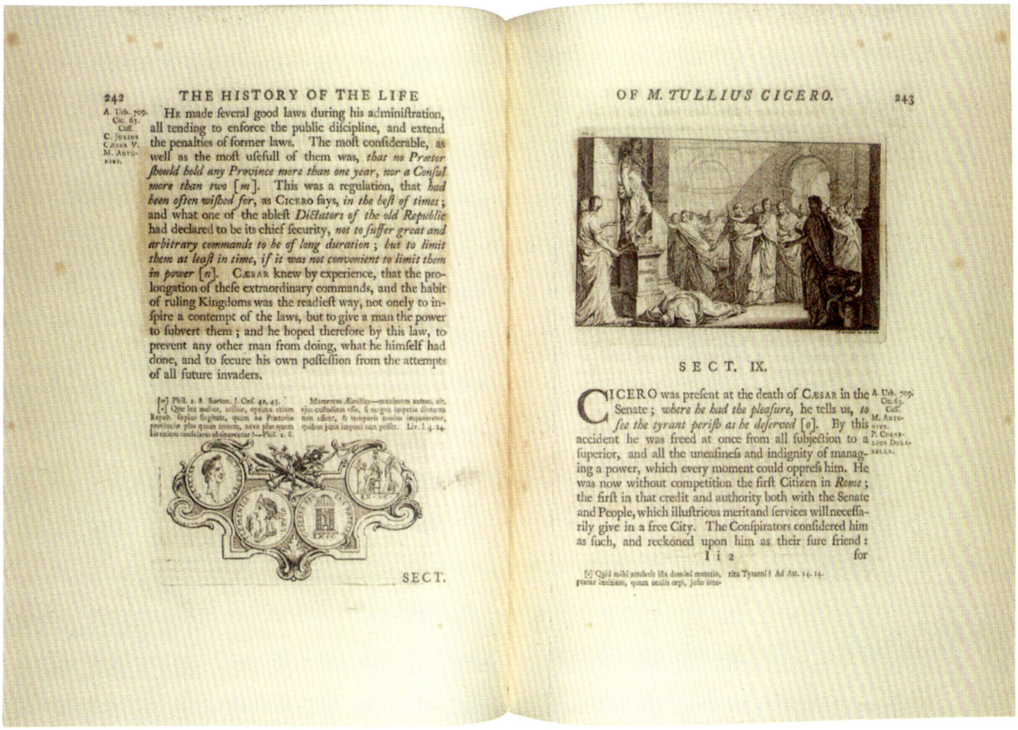

豪华本，也就是用大型纸张印制。这种豪华本的文本排版和普通版本是完全一样的，只是在排版框架固定之后，印刷时，对页框架之间的距离被加大，所用的纸张也比较大。其结果是同样的文本和版式，但是页面上的内外留白会有更多空间。这样的版本能吸引富有的购书者，此类豪华本一度曾非常流行，特别是在18世纪手工印书坊的后期。鉴别豪华版本和普通版本时，最精确的办法是比较它们的订口留白，因为在书籍装订时，翻口留白有可能被裁掉，但订口留白是不可能被裁掉的。

（*左页图及上图*）

对挑剔的顾客来说，用超大的纸张印刷，可以给他们提供一个豪华的选择。和普通纸印刷的版本相比，它们的排版是一样的，只是在排版的框架固定之后，印刷时，两个相邻的框架之间的距离被加大，并用大纸印刷，这样页面之间就有更充裕的留白。这里是1741年出版的英国神学家康尼尔斯·米德尔顿（Conyers Middleton）的《西塞罗传》（*Life of Cicero*）的普通本和豪华本

IV. THE SACRIFICE.

OH all ye, who paſs by, whoſe eyes and mi
  To worldly things are ſharp, but to me b
To me, who took eyes that I might you find:
          Was ever grief like mine?

The Princes of my people make a head
Againſt their Maker: they do wiſh me dead,
Who cannot wiſh, except I give them bread:
          Was ever grief like mine?

Without me each one, who doth now me brav
Had to this day been an Egyptian ſlave.
They uſe that power againſt me, which I gave
          Was ever grief like mine?

Mine own Apoſtle, who the bag did bear,
Though he had all I had, did not forbear
To ſell me alſo, and to put me there:
          Was ever grief like mine?

For thirty pence he did my death deviſe,
Who at three hundred did the ointment prize,
Not half ſo ſweet as my ſweet ſacrifice:
          Was ever grief like mine

Therefore my ſoul melts, and my heart's dear t
Drops blood (the only beads) my words to m
O let this cup paſs, if it be thy pleaſure:
          Was ever grief like mine

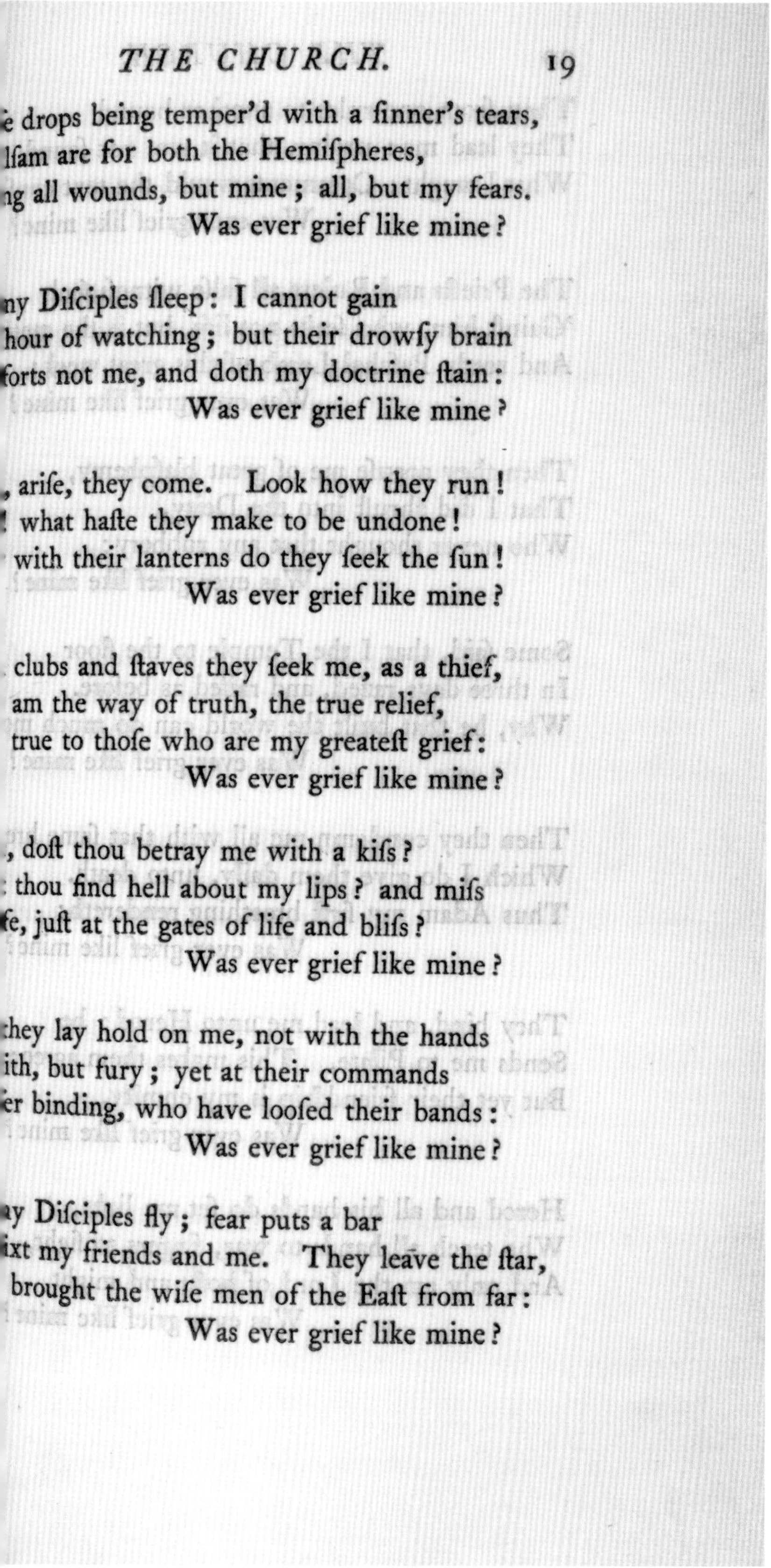

英国出版家威廉·皮克林（William Pickering）1844年版的威尔士诗人乔治·赫伯特的《圣殿》（*The Temple*），其中一些是印刷在牛皮上，为买家提供了豪华的选择，此为一例

Exhortation to auoid hast, and to work by good aduisement.
Epistle of vartuous busines, eschewing idlenesse.
A Ballad to the Sheriffes and Aldermen of London on a May morning.
A disguising before the Mayor of London by the Mercers.
A disguising before the Mayor by the Goldesmithes.
A mumming before the king at Eltham.
A disguising before the king in the castle of Hartford.
A disguising before the great estates of the land.
A mumming before the king at Windsore.
A balad giuen to Hen. the 6. and his mother, on Newyeres day at Hartford.
All thinges are right, so as the Crab goeth forward.
Chusing loues of S. Valentines day.
Of an Esquire that serued in Loues court.
Of a gentlewoman that loued a man of great estate.
Of the ladie of Holland, and Duke of Gloceste[r] before their marriage.
Of Iacke Wat that could pluck the lining out [of] a blacke boll.
Gallaunts, England may waile that euer th[ey] came here.
Æsops Fables moralised in mitre.
The churle and the bird.
The horse, sheepe, and goose.
Gwy Earle of Warwick, & Colbrond the Dan[e].
Prouerbs of Lidgate.
Complaint for departing of T. Chaucer in France embassadour.
Of two mõstrous beasts, Bicorn, & Chichefach[e].
The serpent of diuision.
The temple of Glasse.
The life and martyrdome of S. Edmond King [of] the East Angles.
The roiall receiuing of Hen. the 6. into his n[o]ble citie of London, after his returne out [of] France, Iohn Wells being Maior.
Lidgates Testament.

Heywoods prouerbs, with his, & Sir Thomas Mores Epigrams, may serue for sufficient
supplies of manie of theis deuises. And now translated Petrarch, Ariosto,
Tasso, & Bartas himself deserue curious comparison with Chaucer, Lidgate,
& owre best English, auncient & moderne. Amongst which, the
Countesse of Pembrokes Arcadia, & the Faerie Queene ar now freshest
in request: & Astrophil, & Amyntas ar none of the idlest pastimes of
sum fine humanists. The Earle of Essex much
commendes Albions England: and not unworthily for diuerse
notable pageants, before, & in the Chronicle.
Sum English, & other Histories nowhere more sensibly described,
or more inwardly discouered. The Lord Mountioy ma[kes]
the like account of Daniels peece of the Chronicle, touching th[e]
Usurpation of Henrie of Bullingbrooke. Which in deede is a f[ine]
sententious, & politique peece of Poetrie: as proffitable, as pleasurab[le].
The younger sort takes much delight in Shakespeares Venus, & Adonis:
but his Lucrece, & his tragedie of Hamlet, Prince of Denmarke, hau[e it]
in them, to please the wiser sort. Or such poets: or better: or none.
Vilia miretur vulgus: mihi flauus Apollo
Pocula Castalia plena ministret aqua: quoth Sir Edward Dier, bet[ween]
iest, & earnest. Whose written deuises farr excell most of the Sonets, an[d]
Cantos in print. His Amaryllis, & Sir Walter Raleighs Cynthia
how fine & sweet inuentions? Excellent matter of emulation for Spencer,
Constable, France, Watson, Daniel, Warner, Chapman, Siluester,
Shakespeare, & the rest of owr florishing metricians. I looke for much
aswell in verse, as in prose, from mie two Oxford frends, Doctor Gager, & M. Hac[kluit]
both rarely furnished for the purpose: & I haue a phansie to Owens new Epi[grams]
as pithie as elegant, as plesant as sharp, & sumtime as weightie as breife: & amo[ngst]
so manie gentle, noble, & royall spirits meethinkes I see sum heroicall thing in the
clowdes: mie soueraine hope. Axiophilus shall forgett himself, or will reme[mber]
to leaue sum memorials behinde him: & to make an vse of so manie rhapsodies, can[tos]
hymnes, odes, epigrams, sonets, & discourses, as at idle howers, or at flowing fitt[s]

4

CHAPTER FOUR

VARIETY THROUGH OWNERSHIP

第四章 因藏家而得不同

在印刷过程中，同一版本的书籍会被加入某些个性化的因素，等书籍离开印厂，它们个性化的机会更会倍增。例如，一次印刷某书的一千本，我们看到这一千套尚未装订的书页，因为印刷过程中有意或无意的因素，这一千套书页可能并不完全相同，但你如果把它们看作一千个个体，就知道此时它们正站在同样的起点上，等待被交付给装帧师、书商和读者，它们会走向各自的发展之路。

随着时间的推移，这些书籍都会拥有自己独特的历史。这一千套会被分送到不同的书商手中，会有相似或是不同的装订。等它们一旦被人购买，它们的命运就可能从一位拥有者转移到另一位拥有者的手中，甚至在几代人的手中走过，每本书的旅程都是独一无二的。其中一些可能在私人藏家手中周转，另一些可能会直接进入图书馆等公共机构，也可能在私人收藏之后进入公共机构。有些可能在出版后的几年内，也可能在出版的几百年后被销毁。有史以来，无数书籍已经不复存在，它们的销毁可能是有意的，也可能是意外。如果我们找到同一版本的所有幸存书籍，将它们并排放在一起，我们会看到，它们没有两本是相同的。美国华盛顿的福尔杰莎士比亚图书馆（Folger Shakespeare Library）收藏的八十二册莎士比亚的《第一对开本》（*Shakespeare's First Folio*）闻名于世，这批藏书中的每一本都在印张、装帧、标志、收藏历史等方面有着独一无二之处。

书籍藏家究竟有多重要？这要看他们会在书上留下哪些独特的历史痕迹。书籍影响、塑造并反映人们的兴趣。某本书曾在某个特定阶段被某人拥有，这样的记录可以告诉后人有关藏家以及文本的信息。它可以让我们对藏家的品位、智识和财力进行推断（例如此书是简单还是豪华装帧），也能显示出不同历史时期读者们对某一文本的接受情况。如果某本书被批注过，我们可以进一步分析读者和文本之间的私密关系，以及此书在那个时代的影响。阅读史研究是使用幸存的证据，更好地了解单个读者或一代读者与书籍之间的关系，他们如何互相影响，这种研究已经成为一门很流行的学问。在过去的十年中，已有大量有关阅读史的书籍、文章和网上数据库出现。

研究某本书的个性化历史，我们能依据各种不同的证据，但并不是每本书都留有证据。数百年来，许多藏书家以各种不同的方式在书上标注他们的拥有权，但也有许多没做任何标注。一本 17 世纪的书籍里没有标记、批注、藏书票或任何能够显示它曾被人拥有的证据，这并不罕见。书籍曾被修复、被重新装订，有时还可能不止一次，虽然这些时间点本身也是历史记录的一部分，可能拥有能被解释的信息，但书籍原装帧和扉页的舍弃，肯定会造成关于此书的许多早期信息的丢失。过去许多年，藏书的风尚是倾向于收集干净的版本，不喜欢前任藏家的批注或涂鸦，所以，新主人会特意除去旧主人的标志及题字，或将书中的藏书票取下。图书馆通常更是认为书籍的重要性完全在于文本，所以，它们也只对文本进行关注，传统的图书馆目录主要记录作者和书名，很少会关注前任藏家和装帧的任何信息，这种情况近年来才有所改变。过去，图书修复的首要目的是要为文本的阅读提供一个结实的载体，现在，随着数字文本以及其他复制本的出现，这种观念已经被完全颠覆了。一本 20 世纪装订的 16 世纪出版的《乔叟作品集》，因为重新装订过，上面干干净净的没有任何旧主人的痕迹，也没有任何眉批或题字，虽然它仍是一本历史文献，但是它能为读者和学者提供的，与大量的电子文本和后代的纸质印刷品并没有

最值得一提的是加布里埃尔·哈维所拥有的 1598 年出版的《乔叟作品集》，他在上面题写的笔记中第一次在历史上提到莎士比亚的《哈姆雷特》（86 页插图，左为细部）

区别。这本《乔叟作品集》与另一本同时代出版的经过同样净化处理的也没有不同。但是，英国作家加布里埃尔·哈维（Gabriel Harvey）曾经拥有过的一本 1598 年出版的《乔叟作品集》就大大不同，上面有许多他有关同时代诗人的笔记和评论，其中包括最早提到的关于《哈姆雷特》的文字。显而易见，这本《乔叟作品集》，是独一无二、不可取代的。

— 拥有者的印记 —

人们以很多方式在书籍上留下他们的痕迹，有的在标题页写下了他们的名字，有的贴上他们的藏书票，有的在装帧时标示出他们的姓名或家族徽章，有的在书上记录他们的训诫和箴言。当然，并不是所有的拥有者都在书本上显示自己的身份，他们也可能对文本做出反馈，在空白处写下笔记，或为了突出某一段落，或对作者的某种观点表示不同意，或是补充书中的信息。

标注拥有权方法之一：
个人和机构使用各种方式来表明他们对某本书的拥有权，其中一些容易解释，另一些则不容易。

在书上题字的历史非常悠久。此处三例分别为：杜伦修道院（Durham Priory）的14世纪藏书标记；17世纪王政复辟时期藏书家安格斯列侯爵（Earl of Anglesey，1614—1686）在一本藏书标题页的签名；19世纪一位名叫伯特尔（E. H. Bentall）的先生在标题页的签名，他是“桑姆森号”的一位船员或乘客

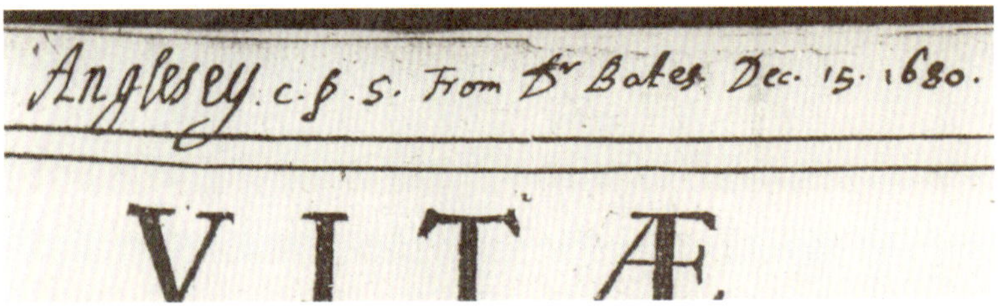

有些书的主人更喜欢密码般的题字。此例为收藏家克拉切罗德（C. M. Cracherode）的签字，他喜欢用姓名的首字母组合，而不是全名。第二例是汉斯·斯隆爵士（Sir Hans Sloane）的藏书符号，这些符号往往代表他购买时所支付的价格，大英博物馆就是在他捐赠的藏品基础上建立起来的

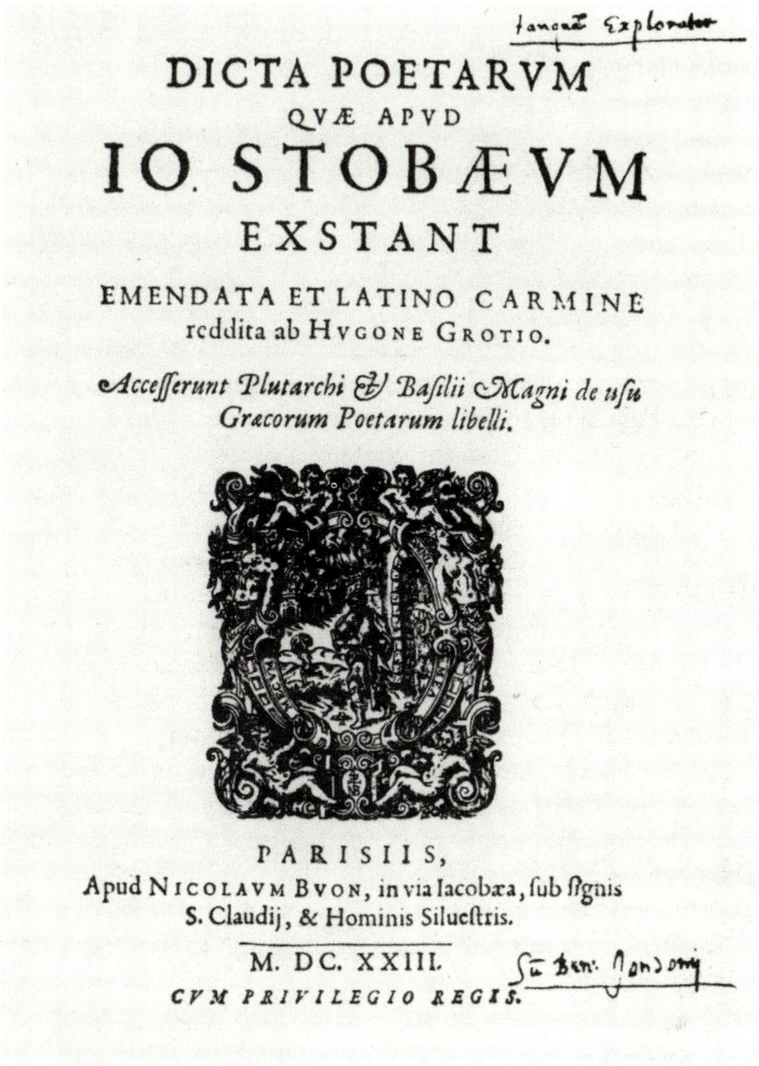

tanquã Explorator

DICTA POETARVM
QVÆ APVD
IO. STOBÆVM
EXSTANT
EMENDATA ET LATINO CARMINE
reddita ab HVGONE GROTIO.

Accesserunt Plutarchi & Basilii Magni de usu Græcorum Poetarum libelli.

PARISIIS,
Apud NICOLAVM BVON, in via Iacobæa, sub signis
S. Claudij, & Hominis Siluestris.

M. DC. XXIII.

CVM PRIVILEGIO REGIS.

Sū Ben: Jonsonij

早期的书籍拥有者们有时会在书上签名并题写他们喜欢的座右铭，例如17世纪早期的剧作家本·琼森（Ben Jonson），他的藏书中除了他的签名外，他还会用拉丁语写上“一位探险家”（tanquam exploratur）

18世纪后期开始，有一些个人和图书馆会在书中盖上图章，如左图医生托马斯·弗莱文（Thomas Frewen）和锡永学院（Sion College)图书馆的印章。18和19世纪的书中，也有人会用镂刻模版在书中印上图案，例如左图中托马斯·克拉克（Thomas Clark）的图案

标注拥有权方法之二：

藏书票有着悠久的历史，可以追溯到15世纪，成千上万的人使用过它们。藏书标签［如此处所示“伊拉斯谟·黑德”（Erasmus Head）］也被广泛使用，如同藏书票一样，藏书标签也是单独印制而成，然后被粘贴到书本上，但是使用凸版印刷而不是雕版印刷

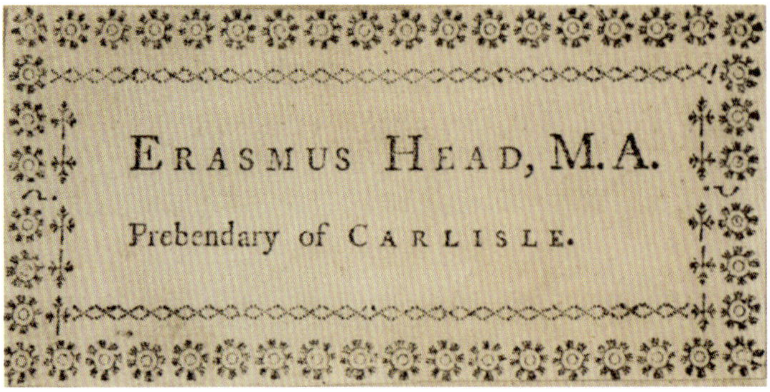

（右页图）

书籍的外表也能告诉我们它们曾经有过的主人，有些书的封面会印上藏家的名字或首字母缩写，有的会使用家族的徽章，从16世纪中叶开始，这些技术在英国就很普遍

A B

WILLIAM
MADAN
1769

"plain the meaning of its contents in words adapted to the "ideas of my thought: then he replied, "The contents are "these: FROM THIS TIME ENTER YE INTO THE MYS-"TERIES OF THE WORD, WHICH BEFORE WAS CLOSED "UP; FOR ALL ITS TRUTHS ARE SO MANY MIRRORS "OF THE LORD."

The doctrine of man's Will in its relations to the divine grace, prevenient and co-operating, is expressed with sufficient accuracy as to the fact, tho' imperfectly grounded & evolved as to the posse, by the spiritual Philagathocalethists who represent the Author's own sentiments. But the worst fault, I can find in the (declared) evil and heretical spirits, amounts to little more, than an inconvenient phraseology.—& the horrid punishments attached the latter solely on account of a supposed error, which is not declared to have influenced their lives or to preclude the love of God or of their neighbor, breathe a spirit of theological Hate akin to persecution.—Swedenborg says. From God the Lord Man receives a ~~power~~ of Will, and thro' God's effective presence he receives the power to exert this Will. The other party, meaning the same thing, says It is God that is within us both to will and to do as far as we will and do righteously.—Without the operations of the Spirit man would be as spiritually dead as a Stock or Stone.— Then (retorts Sw.) he would be no longer a Man.— Be it so! (reply the others) tho' this depends on the choice of the definition—what sound objection can be made to the position, that deserted by God Man would become a Dog, a Brute, or a Devil—according to the kind of the Support withdrawn—from him & from which he had withdrawn?

藏家在书页上写下的文字，可能只是偶尔的旁注，也可能滔滔不绝用尽书页上所有的空白处。在这里，我从流传下来的数以万计的批注中略举几例。英国律师弗朗西斯·哈格雷夫（Francis Hargrave，1741 — 1821）就是一位非常喜欢在书上批注的人物，他的许多藏书现在都在大英图书馆，特别是其中一本有关圣殿教堂（Temple Church）的小册子，空白处被写满了哈格雷夫关于此书的历史和法律方面的笔记。前面我们已经提到过的诗人兼律师加布里埃尔·哈维，他是另一位律师、诗人、讽刺作家托马斯·纳什（Thomas Nashe）的对头，也经常在书中的空白处奋笔疾书。他的私人藏书的许多册都布满了批注和笔记，那本《乔叟作品集》只不过是其中之一。浪漫主义诗人柯勒律治（Samuel Taylor Coleridge）是另一位著名的批注家，文学评论家们对他藏书中的批注和笔记都做过专门研究。

英国都铎王朝早期的伦敦史家罗伯特·法比安（Robert Fabyan，约 1445 — 1513）在他所藏的《纽伦堡编年史》（*Nuremberg Chronicle*，1493）中，写下了大量的笔记和有关当时政府官员的记录，简直就是他有关伦敦历史的个人百科全书。那些喜欢评论的人可能会更进一步，他们会将一些空白的页面和印出的书页装订在一起，以确保有足够进行评论和批注的空间。17 世纪后期英国的一位新教徒牧师约翰·华纳（John Warner），他有一本装订不同寻常的小开本《圣经》，里面有很多空白的页面，他在上面写满了笔记、感想和对前人评论的引用。也有人在课本中加插课堂笔记，例如 19 世纪早期的剑桥大学的学生沃尔特·特里维廉（Walter Trevelyan）的笔记，向我们展示了当时的化学课是如何教授、如何学习的。17 世纪早期的荷兰律师彼得·范·维恩（Peter van Veen）非常欣赏蒙田的著作，他将一本蒙田的《随笔集》送给儿子做礼物，他没有简单地在当中加插进空白的页面，而是在书后写了整整一篇个人回忆录，标注并评点书中的重要段落，还在书页的空白处用钢笔画上素描插图。

如果某本书曾被某位名人收藏过，有时这种连带关系就足以让

（左页图）

诗人柯勒律治曾在他的藏书上写过大量批注，这些文字是研究他思想的窗口，早就受到文学研究者的重视

（下页图）

弗朗西斯·哈格雷夫的藏书中布满了他的批注和评论，这本关于伦敦圣殿教堂的小册子的所有空白处，都被他写满了

and faithful reporter of the decisions of our Courts of Justice,) on the north side of the Church, was repaired and beautified. Dugdale also makes mention of the Effigy, in grey marble, of a Bishop, near the Communion-table, and truly observes that it is most excellently cut: but he adds, that of this Bishop we have no memorial.

Stow speaks of the five Effigies above-mentioned, that are inclosed within the iron-work in the Round Tower, and agrees with the other writers as to some of them, and particularly with Camden, who observes, that the reverence for the holiness of the Knights Templars who were buried there, and for that of the place itself, was such, that King Henry the Third, and many Noblemen of that time, of the highest rank and eminence in the kingdom, were desirous of being buried in this Church.

Accordingly it has been supposed that the following six persons of high rank have been buried in it; namely:—

First.—*Geoffrey de Mandeville*, or, as he is sometimes called, *de Magnaville*, or, in Latin, *de Magnâ villâ*, Earl of Essex; the shield being charged with his arms.

It is expressly stated in an antient manuscript account of the foundation of Walden Abbey, in Essex, by this Geoffrey de Mandeville, that he was buried in the Temple Church. See *Dugdale's Monasticon, Vol. 1*, page 448.

But there seems to be some doubt upon the subject, on account of the time of this Nobleman's death, which is thought to have taken place before the year 1185, in which the Temple Church was consecrated.

Secondly.—*William, Earl of Pembroke*, Earl-Marshal of England; who was Guardian of the Realm in the minority of King Henry the Third. He was, says Camden, "a powerful man in his time." He died in the year 1219, which was thirty-four years after the building of the Temple Church.

On

"On the tomb of this William," says Camden, "I read, *Comes Pembrochiæ*, and this verse :—

Miles eram Martis ; Mars multos vicerat armis.

His arms are on his shield.

Thirdly.—*William, Earl of Pembroke,* Earl-Marshall, son of the former William. He died in the year 1231.

Fourthly.—*Gilbert, Earl of Pembroke,* another son of the first William. He died in the year 1241, being slain in a Tournament at Hertford.

Touching the manner of Gilbert's death, *Weever*, in his *Antient Funeral Monuments*, page 443, observes as follows :—

" *Matthew Paris* recounts, that in the year 1241, Gilbert pro-
" claimed a Tournament in Hertford in scorn of the King's authority,
" by which such sports had been forbidden. It happened that
" himself running was, by the flinging of his horse, cast out of the
" saddle, and the horse gave him such a stroke on the breast that he
" died the same day. His bowels were interred in the Abbey of
" Hertford with the bowels of one *Sir Robert de Say*, a gallant gen-
" tleman slain in the same exercise.

Fifthly.—Here also, say both Stow and Maitland, lies *Robert Rosse*, called *Fursan*. The arms of Rosse are on his shield.

And Weever, in page 443, speaks more particularly of this person, whom he calls *Sir Robert Rosse, Knight*, and mentions the following Epitaph on him, as having formerly been seen in the Temple Church.

HIC REQUIESCIT

R. . . . . . . EQ. . . . . QUONDAM VISITATOR GENERALIS
ORDINIS MILITIÆ TEMPLI IN ANGLIA, FRANCIA, ET IN ITALIA

"This

Ordo grandimōtensis Inicıū habuit anno .1078. p Stephanū.

ORdo grādimōtēsis sb pře stephano. Anno dñi. M. lxxvj. ortū habuit. hic filı⁹ stephani nobilissimi viri de auernie partibus. a pře suo in puericia ductus ē beneuētum. vbi a sancto Milone archiepo xij. annis educatus regulā bñ viuēdi didicit. denıq3 discedens pagratis multis heremis. τ de canonicoꝝ monachoꝝ τ heremitaꝝ vita q̄ imitanda sunt memorie ɔmendans. in aqtania ꝓpe lemonicas ad montem nemorosum. q̄ muretum dr̄ xp̄o duce puenit. vbi fontes repit et rupes terrā desertā. τ iuıā q̄ tota siluestris nouo hospiti suo potū frigidissimū τ domū ventis expositā offerēs. afflictionē corpis τ requıē mētis manifestis indicijs promittebat. Tunc gaudēs stephan⁹. ibi deo se huiturū oñi tp̄e spopōdit. Trigesimū etatis sue annuz agens habitare cepit heremū in ieiunijs vigilijs τ orōnibus ɔtinuis seruiēs deo. cibus ei panis τ aq̄ τ interdū farine siliginee sorbiciūcula atq3 postq3 disponēte deo discipulorum ei⁹ numerus creuit. Insimul nō q̄si vn⁹ ex illis factus est. ß minor oībus illis. Tādem ī infirmitate ɔstitutus in q̄ decessit fratribus ait. Deū vobis relinquo. cui⁹ sunt vniuersa. Si amādo paupertatem ei adheseritis. ipe ꝓuidētia q̄ gubernabat oīa vobis largiet̄ q̄ nouerit expedire. Inde migrauit ad dñm anno etatis sue lxxx. In ordine diaconatus cōstitutus. Pio pře orbati frēs petruz lemonicensis in p̄orem elegerūt. sub eius regimine ꝓfecerūt frēs. monachi sancti augustini locū p̄dictū mureti in quo deo huiebāt ceperūt calūniari. ptendētes ad ius eoꝝ ptinere. Sed q̄ potius aufferenti tunicā τ palliū volebāt dimittere. hře locū aliū pq̄rebant. vbi caput sue religionis instituerent. nulloq3 idoneo repto. Tandē ɔsiliū inierūt. vt locū idoneū deus ostenderet. Et cū ter agn⁹ dei cantatū esset. vox celestis audita ē. In grādi mōte In grādi mōte In grādi mōte. Quā prior τ non nulli frēs audierūt. Finita igitur missa venientes ad locum sibi reuelatum satis mureto vicinū ecclesiam τ domos fecerunt. Et accipiētes sctm̄ corpus in grandi mōtē trāstulerūt. Paucisq3 scıētibus subtus p̄sbiteriuz añ altare recondiderut. vbi post paliticus posit⁹ inscius sanitatē accepit. τ cecus visum. τ alia miracula fecit q̄ prior ne tumultus fieret ei edicto prohibuit.

S. Stephanus

Petrus Damianus

Isaac medicus

Jo. Serapion

Seno τ Arnulphus

37 Philippus pm⁹
Rex francie

PEtrus damianus doctor τ eccie ro. cardinalis eps. in diuinis scripturis eruditissim⁹. Hijs tēporibus eas ob res multo in p̄cio hitus ē. in ytalia vita τ scīa insignis. q̄ τ nōnulla laude digna edidit opuscula. Sermōes q3 elegātes. scripsit τ regulā heremiticā. τ de ordīe vite heremitice. Itē libr̄ ɔ iudeos. narrat τ plura exempla q̄ suis tp̄ibus cōtigerūt. Erat em̄ vir religione τ hūilitate ac sapia noiatissim⁹. Qui cū cardinalis eps esset. vt soli deo hūilitate seruiret epatui cessit. vt deo liberius vacaret. Et cū a gregorio pōtifice eā ob rem rephenderet̄ librū pulcerrimū ad eū scripsit. reddēs roem q̄re epatū dimiserit. Hrıcus ait lorica ferrea vestitus erat ad carnez. duobusq3 ferreis circulis cinctus in corpe τ duos p armos brachiorū.

IOannes medicus cognomēto serapion p idē tēpus claruit. Et de simplicib⁹ medicinis multa cōscripsit ac libruz breuiarij de morbis arcendis. Et qm̄ a ceteris medicis rosas collegit. Serapio cognomīatus ē. Sorapio em̄ roseū sonat vt testis ē Plini⁹ lib. 12. ca. 13.

ISaac Benimirā medicus celeberrim⁹ salomōis medici filius. Et ipe tēpestate istac. in medicina plura scripsit. de dictis vniuersalibus τ pticularibus de febribus de vrina. τ stomacho. In phia q3 de elementis τ diffinitōnibus tractatus composuit.

SEno epus treuerēsis a comite treueroꝝ theoderico capt⁹. τ tercio de rupe p̄cipitato. tandem gladio p cussus interijt.

ARnulph⁹ q3 sctūs cenobio scti medardi signis τ v̄tutib⁹ pollebat sua sctītate elegit ꝓpositū inclusionis. Inde abbas eiusdē monasterij tandē iussu pontificis summi epatum lugdun. rexit.

《纽伦堡编年史》是世界历史汇编，此本曾被英国历史学家罗伯特·法比安收藏，法比安去世之后出版的著作《编年史》（*Cronycle*）是关于中世纪晚期英国历史的重要著作。他在此书里的大量批注将《纽伦堡编年史》变成了个人历史百科全书，也让人窥探到他的工作方式。全书还有大量的木刻插图，都是手工上色，让这本书更为与众不同

一本 1671 年出版的《圣经》，它当时的主人将许多空白页加插进此书中，将其变成了个人的《圣经》学习汇总，他在空白页上记满了他自己及其他学者的注释、评论、说明及观察

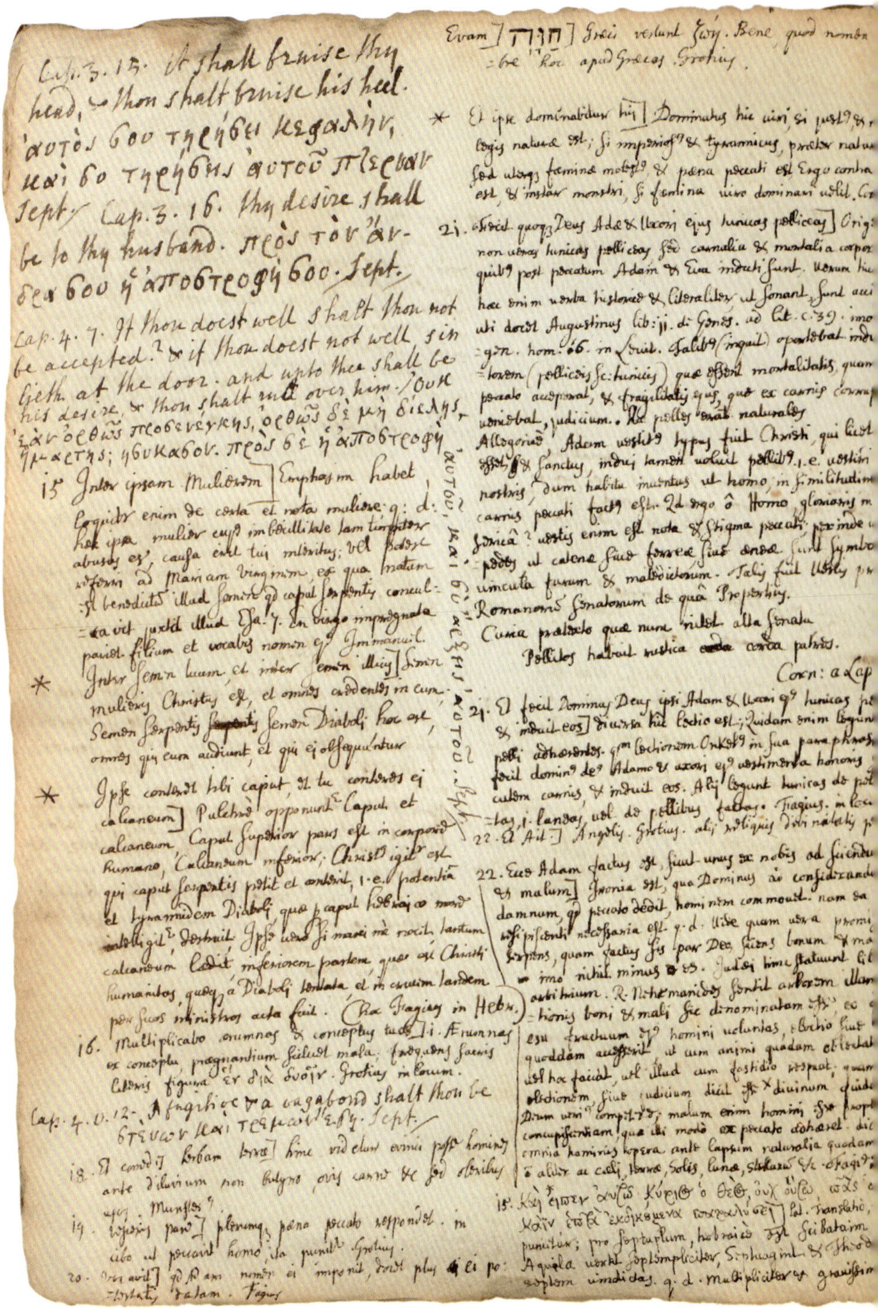

nd ye shall be as gods, know-
nd evil.
when the woman saw that the
ood for food, and that it *was*
the eyes, and a tree to be de-
ake *one* wise; she took of the
of, and did eat, and gave also
usband with her, and he did eat.
e eyes of them both were open-
y knew that they *were* naked:
ewed fig-leaves together, and
selves aprons.
ey heard the voice of the LORD
ng in the garden in the cool of
d Adam and his wife hid them-
n the presence of the LORD
gst the trees of the garden.
e LORD God called unto A-
id unto him, Where *art* thou?
e said, I heard thy voice in the
nd I was afraid, because I *was*
d I hid my self.
he said, Who told thee that
aked? Hast thou eaten of the
eof I commanded thee, that
dest not eat?
the man said, The woman
gavest *to be* with me, she gave
ree, and I did eat.
the LORD God said unto the
hat *is* this *that* thou hast done?
oman said, The serpent beguil-
I did eat.
the LORD God said unto the
ecause thou hast done this, thou
above all cattel, and above
st of the field: upon thy belly
go, and dust shalt thou eat all
f thy life.
I will put enmity between thee
woman, and between thy seed
ed: it shall bruise thy head,
halt bruise his heel.
o the woman he said, I will
ltiply thy sorrow and thy con-
in sorrow thou shalt bring forth
and thy desire *shall be* to thy
and he shall rule over thee.
unto Adam he said, Because
earkened unto the voice of thy
hast eaten of the tree of which
ded thee, saying, Thou shalt
it: cursed *is* the ground for
in sorrow shalt thou eat *of* it
s of thy life.
orns also and thistles shall it
h to thee: and thou shalt eat
f the field.
e sweat of thy face shalt thou eat
thou return unto the ground;
it wast thou taken: for dust
and unto dust thou shalt return.
Adam called his wives name
use she was the mother of all

o Adam also and to his wife did
God make coats of skins, and
em.

22 ¶ And the LORD God said, Behold,
the man is become as one of us, to know
good and evil. And now lest he put forth
his hand, and take also of the tree of life,
and eat, and live for ever:
23 Therefore the LORD God sent him
forth from the garden of Eden, to till the
ground, from whence he was taken.
24 So he drove out the man: and he
placed at the east of the garden of Eden,
cherubims, and a flaming sword, which
turned every way, to keep the way of the
tree of life.

CHAP. IV.

*1 The birth of Cain and Abel. 8 The mur-
der of Abel. 11 The curse of Cain. 19 La-
mech and his two wives.*

AND Adam knew Eve his wife: and she
conceived, and bare Cain, and said,
I have gotten a man from the LORD.
2 And she again bare his brother Abel.
And Abel was a keeper of sheep, but Cain
was a tiller of the ground.
3 And in process of time it came to
pass, that Cain brought of the fruit of the
ground an offering unto the LORD.
4 And Abel, he also brought of the
firstlings of his flock, and of the fat
thereof. And the LORD had respect unto ✱
Abel, and to his offering:
5 But unto Cain and to his offering he
had not respect. And Cain was very
wroth, and his countenance fell.
6 And the LORD said unto Cain, Why
art thou wroth? and why is thy counte-
nance fallen?
7 If thou doest well, shalt thou not be ac-
cepted? and if thou doest not well, sin li-
eth at the door. And unto thee *shall be* his
desire, and thou shalt rule over him.
8 And Cain talked with Abel his bro-
ther: and it came to pass when they were
in the field, that Cain rose up against
Abel his brother, and slew him.
9 And the LORD said unto Cain,
Where *is* Abel thy brother? and he said,
I know not: *Am* I my brothers keeper?
10 And he said, What hast thou done?
the voice of thy brothers bloud crieth un-
to me from the ground.
11 And now *art* thou cursed from the
earth, which hath opened her mouth to
receive thy brothers bloud from thy
hand.
12 When thou tillest the ground, it
shall not henceforth yield unto thee her
strength. A fugitive and a vagabond shalt
thou be in the earth.
13 And Cain said unto the LORD, My
punishment *is* greater then I can bear.
14 Behold, thou hast driven me out
this day from the face of the earth: and
from thy face shall I be hid, and I shall
be a fugitive and a vagabond in the earth
and it shall come to pass, that every one
that findeth me shall slay me.
15 And the LORD said unto him, There-
fore

A 4

...dotion vertit ἐνεπύρισεν inflamavit. i.e. igne de[...]
consumpsit & sic grata esse probavit. vid. Crit: in loco.

... Cain securus est, nec quod puniendus tam gravis a caede
... quemque ad poenam, & omnium exemplum vult superesse,
... aliud quam diu torqueri. Lyran. Abulens. Carthusian.
...ungunt & distinguunt. Omnis qui occiderit Cain, subaudi gra-
...ed ut Symmachus vertit, septimus punietur, Cain scilicet quia
... usque vitae duplicis ad poenam & exemplum. Verum haec dic-
...unt septimum, ut vertit Symmachus, sed septuplum significat.
...ptimum (i.e. septima generatione) longanimitas Dei erga parri-
[τ]οῦ μὴ ἀνελεῖν αὐτὸν πάντα τὸν εὑρίσκοντα αὐτόν
... semper praeunerit ad monstrandam viam qua tuto ingredi
...m ex nomine suo positum in frontem. Alii temporarium signum
...hominibus durabile & perpetuum fuisse putat. Sunt itaque omnia
...laturandum esset, mallem his adstipulari qui sentiunt signum
...orum tremorem. Quod conjiciunt ex eo quod dicitur Vagus &
...od Septuagint. reddiderunt στένων καὶ τρέμων ἔσῃ ἐπὶ τῆς
... hominis [illegible] super terram. Fagius. Corn: a Lap. dicit

+ Cap. 4. 26. οὗτος ἤλπισεν ἐπικα-
...τὸ ὄνομα κυρίου τοῦ Θεοῦ. Sept.
אָז הוּחַל לִקְרֹא בְּשֵׁם. When
...en to call upon the name of the Lord.
...3. Ἔζησε δὲ Ἀδὰμ τριάκοντα καὶ
...ια ἔτη. Sept. Cap. 4. 4. Ἐγένοντο δὲ
...αι Ἀδάμ, ἃς ἔζησε μετὰ τὸ γεννῆ-
...ν τὸν Σήθ, ἔτη ἑπτακόσια. Sept.
Ἔζησε δὲ Σὴθ πέντε καὶ δια-
...τη. Cap. 5. 7. καὶ ἔζησε Σὴθ μετὰ
...σαι αὐτὸν τὸν Ἐνώς, ἑπτὰ ἔ-
...πτακόσια. Sept.

...morti addictus videtur ergo Seth pius ita filium vocasse, ut eum
...peccatum addicti sumus. Secundo homo Enos dici a radice
...ato oblivioni tradendus: ad hoc Etymon alludit Psalm. 8. Quid
ἐπικαλεῖσθαι τὸ ὄνομα [τοῦ Θεοῦ] Septuagint. Hic spe-
...incipere, sed et sperare significat a radice iachal, & spes est
...invocatio nominis Domini, quasi tempore Enos coeperat Idololatria,
...a chol sed a chalal descendit, quod in hiphil habet
...ceptum est. Corn: a Lap: ✱ οὗτος ἤλπισεν etc.] Drusius
..., puto ostendum, tunc inceptum est invocari nomen Domini
...i. i.e. membra verae Ecclesiae, quae in posteris Seth habitasset, multi arti horum
consolabitur nos ab operibus] Firant hunc
...num levasse agriculturae molestias, jungendo
...tro Animalia. (Clarius)

... Cyrillus probat. ut velut Dei ad hominis legatus, propterea Dei
... vocaporet, ut Angeli solent. et ideo infra 6. 2. & 4. Filios Dei
...idem Cyrillus interpretatur Enochi posteros. Aquila videtur hoc hoc voluisse
...um transtulit, τότε ἤρχθη τοῦ καλεῖσθαι ἐν ὀνόματι κυρίου.
...favit huic sensui Irenaeus 4. 30. Grotius

... Adam

...it) Individuam mariti et uxoris societatem
...commendat. Hoc enim dicendi genere signi-
...ficat post ordinatum conjugium fuisse utrumque et
...eorum instar unius hominis. (Clarius id) vocavit
...nomen eorum Adam, ut ipsa appellatione disc-
...erent se insolescere cum se a terra, sanguine vero
...glina constare recordarentur. Significat enim Adam
...terrenus, etiam et rubrum significat.

17世纪早期的荷兰律师彼得·范·维恩，将一本蒙田的《随笔集》个性化，在书页空白处和书后的空白页上写了大量笔记，并在整本书中画了一系列的钢笔画，这是他留给儿子的传家宝

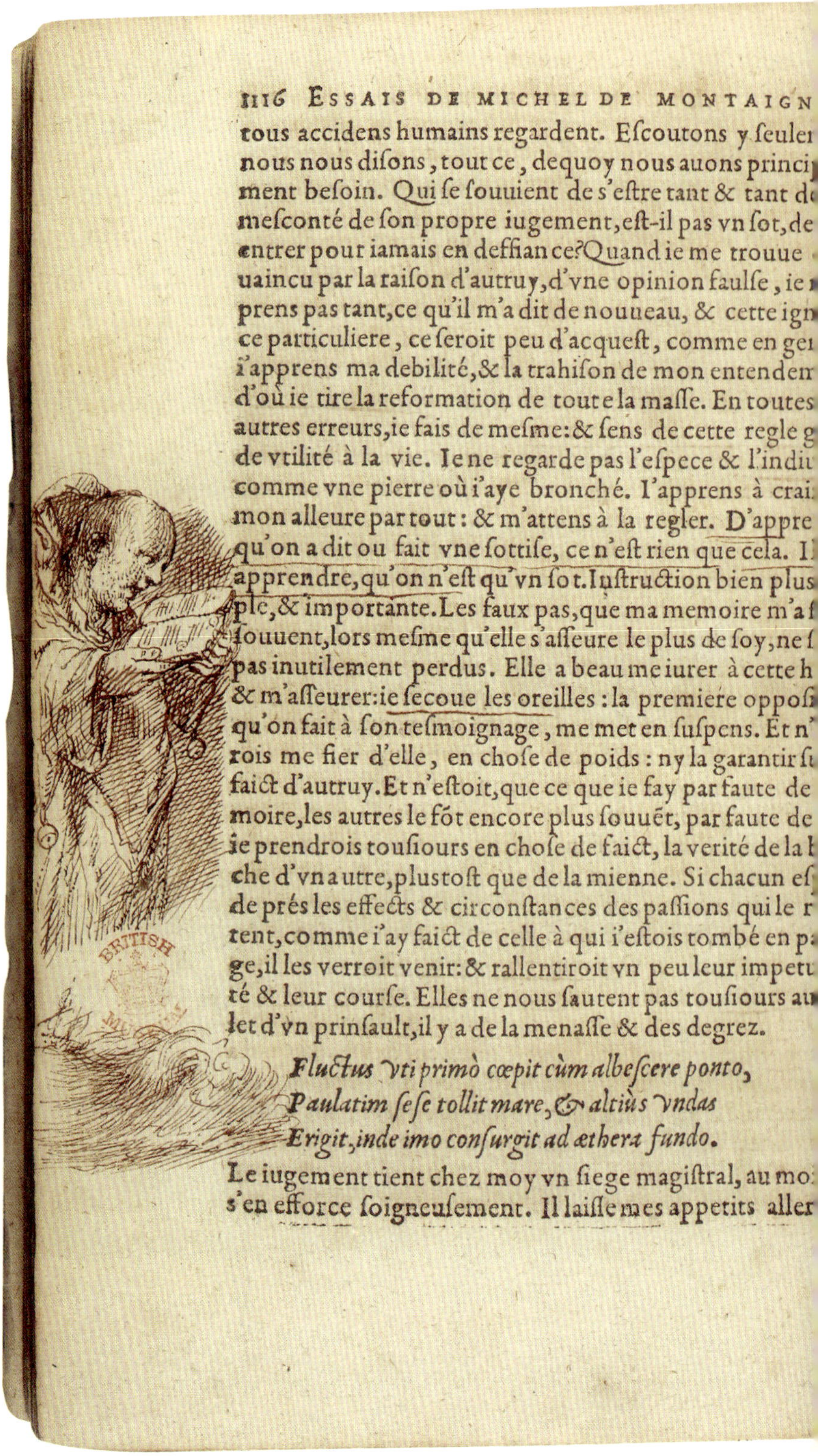
116 ESSAIS DE MICHEL DE MONTAIGN
tous accidens humains regardent. Escoutons y seulem
nous nous disons, tout ce, dequoy nous auons princi
ment besoin. Qui se souuient de s'estre tant & tant d
mesconté de son propre iugement, est-il pas vn sot, de
entrer pour iamais en deffiance? Quand ie me trouue
uaincu par la raison d'autruy, d'vne opinion faulse, ie
prens pas tant, ce qu'il m'a dit de nouueau, & cette ign
ce particuliere, ce seroit peu d'acquest, comme en ge
i'apprens ma debilité, & la trahison de mon entender
d'où ie tire la reformation de toute la masse. En toutes
autres erreurs, ie fais de mesme: & sens de cette regle g
de vtilité à la vie. Ie ne regarde pas l'espece & l'indiu
comme vne pierre où i'aye bronché. I'apprens à crai
mon alleure par tout: & m'attens à la regler. D'appre
qu'on a dit ou fait vne sottise, ce n'est rien que cela. I
apprendre, qu'on n'est qu'vn sot. Instruction bien plus
ple, & importante. Les faux pas, que ma memoire m'a f
souuent, lors mesme qu'elle s'asseure le plus de soy, ne f
pas inutilement perdus. Elle a beau me iurer à cette h
& m'asseurer: ie secoue les oreilles: la premiere oppos
qu'on fait à son tesmoignage, me met en suspens. Et n'
rois me fier d'elle, en chose de poids: ny la garantir s
faict d'autruy. Et n'estoit, que ce que ie fay par faute de
moire, les autres le font encore plus souuent, par faute de
ie prendrois tousiours en chose de faict, la verité de la b
che d'vn autre, plustost que de la mienne. Si chacun e
de prés les effects & circonstances des passions qui le r
tent, comme i'ay faict de celle à qui i'estois tombé en p
ge, il les verroit venir: & rallentiroit vn peu leur impetu
té & leur course. Elles ne nous sautent pas tousiours au
let d'vn prinsault, il y a de la menasse & des degrez.

Fluctus vti primò cœpit cùm albescere ponto,
Paulatim sese tollit mare, & altiùs vndas
Erigit, inde imo consurgit ad æthera fundo.

Le iugement tient chez moy vn siege magistral, au mo
s'en efforce soigneusement. Il laisse mes appetits aller

: & la haine & l'amitié, voire & celle que ie me porte à
-mesme, sans s'en alterer & corrompre. S'il ne peut re-
er les autres parties selõ soy, au moins ne se laisse-il pas
rmer à elles : il fait son jeu à part. L'aduertissement à
un de se cognoistre, doit estre d'vn important effect:
ue ce Dieu de science & de lumiere le fit pláter au frõt
n temple : comme comprenant tout ce qu'il auoit
us conseiller. Platon dit aussi, que prudence n'est
chose, que l'execution de cette ordonnãce : & Socra-
: verifie par le menu en Xenophon. Les difficultez &
curité, ne s'apperçoiuent en chacune science, que par
qui y ont entree. Car encore fault-il quelque degré
elligence, à pouuoir remarquer qu'on ignore : & faut
ser à vne porte, pour sçauoir qu'elle nous est close. D'où
cette Platonique subtilité, que ny ceux qui sçauent,
à s'enquerir, dautant qu'ils sçauẽt: ny ceux qui ne sça-
, dautant que pour s'enquerir, il fault sçauoir, dequoy
enquiert. Ainsi, en cette cy de se cognoistre soy-mes-
e que chacun se void si resolu & satisfait, ce que chacũ
se estre suffisamment entendu, signifie que chacun n'y
ıd rien du tout, comme Socrates apprend à Euthyde-
Moy, qui ne fais autre profession, y trouue vne profon-
& varieté si infinie, que mon apprentissage n'a autre
, que de me faire sentir, combien il me reste à appren-
. ma foiblesse si souuẽt recogneuë, ie dois l'inclination
ay à la modestie: à l'obeïssance des creãces qui me sõt
cites : à vne constante froideur & moderation d'opi-
: & la haine de cette arrogance importune & querel-
se croyant & fiant tout à soy, ennemie capitale de dis-
ıe & de verité. Oyez les regenter. Les premieres sotti-
ıils mettent en auant, c'est au style qu'on establit les
ons & les loix. *Nihil est turpius quam cognitioni & perce-
assertionem approbationémque præcurrere.* Aristarchus disoit,
ciennement, à peine se trouua-il sept sages au monde,
e de son temps à peine se trouua-il sept ignorans. Au-
nous pas plus de raison que luy, de le dire en nostre
s ? L'affirmation & l'opiniastreté, sont signes exprez de

威廉·布莱克对雷诺兹爵士的评价被精确地记录在他在后者文集标题页的题字中，“这个人是被雇来压制艺术的”。布莱克在此书其他页面上的批注更增加了他的负面评价

人倾倒（后文中还会详细谈到）。想象一下，弥尔顿、拜伦，最受崇拜的英雄，或臭名昭著的恶棍，你手中的这本书，曾经被他们拥有过。当然，这些书的价值常常超出名人关系，因为书籍能给我们提供一个窗口，窥探这些人的心智及思维的发展过程。我们知道英国作家威廉·布莱克（William Blake）对画家乔舒亚·雷诺兹爵士（Sir Joshua Reynolds）的评价，因为布莱克在雷诺兹文集的标题页上，留下这样的题字：“这个人是被雇来压制艺术的。”亨利八世的藏书有不少现在被大英图书馆收藏，它们的价值，不仅因为它们曾被亨利八世拿在手上，更因为他在一些与政治或道德有关的段落上做过标记和评论。研究宗教改革那段历史的学者们也很重视亨利八世的坎特伯雷大

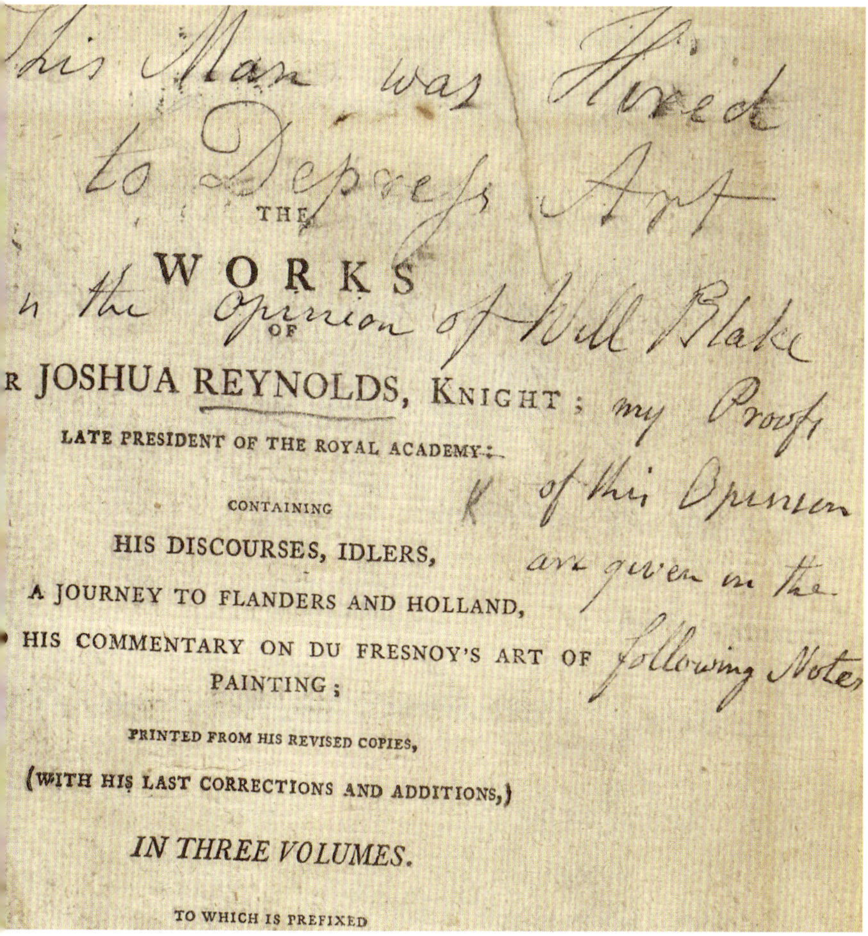

主教托马斯·克兰麦（Thomas Cranmer）个人图书馆中的藏书，一方面是因为这些书籍能让后人洞察到他所阅读的内容，另一方面也因为他的批注和笔记捕捉了他对某些问题的思考和态度。

研究者们向来很重视早期专家们在书上的批注。1774 年，18 世纪的著名藏书家安东尼·艾斯丘（Anthony Askew）的收藏被拍卖时，拍卖目录上特别提到藏品中的许多书籍有古典学者们的批注。批注的传统一直延续到今天，1997 年，历史学家罗斯（A. L. Rowse）的藏书被出售时，书商目录上提到其卖点之一，就是罗斯“评论及批注的习惯随着年龄和智慧而增长，他的藏书的空白处也就越来越布满了他的评论，智慧、讥诮，有时不乏严厉”。那些喜欢批注的人，不需要

（右图）

亨利八世曾在他的许多藏书上题写批注，此为荷兰学者伊拉斯谟（Erasmus）的著作，亨利八世在批注中指出神父们的缺陷

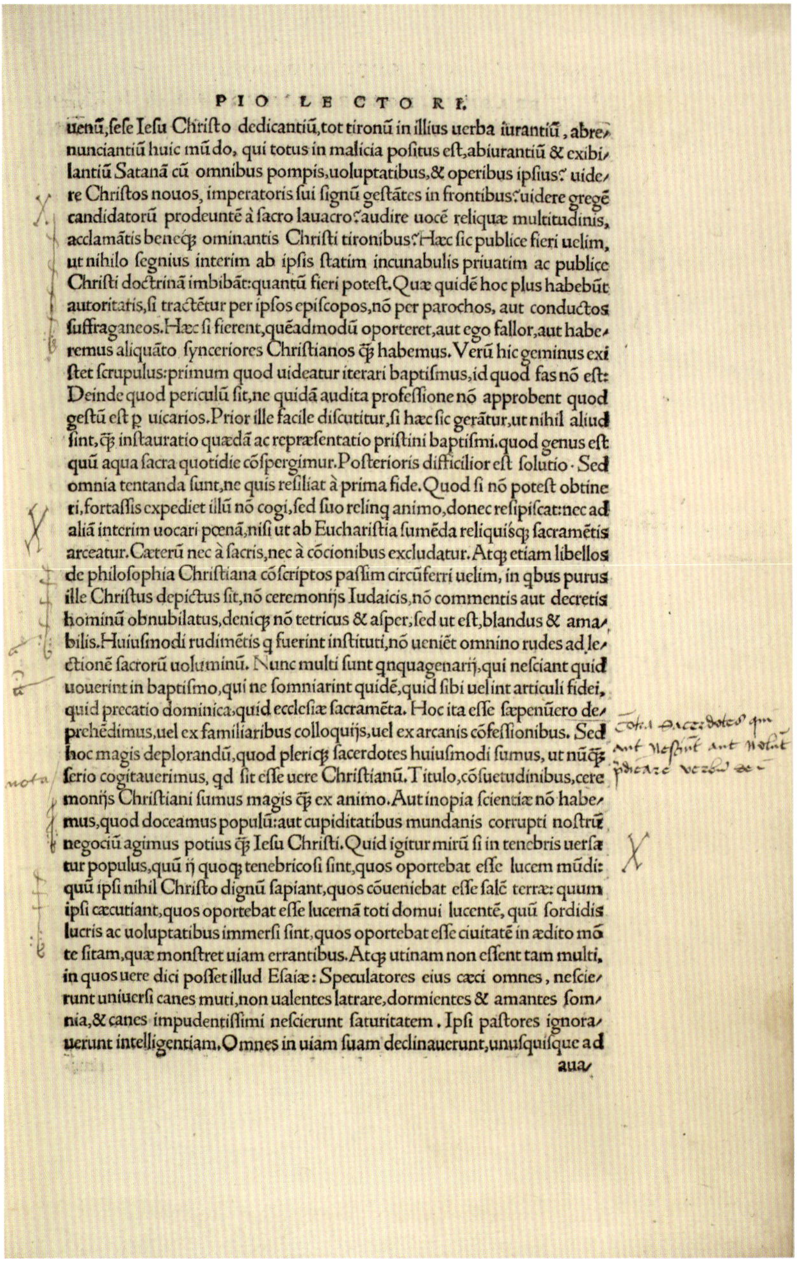
PIO LE CTO RI.

uenū,ſeſe Ieſu Chriſto dedicantiū,tot tironū in illius uerba iurantiū , abre- nunciantiū huic mū do, qui totus in malicia poſitus eſt,abiurantiū & exibi- lantiū Satanā cū omnibus pompis,uoluptatibus,& operibus ipſius: uide- re Chriſtos nouos, imperatoris ſui ſignū geſtātes in frontibus: uidere gregē candidatorū prodeuntē à ſacro lauacro: audire uocē reliquæ multitudinis, acclamātis beneq; ominantis Chriſti tironibus: Hæc ſic publice fieri uelim, ut nihilo ſegnius interim ab ipſis ſtatim incunabulis priuatim ac publice Chriſti doctrinā imbibāt:quantū fieri poteſt. Quæ quidē hoc plus habebūt autoritatis,ſi tractētur per ipſos epiſcopos,nō per parochos, aut conductos ſuffraganeos. Hæc ſi fierent,quēadmodū oporteret,aut ego fallor,aut habe- remus aliquāto ſynceriores Chriſtianos q̄ habemus. Verū hic geminus exi ſtet ſcrupulus:primum quod uideatur iterari baptiſmus,id quod fas nō eſt: Deinde quod periculū ſit,ne quidā audita profeſſione nō approbent quod geſtū eſt p uicarios. Prior ille facile diſcutitur,ſi hæc ſic gerātur,ut nihil aliud ſint, q̄ inſtauratio quædā ac repræſentatio priſtini baptiſmi.quod genus eſt quū aqua ſacra quotidie cōſpergimur. Poſterioris difficilior eſt ſolutio · Sed omnia tentanda ſunt,ne quis reſiliat à prima fide. Quod ſi nō poteſt obtine ri,fortaſſis expediet illū nō cogi,ſed ſuo relinq animo,donec reſipiſcat:nec ad aliā interim uocari pœnā,niſi ut ab Euchariſtia ſumēda reliquiſq; ſacramētis arceatur. Cæterū nec à ſacris,nec à cōcionibus excludatur. Atq; etiam libellos de philoſophia Chriſtiana cōſcriptos paſſim circūferri uelim, in qbus purus ille Chriſtus depictus ſit,nō ceremonijs Iudaicis,nō commentis aut decretis hominū obnubilatus,deniq; nō tetricus & aſper,ſed ut eſt,blandus & ama- bilis. Huiuſmodi rudimētis q fuerint inſtituti,nō uenient omnino rudes ad le- ctionē ſacrorū uoluminū. Nunc multi ſunt qnquagenarij,qui neſciant quid uouerint in baptiſmo,qui ne ſomniarint quidē,quid ſibi uelint articuli fidei, quid precatio dominica,quid eccleſiæ ſacramēta. Hoc ita eſſe ſæpenūero de- prehēdimus,uel ex familiaribus colloquijs,uel ex arcanis cōfeſſionibus. Sed hoc magis deplorandū,quod pleriq; ſacerdotes huiuſmodi ſumus, ut nūq; ſerio cogitauerimus, qd ſit eſſe uere Chriſtianū. Titulo,cōſuetudinibus,cere monijs Chriſtiani ſumus magis q̄ ex animo. Aut inopia ſcientiæ nō habe- mus,quod doceamus populū:aut cupiditatibus mundanis corrupti noſtrū negociū agimus potius q̄ Ieſu Chriſti. Quid igitur mirū ſi in tenebris uerſa tur populus,quū ij quoq; tenebricoſi ſint,quos oportebat eſſe lucem mūdi: quū ipſi nihil Chriſto dignū ſapiant,quos cōueniebat eſſe ſalē terræ: quum ipſi cæcutiant,quos oportebat eſſe lucernā toti domui lucentē, quū ſordidis lucris ac uoluptatibus immerſi ſint,quos oportebat eſſe ciuitatē in ædito mō te ſitam,quæ monſtret uiam errantibus. Atq; utinam non eſſent tam multi, in quos uere dici poſſet illud Eſaiæ: Speculatores eius cæci omnes , neſcie- runt uniuerſi canes muti,non ualentes latrare,dormientes & amantes ſom- nia,& canes impudentiſſimi neſcierunt ſaturitatem . Ipſi paſtores ignora- uerunt intelligentiam. Omnes in uiam ſuam declinauerunt,unuſquiſque ad

aua-

（右页图）

研究宗教改革史的学生们看到有“托马斯·坎图良”（Thomas Cantuarien）签名的书时，就会意识到这本书的重要性，因为这些书都曾是亨利八世的坎特伯雷大主教托马斯·克兰麦的藏书，有些书中还会有他的题注和眉批，那么就更值得重视了

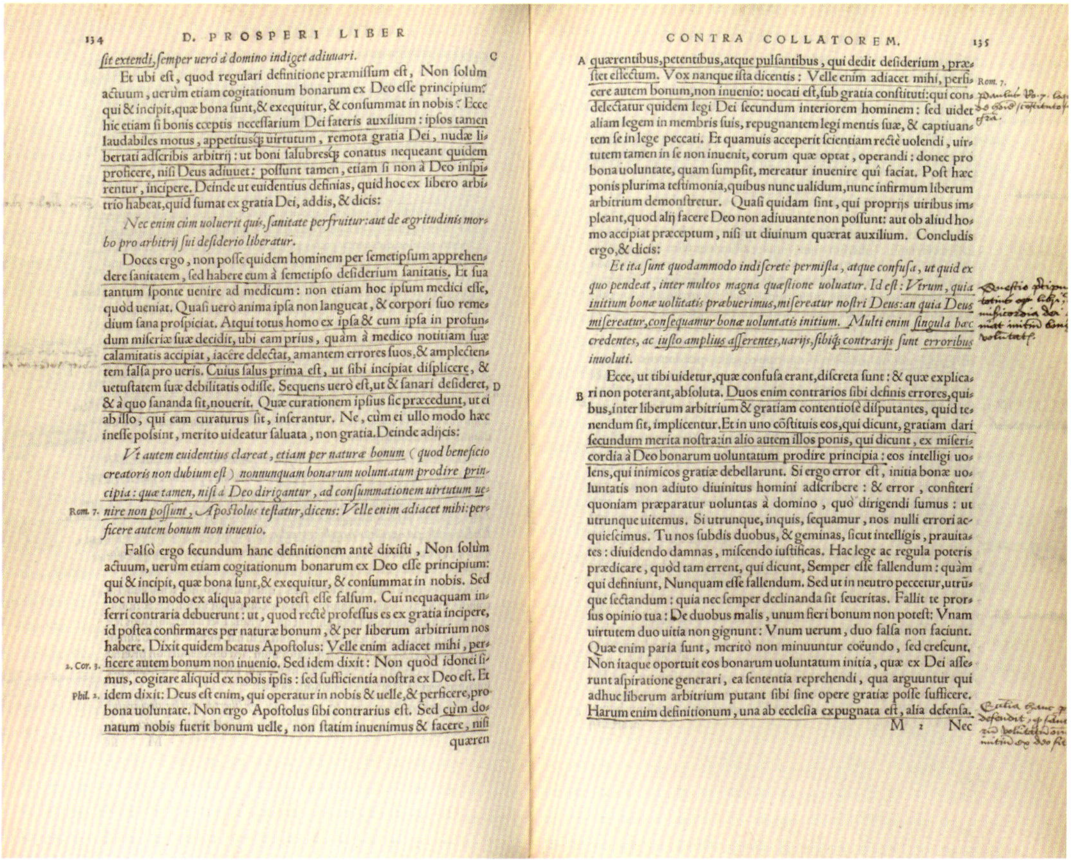

134 D. PROSPERI LIBER

sit extendi, semper uerò à domino indiget adiuuari. C

Et ubi est, quod regulari definitione præmissum est, Non solùm actuum, uerùm etiam cogitationum bonarum ex Deo esse principium: qui & incipit, quæ bona sunt, & exequitur, & consummat in nobis? Ecce hic etiam si bonis cœptis necessarium Dei fateris auxilium: ipsos tamen laudabiles motus, appetitusq; uirtutum, remota gratia Dei, nudæ libertati adscribis arbitrij: ut boni salubresq; conatus nequeant quidem proficere, nisi Deus adiuuet: possunt tamen, etiam si non à Deo inspirentur, incipere. Deinde ut euidentius definias, quid hoc ex libero arbitrio habeat, quid sumat ex gratia Dei, addis, & dicis:

Nec enim cùm uoluerit quis, sanitate perfruitur: aut de ægritudinis morbo pro arbitrij sui desiderio liberatur.

Doces ergo, non posse quidem hominem per semetipsum apprehendere sanitatem, sed habere eum à semetipso desiderium sanitatis. Et sua tantum sponte uenire ad medicum: non etiam hoc ipsum medici esse, quòd ueniat. Quasi uerò anima ipsa non langueat, & corpori suo remedium sana prospiciat. Atqui totus homo ex ipsa & cum ipsa in profundum miseriæ suæ decidit, ubi eam prius, quàm à medico notitiam suæ calamitatis accipiat, iacêre delectat, amantem errores suos, & amplectentem falsa pro ueris. Cuius salus prima est, ut sibi incipiat displicere, & uetustatem suæ debilitatis odisse. Sequens uerò est, ut & sanari desideret, D & à quo sananda sit, nouerit. Quæ curationem ipsius sic præcedunt, ut ei ab illo, qui eam curaturus sit, inserantur. Ne, cùm ei ullo modo hæc inesse posint, merito uideatur saluata, non gratia. Deinde adijcis:

Vt autem euidentius clareat, etiam per naturæ bonum (quod beneficio creatoris non dubium est) nonnunquam bonarum uoluntatum prodire principia: quæ tamen, nisi à Deo dirigantur, ad consummationem uirtutum uenire non possunt,
Rom. 7. *Apostolus testatur, dicens: Velle enim adiacet mihi: perficere autem bonum non inuenio.*

Falsò ergo secundum hanc definitionem antè dixisti, Non solùm actuum, uerùm etiam cogitationum bonarum ex Deo esse principium: qui & incipit, quæ bona sunt, & exequitur, & consummat in nobis. Sed hoc nullo modo ex aliqua parte potest esse falsum. Cui nequaquam inferri contraria debuerunt: ut, quod rectè professus es ex gratia incipere, id postea confirmares per naturæ bonum, & per liberum arbitrium nos habere. Dixit quidem beatus Apostolus: Velle enim adiacet mihi, per-
2. Cor. 3. ficere autem bonum non inuenio. Sed idem dixit: Non quòd idonei simus, cogitare aliquid ex nobis ipsis: sed sufficientia nostra ex Deo est. Et
Phil. 2. idem dixit: Deus est enim, qui operatur in nobis & uelle, & perficere, pro bona uoluntate. Non ergo Apostolus sibi contrarius est. Sed cùm donatum nobis fuerit bonum uelle, non statim inuenimus & facere, nisi

quæren

CONTRA COLLATOREM. 135

A quærentibus, petentibus, atque pulsantibus, qui dedit desiderium, præstet effectum. Vox nanque ista dicentis: Velle enim adiacet mihi, perfi- Rom. 7.
cere autem bonum, non inuenio: uocati est, sub gratia constituti: qui condelectatur quidem legi Dei secundum interiorem hominem: sed uidet aliam legem in membris suis, repugnantem legi mentis suæ, & captiuantem se in lege peccati. Et quamuis acceperit scientiam rectè uolendi, uirtutem tamen in se non inuenit, eorum quæ optat, operandi: donec pro bona uoluntate, quam sumpsit, mereatur inuenire quî faciat. Post hæc ponis plurima testimonia, quibus nunc ualidum, nunc infirmum liberum arbitrium demonstretur. Quasi quidam sint, qui proprijs uiribus impleant, quod alij facere Deo non adiuuante non possunt: aut ob aliud homo accipiat præceptum, nisi ut diuinum quærat auxilium. Concludis ergo, & dicis:

Et ita sunt quodammodo indiscretè permista, atque confusa, ut quid ex quo pendeat, inter multos magna quæstione uoluatur. Id est: Vtrum, quia initium bonæ uolũtatis præbuerimus, misereatur nostri Deus: an quia Deus misereatur, consequamur bonæ uoluntatis initium. Multi enim singula hæc credentes, ac iusto amplius asserentes, uarijs, sibiq; contrarijs sunt erroribus inuoluti.

Ecce, ut tibi uidetur, quæ confusa erant, discreta sunt: & quæ explica-
B ri non poterant, absoluta. Duos enim contrarios sibi definis errores, quibus, inter liberum arbitrium & gratiam contentiosè disputantes, quid tenendum sit, implicentur. Et in uno cõstituis eos, qui dicunt, gratiam dari secundum merita nostra; in alio autem illos ponis, qui dicunt, ex misericordia à Deo bonarum uoluntatum prodire principia: eos intelligi uolens, qui inimicos gratiæ debellarunt. Si ergo error est, initia bonæ uoluntatis non adiuto diuinitus homini adscribere: & error, confiteri quoniam præparatur uoluntas à domino, quò dirigendi sumus: ut utrunque uitemus. Si utrunque, inquis, sequamur, nos nulli errori acquiescimus. Tu nos subdis duobus, & geminas, sicut intelligis, prauitates: diuidendo damnas, miscendo iustificas. Hac lege ac regula poteris prædicare, quòd tam errent, qui dicunt, Semper esse fallendum: quàm qui definiunt, Nunquam esse fallendum. Sed ut in neutro peccetur, utrũque sectandum: quia nec semper declinanda sit seueritas. Fallit te prorsus opinio tua: De duobus malis, unum fieri bonum non potest: Vnam uirtutem duo uitia non gignunt: Vnum uerum, duo falsa non faciunt. Quæ enim paria sunt, meritò non minuuntur coëundo, sed crescunt. Non itaque oportuit eos bonarum uoluntatum initia, quæ ex Dei asserunt aspiratione generari, ea sententia reprehendi, qua arguuntur qui adhuc liberum arbitrium putant sibi sine opere gratiæ posse sufficere. Harum enim definitionum, una ab ecclesia expugnata est, alia defensa.

M 2 Nec

（右页图）
17世纪早期，伦敦外科医生约瑟夫·芬顿利用书中空白页记录他所拥有的外科书籍

多有名或多重要，他们的文字同样可以充满趣味。前辈读者中的那些无名之辈所做的批注也能为后人提供有价值的证据，说明历代读者们对当时的出版物的吸收和反馈。

人们在书上留下的文字并不局限于和此书有关的内容，每本书前后空白的页面是可以利用的空间，许多人在上面记录其他重要事件。约瑟夫·芬顿（Joseph Fenton，1634年去世）是17世纪早期伦敦圣巴塞洛缪医院（St Bartholomew's Hospital）的外科医生，与英国著名医生威廉·哈维（William Harvey）是同代人，他用一本医学文献的空白页记录了他“书房中所有的外科医学著作”。约翰·罗巴茨（John Robartes），第二代罗巴茨爵士（Lord Robartes，1606—1685），是建立了康沃尔郡的林翰德洛克庄园（Lanhydrock House）非凡图书馆的重要人物，他在一些书的扉页上，记录了与此书毫无关联的庄园事件，例如鹿群的情况，某一年猎杀了多少头鹿，等等。学校教科书中封底扉页上的涂写也往往能见证前代学生们上课开小差的能力，例如罗切斯特修道院的一位修士所收藏的小册子上，有不少手书的言语污秽的打油诗，证明了修道院的学生们拥有充足的世俗知识。批注不只限于文字，有人会在书页上描画抽象符号，这些符号与文本内容是否有直接关系也可待商榷。约翰逊博士在编纂他的《词典》时使用过许多书籍，这些书上也注有各种符号，标出《词典》中解释词语用法时会用到的引文。

人们在阅读过的书籍上留下各种标记，有的很容易理解，有的则不然。文字批注比较直截了当，它们可能与文本内容有关系，也可能没有，这些文字往往是读者的评论、索引、总结或翻译。另一些常见的批注是在文本下方或边上画线，或使用各种符号，例如星号、打钩或箭头等。研究阅读史的学者们越来越多地关注读者与书本之间的互动关系，对它们进行分类和区别。批注和标识有些像作者和读者之间的乒乓球游戏，他们交流思想，有时候会碰撞合成出一些有趣的东西，读者的批注可以自成一体，为其他读者提供参考。

A note of all the Bookes of Chyrurgerye
that I have in my studye.

...ipporrates
...ulus Ægineta
...tius
...ido to the
...ker onlie Chy
...rgions bonnde.
...aultius
...reus.
...lloppius
...nelius Celsus
...dreas a Cruce
...zonius
...yrurgia Chyrurgice
...lmoteus.
...græus.
...dreas Alchazar.
...britius ab Aqua=
...ndente.
...anthus
...racelsus.
...ridanus Sanctus.
...taeus.
...uercitanus.
...buralis
...rus de Argillata.
...rnaldus de
...illa noua
...dus Vidius
...liacotius
...rmelinus
...lielmus Fabritius
...atheus Roßius

Feßennius
Andreas Vesalius
Andreas Laurentius
de strumis

基督教牧师和神学家艾萨克·沃茨（Isaac Watts）出版于18世纪中期的著作，上有约翰逊博士所注的符号，他编纂的《词典》中，有些字例出自此书

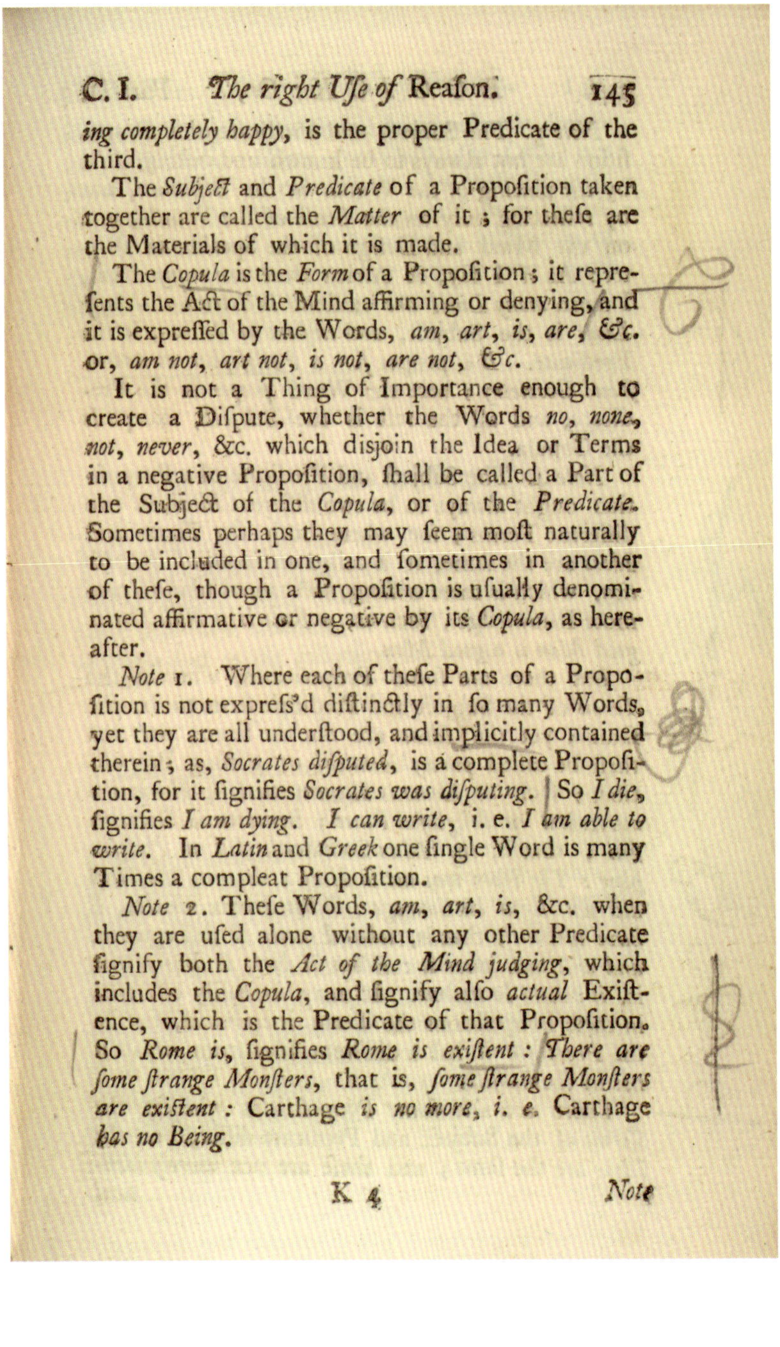

C. I. *The right Uſe of* Reaſon. 145

ing completely happy, is the proper Predicate of the third.

The *Subject* and *Predicate* of a Propoſition taken together are called the *Matter* of it; for theſe are the Materials of which it is made.

The *Copula* is the *Form* of a Propoſition; it repreſents the Act of the Mind affirming or denying, and it is expreſſed by the Words, *am*, *art*, *is*, *are*, *&c.* or, *am not*, *art not*, *is not*, *are not*, *&c.*

It is not a Thing of Importance enough to create a Diſpute, whether the Words *no*, *none*, *not*, *never*, &c. which disjoin the Idea or Terms in a negative Propoſition, ſhall be called a Part of the Subject of the *Copula*, or of the *Predicate*. Sometimes perhaps they may ſeem moſt naturally to be included in one, and ſometimes in another of theſe, though a Propoſition is uſually denominated affirmative or negative by its *Copula*, as hereafter.

Note 1. Where each of theſe Parts of a Propoſition is not expreſs'd diſtinctly in ſo many Words, yet they are all underſtood, and implicitly contained therein; as, *Socrates diſputed*, is a complete Propoſition, for it ſignifies *Socrates was diſputing*. So *I die*, ſignifies *I am dying*. *I can write*, i. e. *I am able to write*. In *Latin* and *Greek* one ſingle Word is many Times a compleat Propoſition.

Note 2. Theſe Words, *am*, *art*, *is*, &c. when they are uſed alone without any other Predicate ſignify both the *Act of the Mind judging*, which includes the *Copula*, and ſignify alſo *actual* Exiſtence, which is the Predicate of that Propoſition. So *Rome is*, ſignifies *Rome is exiſtent*: *There are ſome ſtrange Monſters*, that is, *ſome ſtrange Monſters are exiſtent*: Carthage *is no more*, *i. e.* Carthage *has no Being*.

K 4 Note

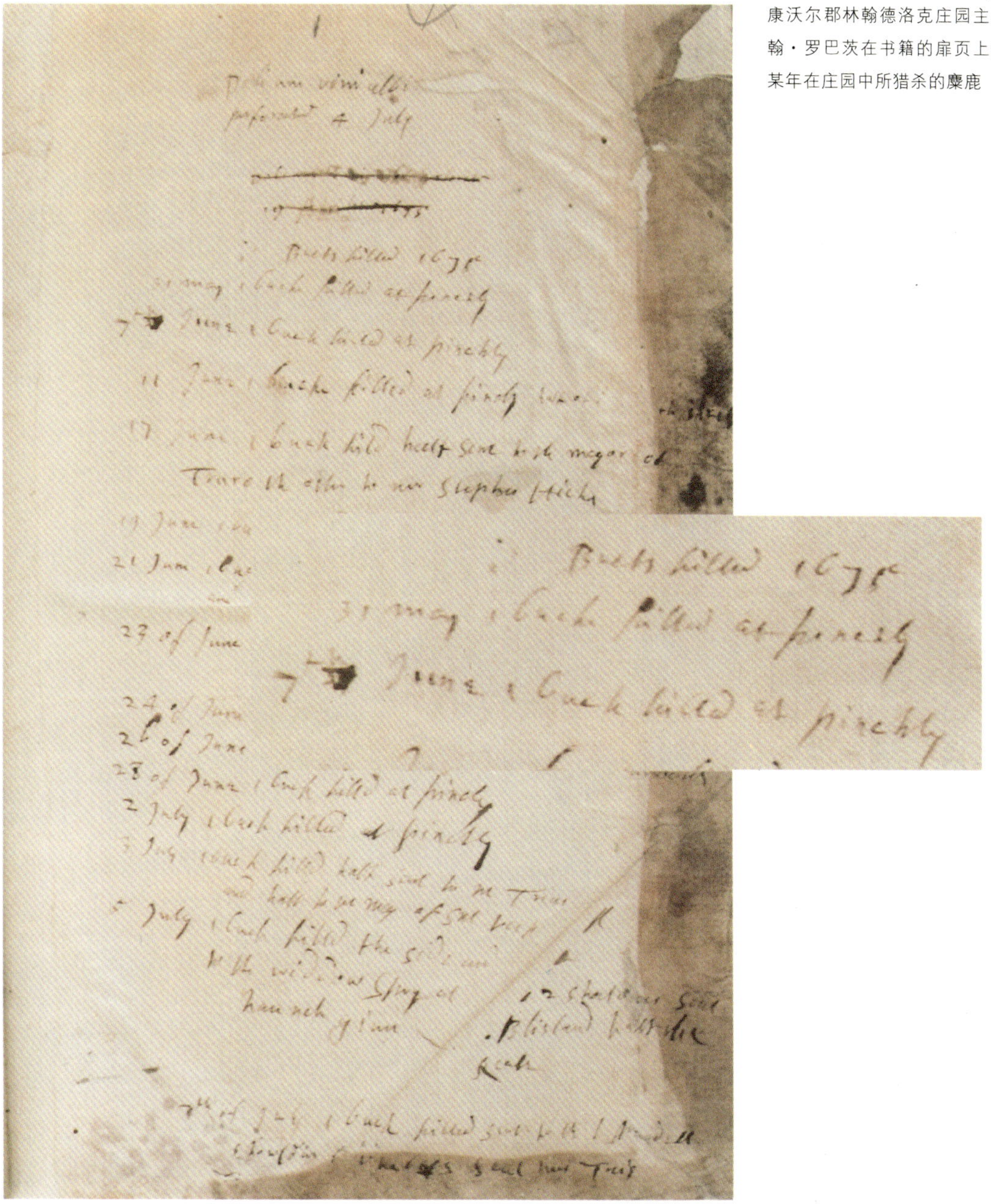

康沃尔郡林翰德洛克庄园主人约翰·罗巴茨在书籍的扉页上记录某年在庄园中所猎杀的麋鹿

M. T. Ciceronis Oratio[illegible] xii. Selectarum Liber. Editio cum Olivet, aliiſque notæ melioris Exemplaribus collata, et in uſum ſtudioſæ Juventutis edita, 1785. 2s. 6d.

M. T. Ciceronis Opuscula; hoc eſt, Cato Major, ſeu, de Senectute; Lælius, ſeu, de Amicitia; Paradoxa; Somnium Scipionis. Præfigitur ejuſdem M. T. Ciceronis Vita Literaria nunc primùm in lucem data. Editio nova. 2s.

De Fide et Officiis Chriſtianorum, ex cl. Burneti et Grotii libellis, in uſum Juventutis Chriſtianæ. Editio altera. 1s. 6d.

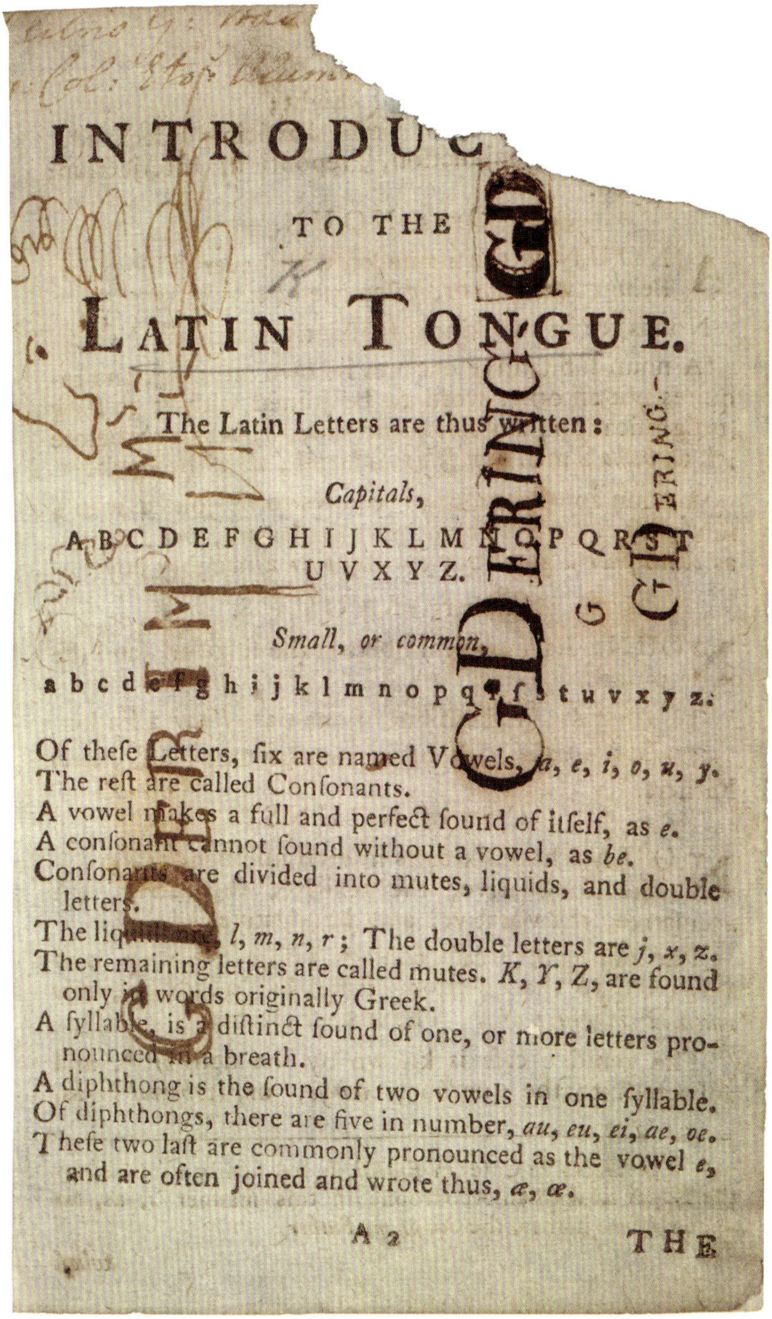
INTRODUC

TO THE

LATIN TONGUE.

The Latin Letters are thus written:

Capitals,

A B C D E F G H I J K L M N O P Q R S T U V X Y Z.

Small, or common,

a b c d e f g h i j k l m n o p q r ſ s t u v x y z.

Of theſe Letters, ſix are named Vowels, *a, e, i, o, u, y.*
The reſt are called Conſonants.
A vowel makes a full and perfect ſound of itſelf, as *e.*
A conſonant cannot ſound without a vowel, as *be.*
Conſonants are divided into mutes, liquids, and double letters.
The liquids are, *l, m, n, r*; The double letters are *j, x, z.*
The remaining letters are called mutes. *K, Y, Z,* are found only in words originally Greek.
A ſyllable, is a diſtinct ſound of one, or more letters pronounced in a breath.
A diphthong is the ſound of two vowels in one ſyllable.
Of diphthongs, there are five in number, *au, eu, ei, ae, oe.*
Theſe two laſt are commonly pronounced as the vowel *e,* and are often joined and wrote thus, *æ, œ.*

A 2 THE

这本拉丁语语法书上的涂鸦是惠灵顿公爵（Duke of Wellington）和他的朋友乔治·哈蒙德（George Hammond）在伊顿公学读书时所写

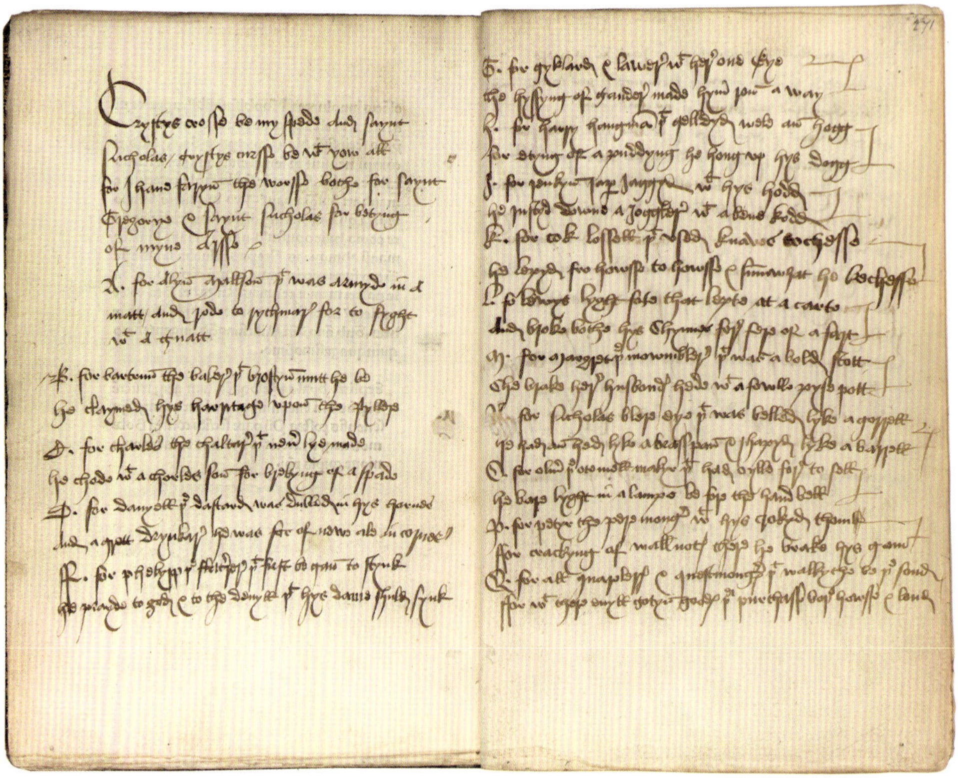

在戏剧表演彩排或提词时使用的戏剧脚本，上面经常会有各种记号，或是标记需要修改或删节的地方，或是注明表演者在舞台上的位置以及导演的要求。《圣经》上经常也会见到一些特殊的批注，例如记录家庭生活中的重大事件，或是对某段祷语的特别理解，《圣经》似乎是记录这些细节最合适的场所。19 世纪初英国布伦德里特（Brundrit）家族所藏的《圣经・新约全书》的开头，记录着这一家族许多人的出生与死亡。历史上，无数普通人家的《圣经》上都有这样的记载。

书中批注的重要性，不仅因为它们可以告诉我们批注者的观点，而且因为它们可能包含别处没有的有关此书文本和出版的重要信息。英国内战期间，伦敦书商乔治・托马森（George Thomason，1600？—1666），收集了大约二万三千种小册子、传单、海报、新闻

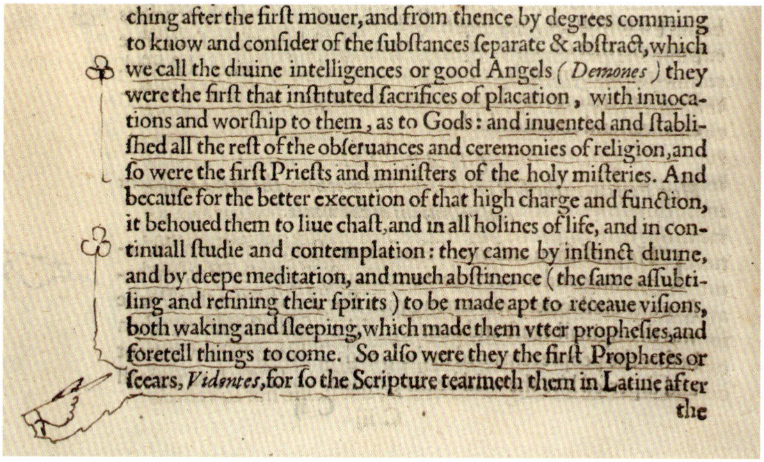
ching after the firſt mouer,and from thence by degrees comming
to know and conſider of the ſubſtances ſeparate & abſtract,which
we call the diuine intelligences or good Angels (*Demones*) they
were the firſt that inſtituted ſacrifices of placation, with inuoca-
tions and worſhip to them, as to Gods: and inuented and ſtabli-
ſhed all the reſt of the obſeruances and ceremonies of religion,and
ſo were the firſt Prieſts and miniſters of the holy miſteries. And
becauſe for the better execution of that high charge and function,
it behoued them to liue chaſt,and in all holines of life, and in con-
tinuall ſtudie and contemplation: they came by inſtinct diuine,
and by deepe meditation, and much abſtinence (the ſame aſſubti-
ling and refining their ſpirits) to be made apt to receaue viſions,
both waking and ſleeping,which made them vtter propheſies,and
foretell things to come. So alſo were they the firſt Prophetes or
ſeears, *Videntes*, for ſo the Scripture tearmeth them in Latine after
the

（左页图）

此书为15世纪后期印刷的一些小册子的合集，由罗切斯特修道院的僧侣约翰·诺布尔（John Noble）收藏，后来进入亨利八世的图书馆，在它的扉页上有一首手书的淫秽打油诗。一位20世纪的编辑这样评论："作为当时的普通读者所喜欢的幽默的例子，这首诗的重要性远远胜过它在文学上的价值。"

（左上图）

人们会用各种符号和线条在自己的藏书上做标记

报道，这个收藏是独一无二的。更重要的是，托马森习惯于每天都在这些出版物上标注日期，这使它们作为历史文献的价值大大增加，后代历史学家们能依此推断在这个政局动乱的时期，那些喋喋不休的争吵的来龙去脉。许多世纪以来，不少书籍因其内容的争议性，作者们不愿暴露身份，将它们匿名或以笔名出版，但他们同时代的读者有的可能知道或猜测作者的身份，所以，他们会在标题页上注明他们认为的作者的名字，这样的书籍并不少见。关于匿名书籍的最重要的多卷本参考书是英国学者哈尔凯特和朗恩（Samuel Halkett & John Laing）编辑的《英文匿名笔名出版物字典》（*Dictionary of Anonymous and Pseudonymous Publications in the English Language*），在进行作者鉴别时，广泛依据了那些有批注的版本。这些作者同代人的批注有时是正确的，有时则是错误的，但无论如何，它们都让我们认识到这些出版物同代人的视角和观点。

有的作者会在他们出版的著作上记录后来的看法，这就非常有意思。一旦印刷之后，文本就会冻结而不可改变（不像如今的电子文本），作者可能在书上更正、添加或改变他们的观点，希望此书重印时可以进行修正，当然，也有许多书没有再被重印。

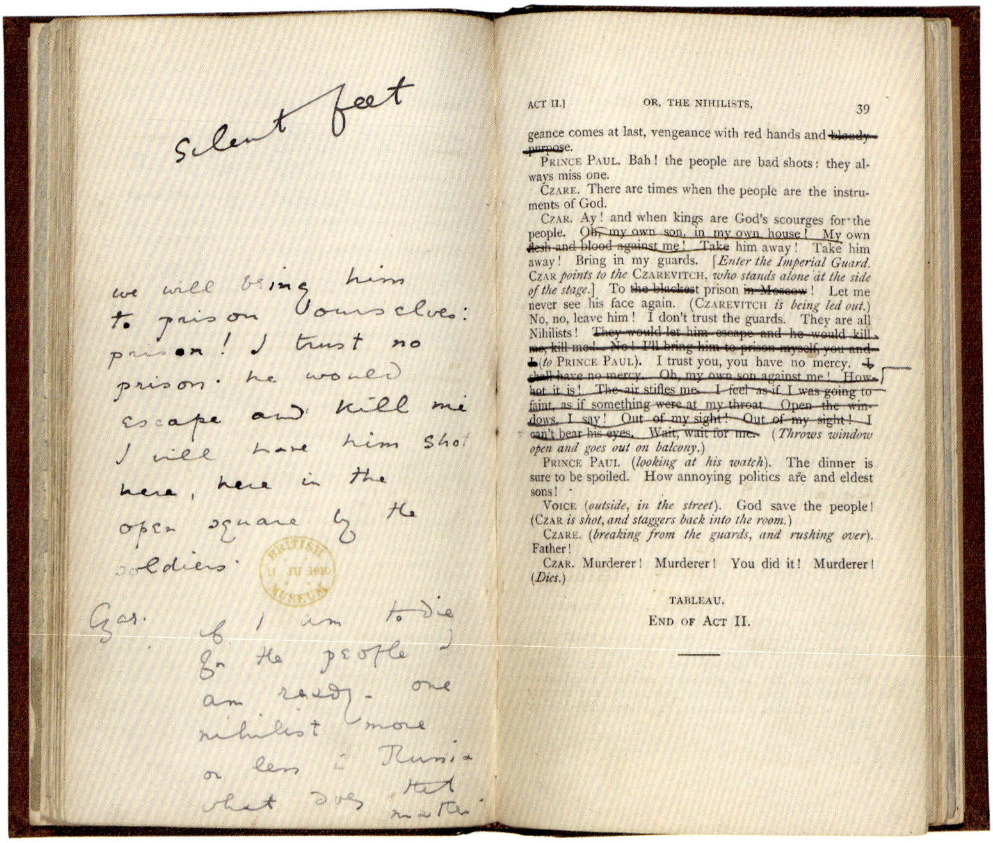
ACT II.] OR, THE NIHILISTS. 39

geance comes at last, vengeance with red hands and bloody purpose.

PRINCE PAUL. Bah! the people are bad shots: they always miss one.

CZARE. There are times when the people are the instruments of God.

CZAR. Ay! and when kings are God's scourges for the people. Oh, my own son, in my own house! My own flesh and blood against me! Take him away! Take him away! Bring in my guards. [*Enter the Imperial Guard.* CZAR *points to the* CZAREVITCH, *who stands alone at the side of the stage.*] To the blackest prison in Moscow! Let me never see his face again. (CZAREVITCH *is being led out.*) No, no, leave him! I don't trust the guards. They are all Nihilists! They would let him escape and he would kill me, kill me! No! I'll bring him to prison myself, you and I (*to* PRINCE PAUL). I trust you, you have no mercy. I shall have no mercy. Oh, my own son against me! How hot it is! The air stifles me. I feel as if I was going to faint, as if something were at my throat. Open the windows, I say! Out of my sight! Out of my sight! I can't bear his eyes. Wait, wait for me. (*Throws window open and goes out on balcony.*)

PRINCE PAUL (*looking at his watch*). The dinner is sure to be spoiled. How annoying politics are and eldest sons!

VOICE (*outside, in the street*). God save the people! (CZAR *is shot, and staggers back into the room.*)

CZARE. (*breaking from the guards, and rushing over*). Father!

CZAR. Murderer! Murderer! You did it! Murderer! (*Dies.*)

TABLEAU.

END OF ACT II.

奥斯卡·王尔德（Oscar Wilde）的第一部剧本《维拉》(*Vera*)，此本曾在 1882 年纽约演出时用来为演员提词，上面标注出实际演出时对原剧本的一些修改

人们对书籍的补充不限于文字，也包含图像，他们在书中可写可画（例如我们前文提到的荷兰律师彼得·范·维恩）。有时除了书中原来的插图外，后人也可以在书中加插进新的插图。因为以前出版物的印刷和装订是由不同人完成的分开的工序，书页被印刷出来后，会根据出版社或购书者的要求进行装订。所以，在装订之前，很容易加入新的文本或插图的书页。这一过程之所以流行，一部分原因是因为版画的繁荣。那些木刻或蚀刻的版画作品被印出许多份，它们可以作为单张图片或画集来保存，可以被挂在墙上，也可以被装订进书籍中。例如，17 和 18 世纪期间，描绘《圣经》故事的版画非常流行，所以，根据购书者的意愿，将这些版画装订进《圣经》中的情况很常见。书

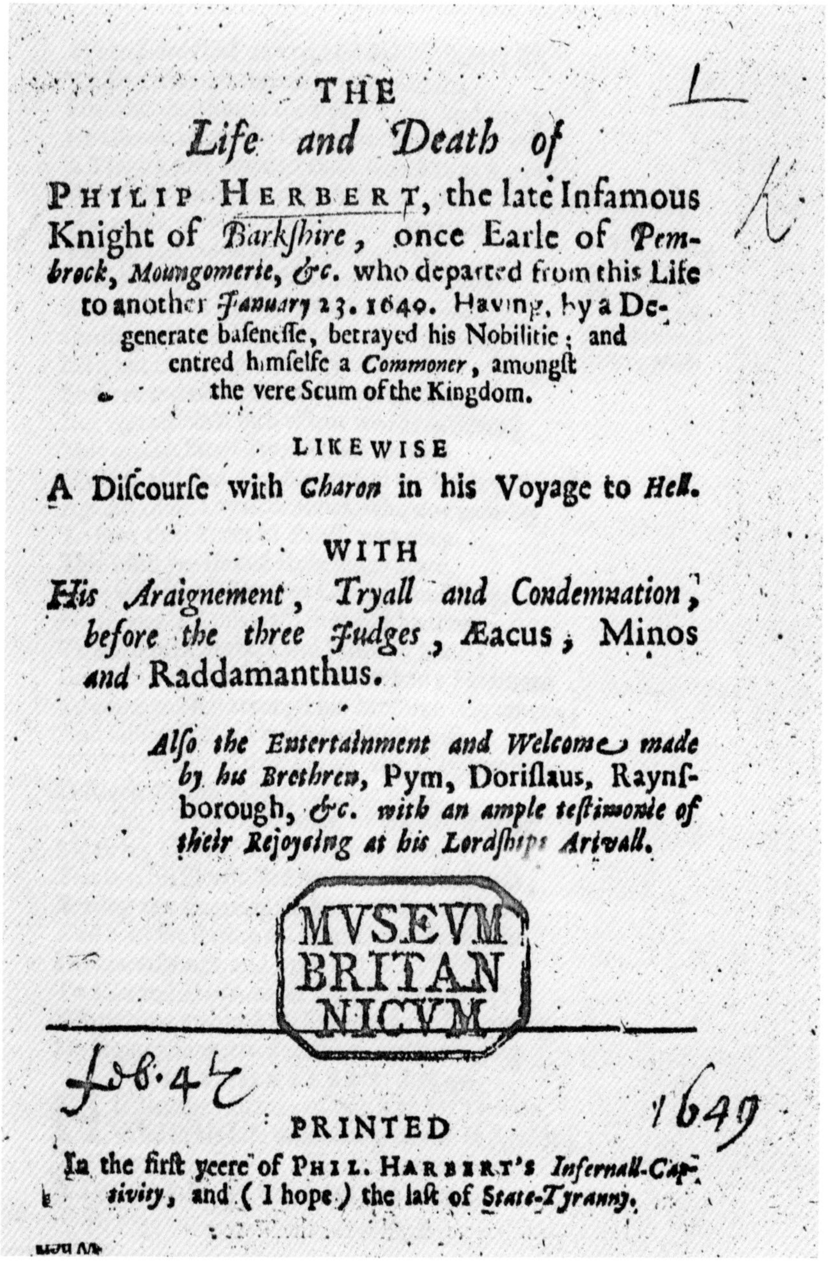

THE

Life and Death of

PHILIP HERBERT, the late Infamous Knight of *Barkshire*, once Earle of *Pembrock*, *Moungomerie*, *&c.* who departed from this Life to another *January* 23. 1640. Having, by a Degenerate basenesse, betrayed his Nobilitie; and entred himselfe a *Commoner*, amongst the vere Scum of the Kingdom.

LIKEWISE

A Discourse with *Charon* in his Voyage to *Hell*.

WITH

His Araignement, Tryall and Condemnation, before the three Judges, Æacus, Minos *and* Raddamanthus.

Also the Entertainment and Welcome made by his Brethren, Pym, Dorislaus, Raynsborough, *&c. with an ample testimonie of their Rejoycing at his Lordships Arivall.*

PRINTED

In the first yeere of PHIL. HARBERT'S *Infernall-Captivity*, and (I hope) the last of *State-Tyranny*.

英国内战时的书商乔治·托马森，他不仅收集了16世纪四五十年代一系列独特的新闻传单和小册子，还在这些出版物上注明了具体日期，对后人来说，他精确地记录历史，功不可没

（下页图）

19世纪初布伦德里特家族的出生、婚嫁、死亡，都记录在这本《圣经》的开头，许多普通家庭在他们的《圣经》或祈祷书中都有这样的记载

Ann Owen Browndrit
Born 22nd August 1820
at 5 Oclock in the Aftern
Died Oct 19th 1826 at half past three in Mo

Elizabeth Browndrit
Born 7th of February 1823
at half past 9 Oclock at nig

Ellen Browndrit Born Jany 28
1826 at ½ past two in the Morn
Died July 4th 1826 at ½ past three in the M

William Wright Browndrit
born 13th September 1827 at half
past three in the Morning

Robt Wright Browndrit born Apr
18th 1830 at eleven Oclock in the forno

John Browndrit Born Jany 4th 183[illegible]
at ¼ before 1 Oclock in the Morning

Joseph Brundrit born 16th May 1835.
Died December 19 1835.

THE GOSPEL according to St. MATTHEW.

CHAP. I.

1 The genealogy of Christ: 18 His conception and birth: 21, 23 His names.

THE book of the generation of Jesus
Christ, the son of David, the son of
Abraham.
2 ¶ Abraham begat Isaac; and Isaac
begat Jacob; and Jacob begat Judas
and his brethren;
3 And Judas begat Phares and Zara of
Thamar; and Phares begat Esrom; and
Esrom begat Aram;
4 And Aram begat Aminadab; and
Aminadab begat Naasson; and Naasson
begat Salmon;
5 And Salmon begat Booz of Rachab;
and Booz begat Obed of Ruth; and Obed
begat Jesse;
6 And Jesse begat David the king;
and David the king begat Solomon of
her *that had been the wife* of Urias;
7 And Solomon begat Roboam; and Ro-
boam begat Abia; and Abia begat Asa;
8 And Asa begat Josaphat; and Josa-
phat begat Joram; and Joram begat
Ozias;
9 And Ozias begat Joatham; and
Joatham begat Achaz; and Achaz begat
Ezekias;
10 And Ezekias begat Manasses; and
Manasses begat Amon; and Amon begat
Josias;
11 And Josias begat Jechonias and his
brethren, about the time they were
carried away to Babylon;
12 And after they were brought to
Babylon, Jechonias begat Salathiel; and
Salathiel begat Zorobabel;
13 And Zorobabel begat Abiud; and
Abiud begat Eliakim; and Eliakim
begat Azor;
14 And Azor begat Sadoc; and Sadoc
begat Achim; and Achim begat Eliud;
15 And Eliud begat Eleazar; and
Eleazar begat Matthan; and Matthan
begat Jacob.
16 And Jacob begat Joseph the husband
of Mary, of whom was born Jesus, who
is called Christ.
17 So all the generations from Abraham
to David *are* fourteen generations; and
from David until the carrying away into
Babylon *are* fourteen generations; and
from the carrying away into Babylon
unto Christ *are* fourteen generations.
18 ¶ Now the birth of Jesus Christ was
on this wise: When as his mother Mary
was espoused to Joseph, before they
came together, she was found with child
of the Holy Ghost.
19 Then Joseph her husband, being
a just *man*, and not willing to make her
a public example, was minded to put
her away privily.
20 But while he thought on these things,
behold, the angel of the LORD appeared
unto him in a dream, saying, Joseph,
thou son of David, fear not to take unto
thee Mary thy wife; for that which is
conceived in her is of the Holy Ghost.
21 And she shall bring forth a son,
and thou shalt call his name JESUS: for
he shall save his people from their sins.
22 Now all this was done, that it
might be fulfilled which was spoken of
the Lord by the prophet, saying,
23 Behold, a virgin shall be with child,
and shall bring forth a son, and they shall
call his name Emmanuel; which being
interpreted, is, God with us.
24 Then Joseph, being raised from
sleep, did as the angel of the Lord had
bidden him, and took unto him his wife:
25 And knew her not till she had
brought forth her first-born son: and he
called his name JESUS.

CHAP. II.

1 The wise men coming to Christ, 11 worship him. 14 Joseph fleeth into Egypt.

NOW when Jesus was born in Beth-
lehem of Judea, in the days of
Herod the king, behold, there came wise
men from the east to Jerusalem,
2 Saying, Where is he that is born King
of the Jews? for we have seen his star
in the east, and are come to worship him.
3 When Herod the king had heard
these things, he was troubled, and all
Jerusalem with him.
4 And when he had gathered all the
chief priests and scribes of the people
together, he demanded of them where
Christ should be born.
5 And they said unto him, In Bethle-
hem of Judea: for thus it is written by
the prophet,
6 And thou Bethlehem, *in* the land of
Juda, art not the least among the princes
of Juda: for out of thee shall come
a Governor, that shall rule my people
Israel.
7 Then Herod, when he had privily
called the wise men, inquired of them
diligently what time the star appeared.
8 And he sent them to Bethlehem;
and said, Go and search diligently for
the young child; and when ye have found
him, bring me word again, that I may
come and worship him also.
9 When they had heard the king, they
departed: and, lo, the star, which they
saw in the east, went before them, till it

Mary Jane Brundrit, born 10 March 1837.
at half past nine in the morning

作者希望隐藏身份而匿名或用笔名出版书籍，但有时他们的同时代人会在书页上记录作者的名字（有些只是猜测），这对后人来说非常有用

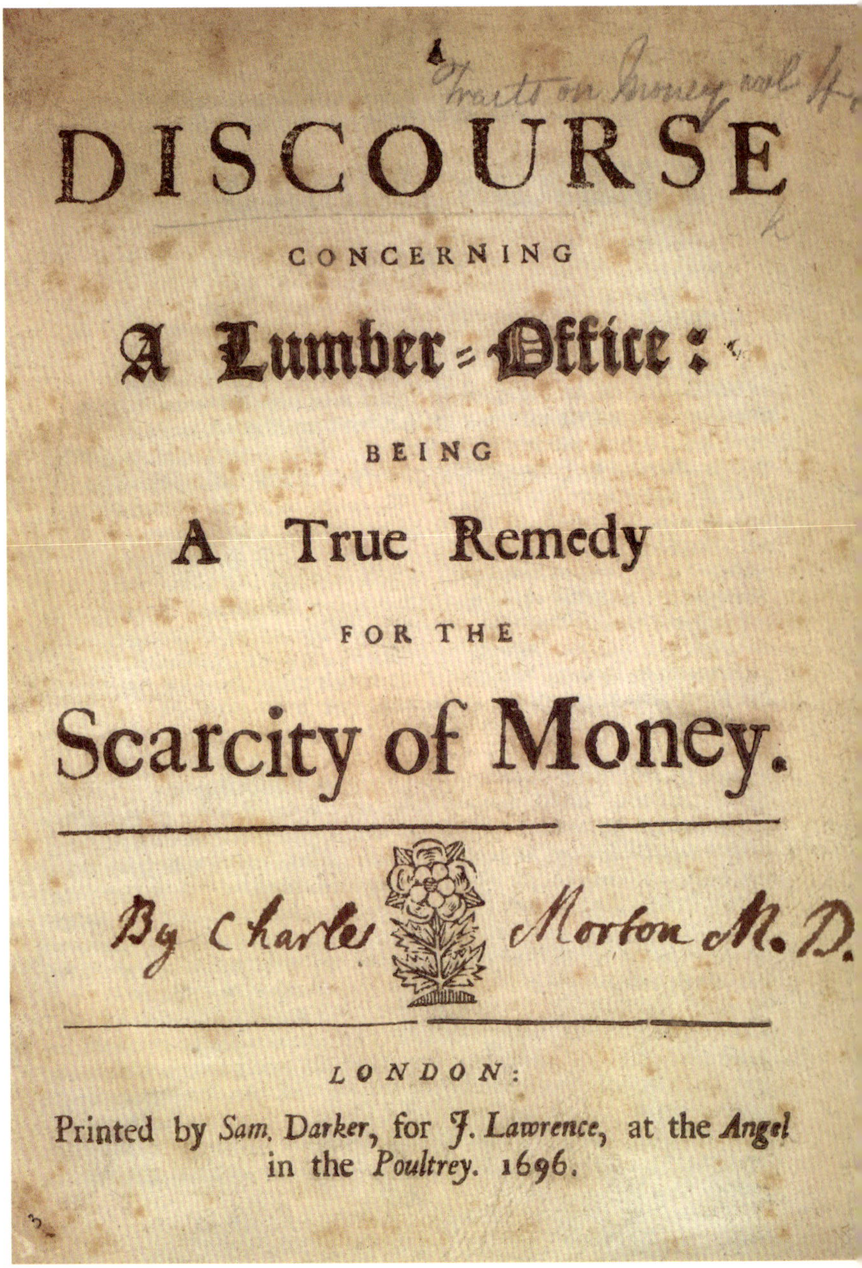
A
DISCOURSE
CONCERNING
A Lumber-Office:
BEING
A True Remedy
FOR THE
Scarcity of Money.

By Charles Morton M.D.

LONDON:
Printed by *Sam. Darker*, for *J. Lawrence*, at the *Angel* in the *Poultrey*. 1696.

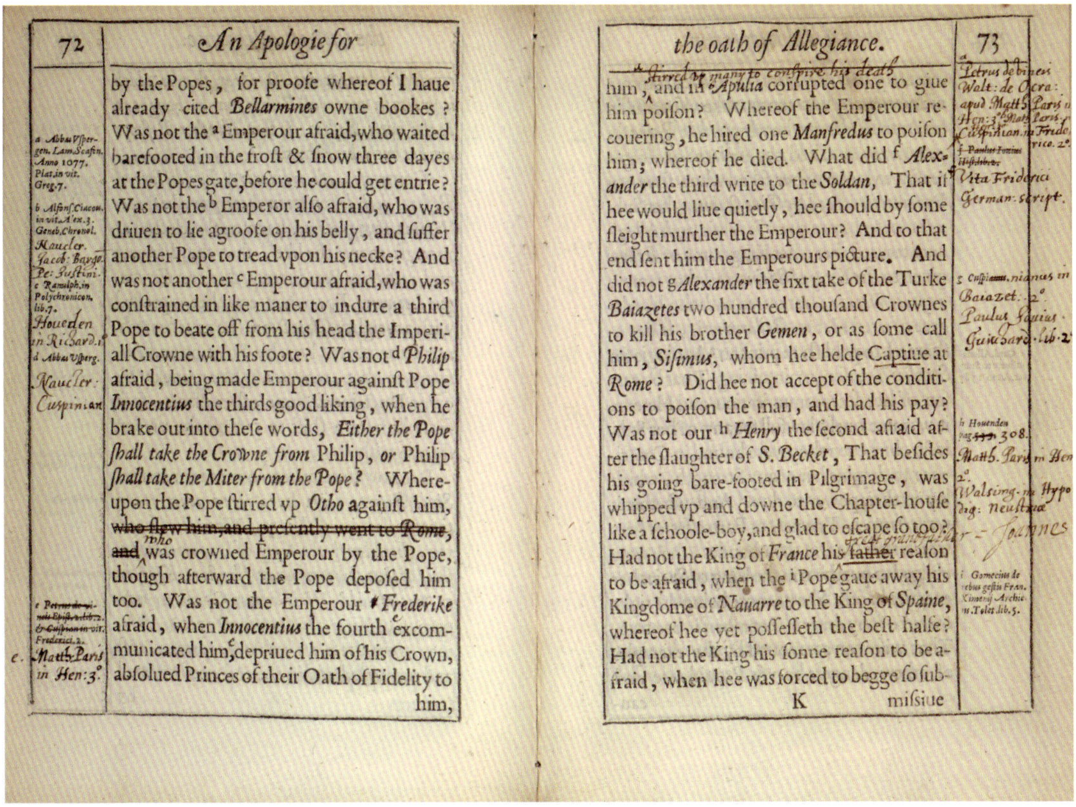

72 An Apologie for

by the Popes, for proofe whereof I haue already cited *Bellarmines* owne bookes? Was not the a Emperour afraid, who waited barefooted in the frost & snow three dayes at the Popes gate, before he could get entrie? Was not the b Emperor also afraid, who was driuen to lie agroofe on his belly, and suffer another Pope to tread vpon his necke? And was not another c Emperour afraid, who was constrained in like maner to indure a third Pope to beate off from his head the Imperiall Crowne with his foote? Was not d *Philip* afraid, being made Emperour against Pope *Innocentius* the thirds good liking, when he brake out into these words, *Either the Pope shall take the Crowne from* Philip, *or* Philip *shall take the Miter from the Pope?* Whereupon the Pope stirred vp *Otho* against him, who slew him, and presently went to *Rome*, and was crowned Emperour by the Pope, though afterward the Pope deposed him too. Was not the Emperour e *Frederike* afraid, when *Innocentius* the fourth excommunicated him, depriued him of his Crown, absolued Princes of their Oath of Fidelity to him,

a Abbas Vsperg. Lam. Scafn. Anno 1077. Plat. in vit. Greg. 7.
b Alfons. Ciacon. in vit. Alex. 3. Geneb. Chronol.
c Ranulph. in Polychronicon. lib. 7.
d Abbas Vsperg.

the oath of Allegiance. 73

him, and in *Apulia* corrupted one to giue him poison? Whereof the Emperour recouering, he hired one *Manfredus* to poison him, whereof he died. What did f *Alexander* the third write to the *Soldan*, That if hee would liue quietly, hee should by some sleight murther the Emperour? And to that end sent him the Emperours picture. And did not g *Alexander* the sixt take of the Turke *Baiazetes* two hundred thousand Crownes to kill his brother *Gemen*, or as some call him, *Sisimus*, whom hee helde Captiue at *Rome*? Did hee not accept of the conditions to poison the man, and had his pay? Was not our h *Henry* the second afraid after the slaughter of *S. Becket*, That besides his going bare-footed in Pilgrimage, was whipped vp and downe the Chapter-house like a schoole-boy, and glad to escape so too? Had not the King of *France* his father reason to be afraid, when the i Pope gaue away his Kingdome of *Nauarre* to the King of *Spaine*, whereof hee yet possesseth the best halfe? Had not the King his sonne reason to be afraid, when hee was forced to begge so submissiue

K

h Houenden pag. 308.
i Gomecius de rebus gestis Fran. Ximenij Archie. Tolet. lib. 5.

籍根据藏家的意愿加入新的插图，这往往被称为是“额外插图”，或被称为“格兰杰式插入法”，这个说法是为了纪念英国18世纪传记作家和收藏家詹姆斯·格兰杰（James Granger，1723—1776），他1769年的著作《英格兰的传记史》（*Biographical history of England*）就是以购书者们在装订时要求加插肖像画而著名。这种加插图画的做法早在格兰杰之前就已存在，在15和16世纪的手抄或印刷书籍中，就有很多它们早期藏家在书中粘贴图片的例子，而且，有时还不仅仅是图片，藏家们也会插入与文本内容有关的签名和手稿资料。

读者通过在书本中批注而增加书的内容，但有时，读者也会删除他们不喜欢或觉得不合适的东西，书的内容因此而减少。污损一本书，虽然是负面的举动，但也赋予了某本书个性化的特征。16世纪英国

英国国王詹姆士一世所写《三个绳节对三个楔或为效忠宣誓辩护》（*Triplici nodo, triplex cuneus or an Apologie for Oath of Allegiance*），是当时新教和天主教教徒之间激烈论战的小册子之一。此本由国王亲笔题写，标注出下次印刷时要做的修改

1532年出版的英文祈祷书中的一页，上面贴有耶稣和跪拜修女的木刻版画。这本书属于圣毕哲修会的赛恩修道院（Syon Abbey）中的一位修士或修女

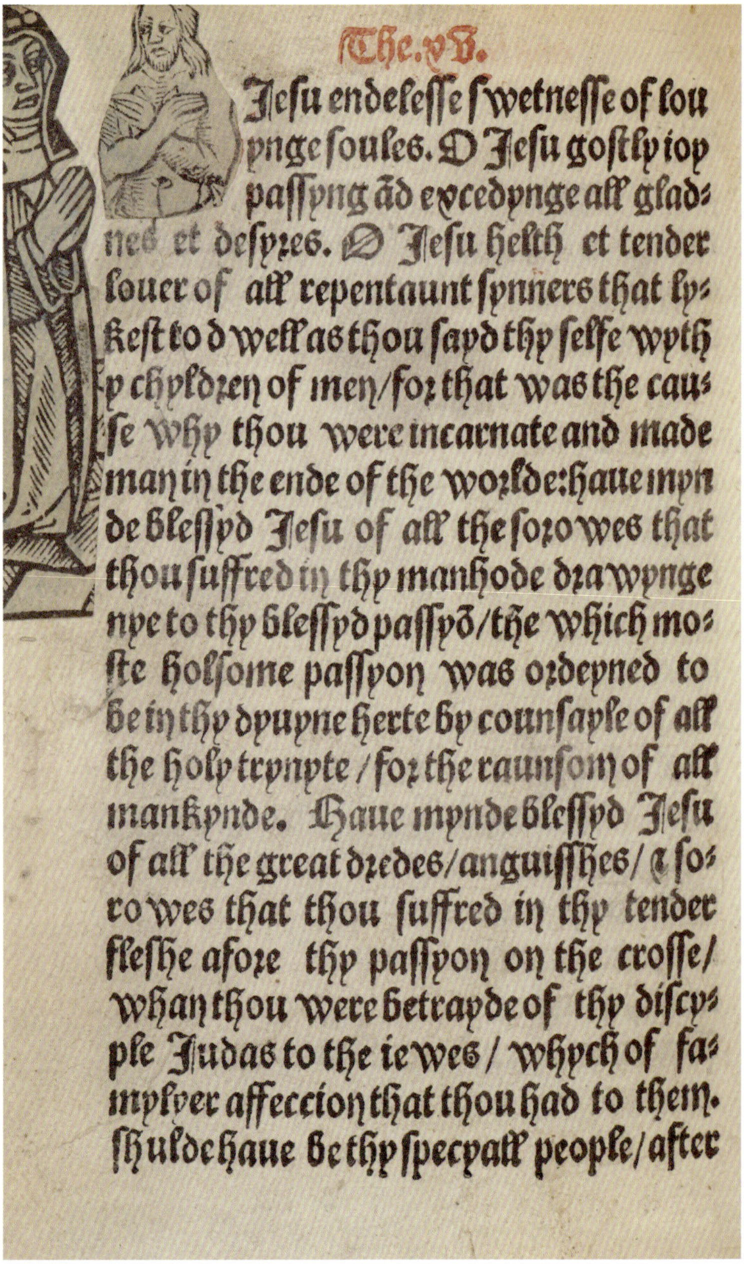
The.vi.
Jesu endelesse swetnesse of lou
ynge soules. O Jesu gostly ioy
passyng ād excedynge all glad-
nes et desyres. O Jesu helth et tender
louer of all repentaunt synners that ly-
kest to dwell as thou sayd thy selfe wyth
ẏ chyldren of men/for that was the cau-
se why thou were incarnate and made
man in the ende of the worlde: haue myn
de blessyd Jesu of all the sorowes that
thou suffred in thy manhode drawynge
nye to thy blessyd passyō/the which mo-
ste holsome passyon was ordeyned to
be in thy dyuyne herte by counsayle of all
the holy trynyte/for the raunsom of all
mankynde. Haue mynde blessyd Jesu
of all the great dredes/anguisshes/& so-
rowes that thou suffred in thy tender
fleshe afore thy passyon on the crosse/
whan thou were betrayde of thy discy-
ple Judas to the iewes/whych of sa-
myler affeccion that thou had to them.
shulde haue be thy specyall people/after

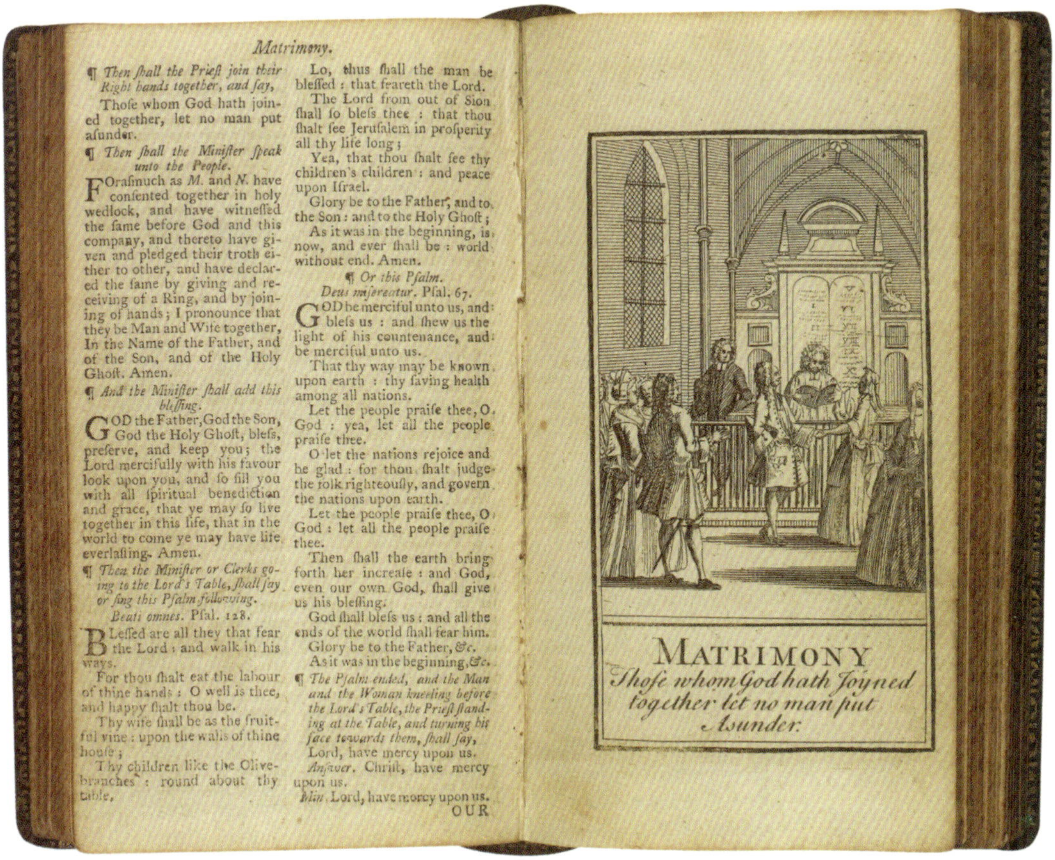
Matrimony.

¶ Then ſhall the Prieſt join their Right hands together, and ſay,

Thoſe whom God hath joined together, let no man put aſunder.

¶ Then ſhall the Miniſter ſpeak unto the People.

FOraſmuch as M. and N. have conſented together in holy wedlock, and have witneſſed the ſame before God and this company, and thereto have given and pledged their troth either to other, and have declared the ſame by giving and receiving of a Ring, and by joining of hands; I pronounce that they be Man and Wife together, In the Name of the Father, and of the Son, and of the Holy Ghoſt. Amen.

¶ And the Miniſter ſhall add this bleſſing.

GOD the Father, God the Son, God the Holy Ghoſt, bleſs, preſerve, and keep you; the Lord mercifully with his favour look upon you, and ſo fill you with all ſpiritual benediction and grace, that ye may ſo live together in this life, that in the world to come ye may have life everlaſting. Amen.

¶ Then the Miniſter or Clerks going to the Lord's Table, ſhall ſay or ſing this Pſalm following.

Beati omnes. Pſal. 128.

BLeſſed are all they that fear the Lord : and walk in his ways.

For thou ſhalt eat the labour of thine hands : O well is thee, and happy ſhalt thou be.

Thy wife ſhall be as the fruitful vine : upon the walls of thine houſe;

Thy children like the Olive-branches : round about thy table.

Lo, thus ſhall the man be bleſſed : that feareth the Lord.

The Lord from out of Sion ſhall ſo bleſs thee : that thou ſhalt ſee Jeruſalem in proſperity all thy life long;

Yea, that thou ſhalt ſee thy children's children : and peace upon Iſrael.

Glory be to the Father, and to the Son : and to the Holy Ghoſt;

As it was in the beginning, is now, and ever ſhall be : world without end. Amen.

¶ Or this Pſalm.

Deus miſereatur. Pſal. 67.

GOD be merciful unto us, and bleſs us : and ſhew us the light of his countenance, and be merciful unto us.

That thy way may be known upon earth : thy ſaving health among all nations.

Let the people praiſe thee, O God : yea, let all the people praiſe thee.

O let the nations rejoice and be glad : for thou ſhalt judge the folk righteouſly, and govern the nations upon earth.

Let the people praiſe thee, O God : let all the people praiſe thee.

Then ſhall the earth bring forth her increaſe : and God, even our own God, ſhall give us his bleſſing.

God ſhall bleſs us : and all the ends of the world ſhall fear him.

Glory be to the Father, &c.

As it was in the beginning, &c.

¶ The Pſalm ended, and the Man and the Woman kneeling before the Lord's Table, the Prieſt ſtanding at the Table, and turning his face towards them, ſhall ſay,

Lord, have mercy upon us.

Anſwer. Chriſt, have mercy upon us.

Min. Lord, have mercy upon us.

OUR

一本 18 世纪的祈祷书，书的主人通过加插一组插图来让此书个性化。原版书并非如此，插图是另外购买后与书页装订在一起的。当时有一系列类似的插图出售

的一些教堂用书，在经历了宗教改革的剧变之后，常常系统地按照亨利八世 1542 年颁布的诏谕而被清理，将所有提及罗马教皇和圣托马斯·贝克特（Saint Thomas à Becket）的内容删除。那些冒犯的话语或是被画掉，或是被剪裁，“洁本”依然可以继续使用。

有史以来，由于政治或宗教的原因，对书籍历来就有各种各样的审查制度。还有另一种对书籍的污损行为可能会被法律制裁。例如，1959 年 1 月，年轻的作家乔·奥顿（Joe Orton）和他的同性恋人肯尼斯·哈利韦尔（Kenneth Halliwell）将伦敦伊斯灵顿公共图书馆的一些书籍偷出来进行污损，他们对护封和内容进行描画和涂写，添加了玩笑或淫秽的内容，然后他们将这些书偷偷放回图书馆书架上，图

1962年，乔·奥顿和肯尼斯·哈利韦尔被判刑入狱，因为他们对伊斯灵顿公共图书馆的一些书籍加以污损，法官在判决时说他们的举动是“纯粹的恶意和破坏，我们必须保护公众”。这些书现在都被保存在伊斯灵顿图书馆，成为当时历史的一部分。奥顿解释他们之所以这么做，是因为伊斯灵顿图书馆中充满了垃圾小说

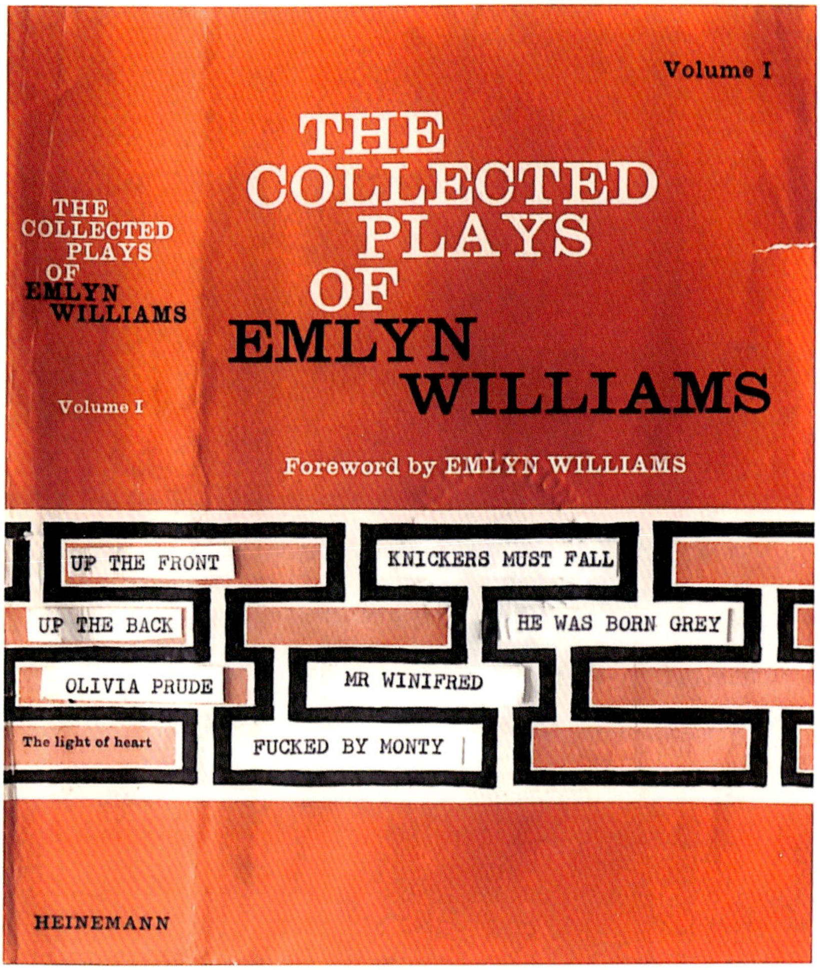

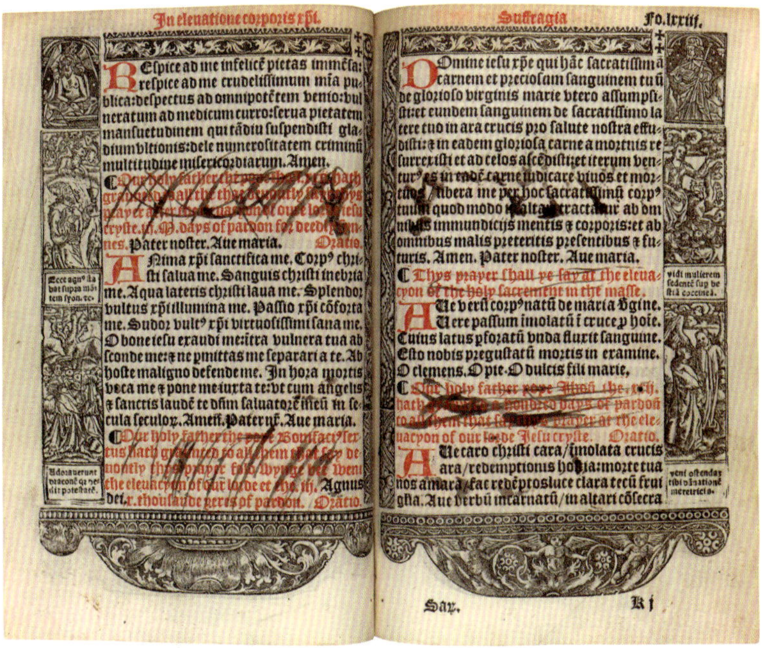
In eleuatione corporis xpi.　　Suffragia　　Fo.lxxiii.

此为 1527 年为英国市场出版的《时段祈祷书》，此书的主人服从亨利八世的诏谕，在祈祷书中画掉了所有提及罗马教皇和圣父的文字

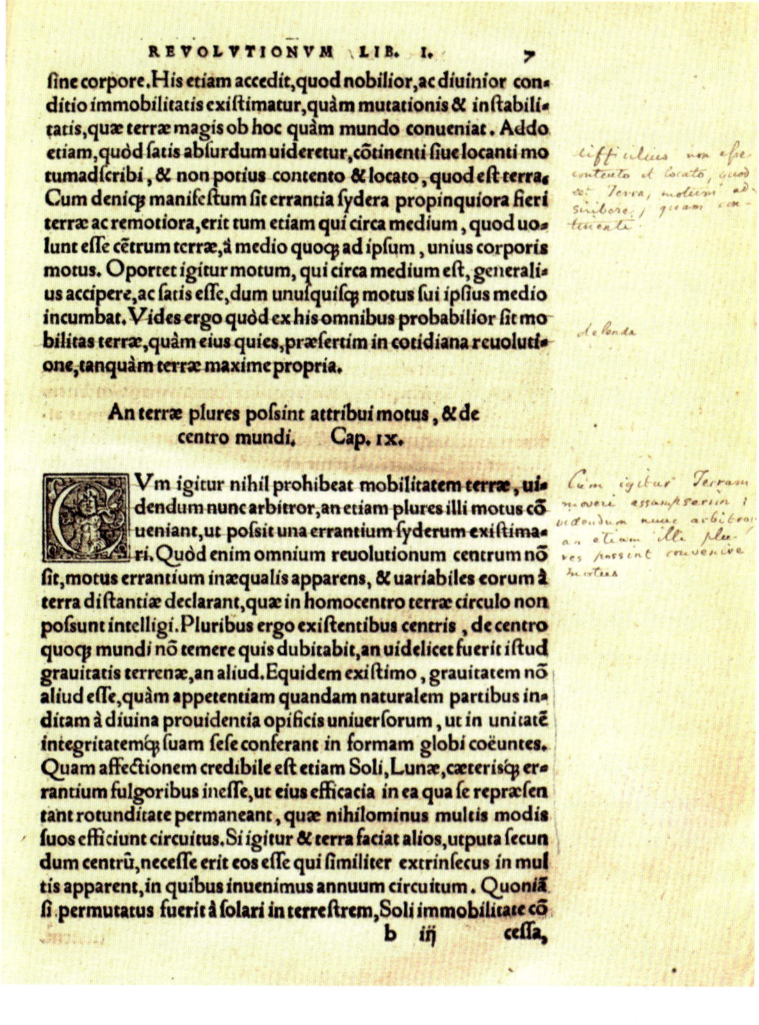
REVOLVTIONVM LIB. I. 7

fine corpore. His etiam accedit, quod nobilior, ac diuinior conditio immobilitatis existimatur, quàm mutationis & instabilitatis, quæ terræ magis ob hoc quàm mundo conueniat. Addo etiam, quòd satis absurdum uideretur, cõtinenti siue locanti motum adscribi, & non potius contento & locato, quod est terra. Cum deniq; manifestum sit errantia sydera propinquiora fieri terræ ac remotiora, erit tum etiam qui circa medium, quod uolunt esse cẽtrum terræ, à medio quoq; ad ipsum, unius corporis motus. Oportet igitur motum, qui circa medium est, generalius accipere, ac satis esse, dum unusquisq; motus sui ipsius medio incumbat. Vides ergo quòd ex his omnibus probabilior sit mobilitas terræ, quàm eius quies, præsertim in cotidiana reuolutione, tanquàm terræ maxime propria.

An terræ plures possint attribui motus, & de centro mundi. Cap. IX.

CVm igitur nihil prohibeat mobilitatem terræ, uidendum nunc arbitror, an etiam plures illi motus cõueniant, ut possit una errantium syderum existimari. Quòd enim omnium reuolutionum centrum nõ sit, motus errantium inæqualis apparens, & uariabiles eorum à terra distantiæ declarant, quæ in homocentro terræ circulo non possunt intelligi. Pluribus ergo existentibus centris, de centro quoq; mundi nõ temere quis dubitabit, an uidelicet fuerit istud grauitatis terrenæ, an aliud. Equidem existimo, grauitatem nõ aliud esse, quàm appetentiam quandam naturalem partibus inditam à diuina prouidentia opificis uniuersorum, ut in unitatẽ integritatemq; suam sese conferant in formam globi coeuntes. Quam affectionem credibile est etiam Soli, Lunæ, cæterisq; errantium fulgoribus inesse, ut eius efficacia in ea qua se repræsentant rotunditate permaneant, quæ nihilominus multis modis suos efficiunt circuitus. Si igitur & terra faciat alios, utputa secundum centrũ, necesse erit eos esse qui similiter extrinsecus in multis apparent, in quibus inuenimus annuum circuitum. Quoniã si permutatus fuerit à solari in terrestrem, Soli immobilitate cõcessa,

b iij

哥白尼著名的有关地球围着太阳公转的著作，在 1620 年受到罗马天主教会的审查，教皇传下诏令要求删除书中的许多段落。此为 1543 年的初版本，书的主人根据诏令在上面进行删除和修改

书馆特地雇用了额外的工作人员，花了很长时间才将他们抓获。1962年5月，奥顿和哈利韦尔被判六个月监禁，在今天看来，这个处罚是有些严重了。奥顿后来说这几个月的监狱生活是他文学创作生涯的突破点，让他成为一位成功的剧作家。现在，被这二位污损的书籍已经成为20世纪60年代文化史的一部分，当年将他们送进监狱的伊斯灵顿图书馆还特地为这些书举办过特展。

传说中圣波尼法爵用来抵御杀人凶手的手抄书，书页被宝剑划破。此书为福尔达大教堂珍藏（右页图）。圣波尼法爵的画像经常是手执宝剑，剑上刺挑着此书（上图）

— 因关联而崇拜 —

长期以来，人们一直认为与某位历史名人或历史事件有关联的书籍有特殊的收藏价值，这也是最早人们对于书籍历史来源的兴趣。德国的福尔达大教堂（The Cathedral of Fulda）藏有一本6世纪的手抄福音书，此书的木制封面上有被宝剑划破的痕迹，传说8世纪德国传教士圣波尼法爵（St Boniface）曾用此书作为抵御异教徒攻击的盾牌。它的盾牌功能显然不到位，所以圣波尼法爵还是被杀死了，但从那以后，这本书就成了宝藏。

现藏于剑桥大学基督圣体学院（Corpus Christi College, Cambridge）的6世纪的《圣奥古斯丁福音书》（*Gospels of St Augustine*）极为珍贵，因为它是现存最古老的福音书。公元597年，圣奥古斯丁前来英国布道，亲自将此书带来，这就让这本福音书更为特殊。 我们知道，无数个世纪以来，这样的书籍因为它们与圣人的关联，格外被人崇拜。在一幅15世纪描绘坎特伯雷圣奥古斯丁大教堂圣坛的画中，我们能看到这本书也在画上。此书和其他被认为曾经属于圣奥古斯丁的珍贵文物一起，被陈列在圣坛前。当时还有一个传说：一位当地农民在这些书上宣了假誓，结果变得双目失明。

书籍并不都需要与圣人有所关联才能变得特殊。任何一本曾被有些名气的历史人物拥有过或使用过的书籍，无论那人是英雄还是恶

棍，都能沾上灵气，被视为收藏真品。一本二手或古旧书籍，其价格会因它的连带关系而上升，与它的前任拥有者的名声以及后人对他们的兴趣成正比。某本普通的二手书店中的低价书，如果扉页上有丘吉尔或约翰·列侬的签名，那价格就会飙升。在一些重要的科学论文的单印本中，这一现象更为鲜明。例如，1953 年的《自然》上发表了首次揭示 DNA 结构的论文，此论文的单印本，上有两位科学家克里克（Crick）和沃森（Watson）的亲笔签名，转手价格为数万英镑，虽然这三页纸的论文可以随意从网上下载打印。

有些书籍，如果是与某个特定的历史事件有关，那就更有意思。英国九日女王简·格雷（Lady Jane Grey）有一本手抄的祈祷书，上有她手书的关于“生之日，死之时”的语句，据说，1554 年她在伦敦塔被处决时，她曾把这本书带上了断头台。有了这种关联，此书也就特别让人感动。还有另一种连带关系特别有价值，那就是作者送给朋友或同仁的签名本。

这本6世纪的《圣奥古斯丁福音书》是圣奥古斯丁于公元597年带到英国的，因为它的历史关联，所以格外宝贵。至今，坎特伯雷大主教宣誓就职时，仍然使用此书（左页图）。此为中世纪末期描绘坎特伯雷圣奥古斯丁大教堂圣坛的图画，画上就有这本《圣奥古斯丁福音书》，此书和其他一些被认为属于圣奥古斯丁的神圣文物一起，被展放在大教堂的圣坛前（左图）

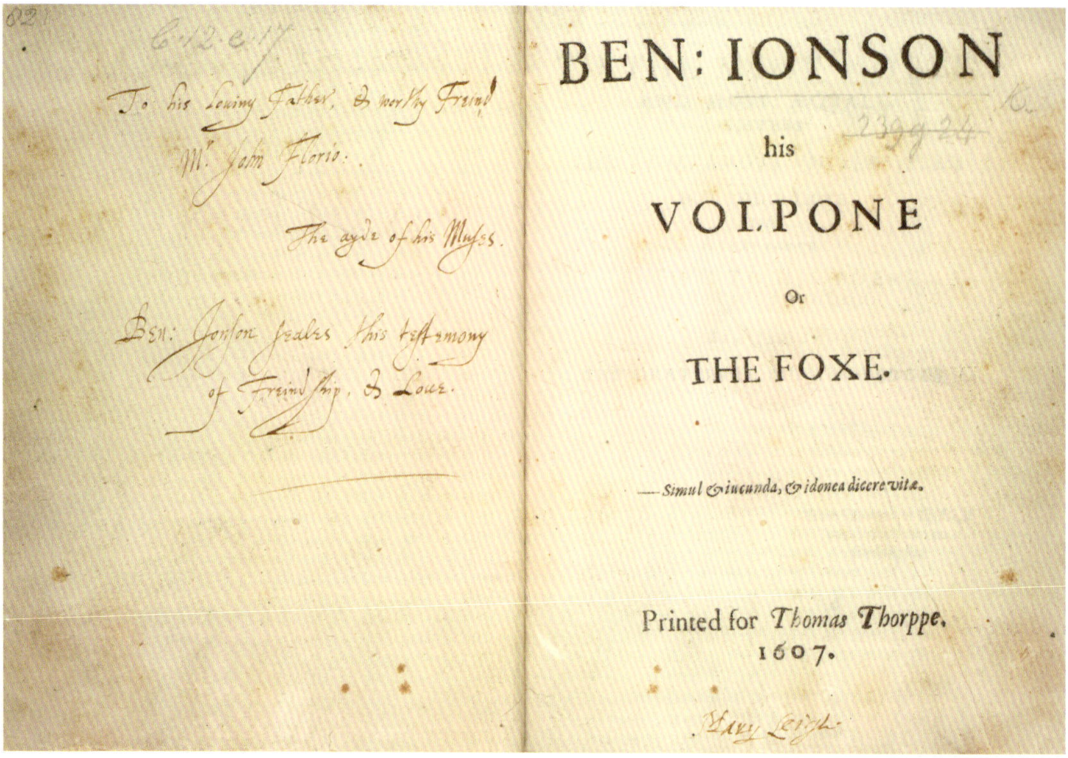

（上图）

英国文艺复兴时的剧作家本·琼森的作品《福尔蓬奈》（*Volpone*）初版本，由剧作家签赠给他同时代的作家和词典编纂者约翰·弗洛里奥（John Florio）

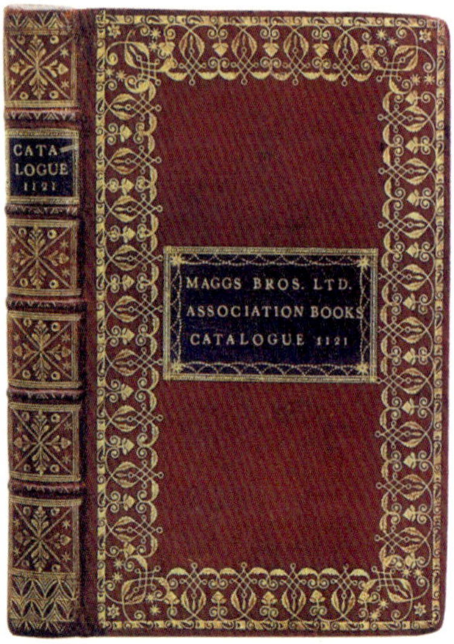

（右图）

与著名人物有关联的书籍一直是人们喜欢收藏的，书商的目录也常常会强调这种关联

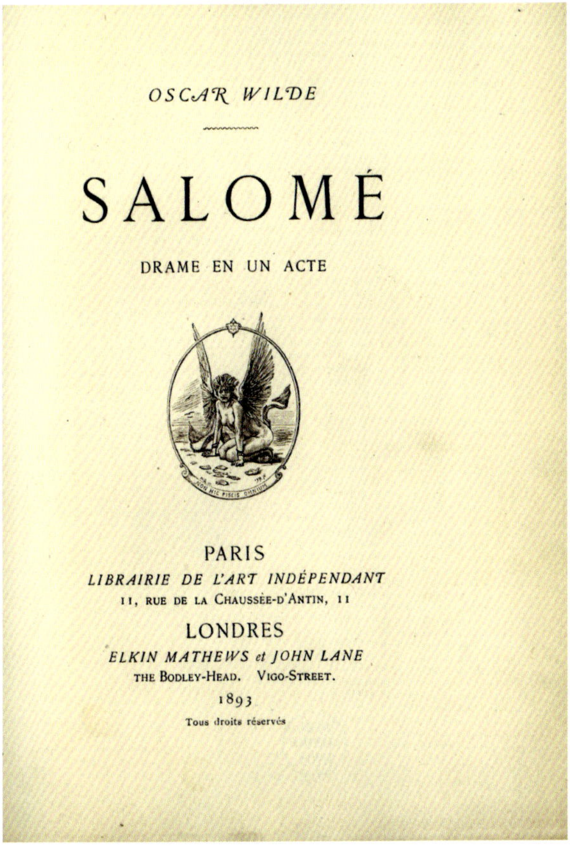

OSCAR WILDE

SALOMÉ

DRAME EN UN ACTE

PARIS
LIBRAIRIE DE L'ART INDÉPENDANT
11, RUE DE LA CHAUSSÉE-D'ANTIN, 11

LONDRES
ELKIN MATHEWS et JOHN LANE
THE BODLEY-HEAD. VIGO-STREET.
1893

Tous droits réservés

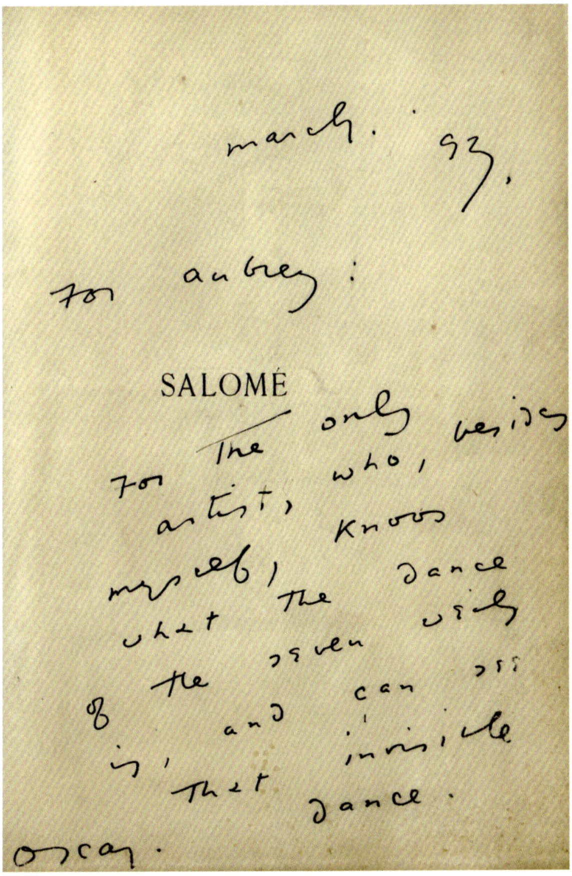

march. 93.

for aubrey:

SALOMÉ

for the only artist, who, besides myself, knows what the dance of the seven veils is, and can see that invisible dance.

oscar.

奥斯卡·王尔德的《莎乐美》（*Salomé*），此本由作者签赠给另一位世纪末的作家奥伯利·比亚兹莱（Aubrey Beardsley），扉页上的赠言写道：“给奥伯利：除了我以外，你是唯一知道什么是七层面纱舞蹈的艺术家，而且能够看到那种无形的舞蹈。奥斯卡。”

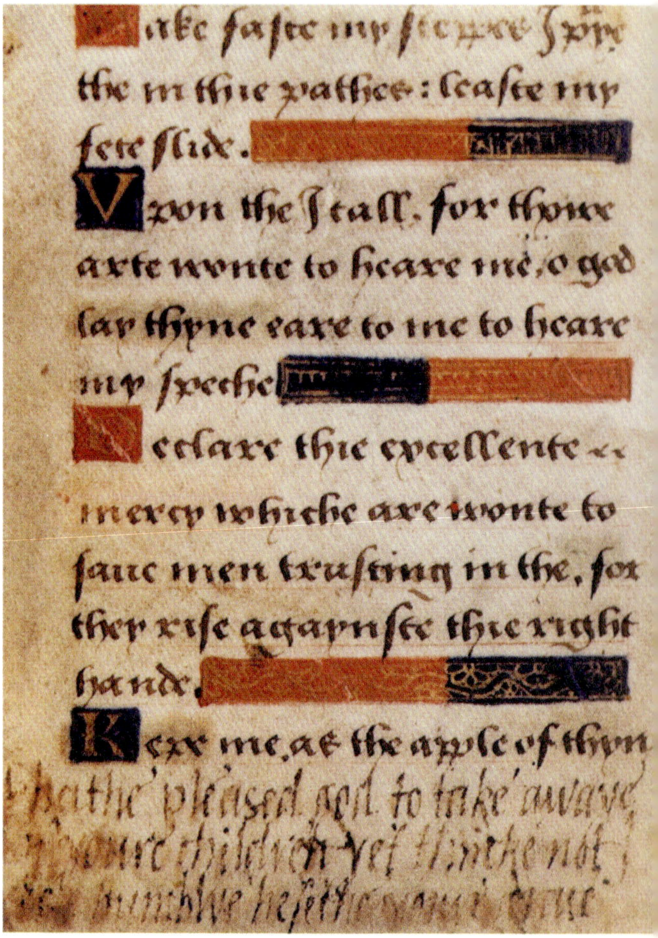

Make faste my steppes

the in thine pathes: leaste my

fete slide.

Vpon the I call. for thowe

arte wonte to heare me, o god

lay thyne eare to me to heare

my speche

Declare thie excellente

mercy whiche are wonte to

saue men trusting in the. for

they rise agaynste thie right

hande.

Kepe me, as the apple of thyn

it hathe pleased god to take awaye

your children yet thinke not

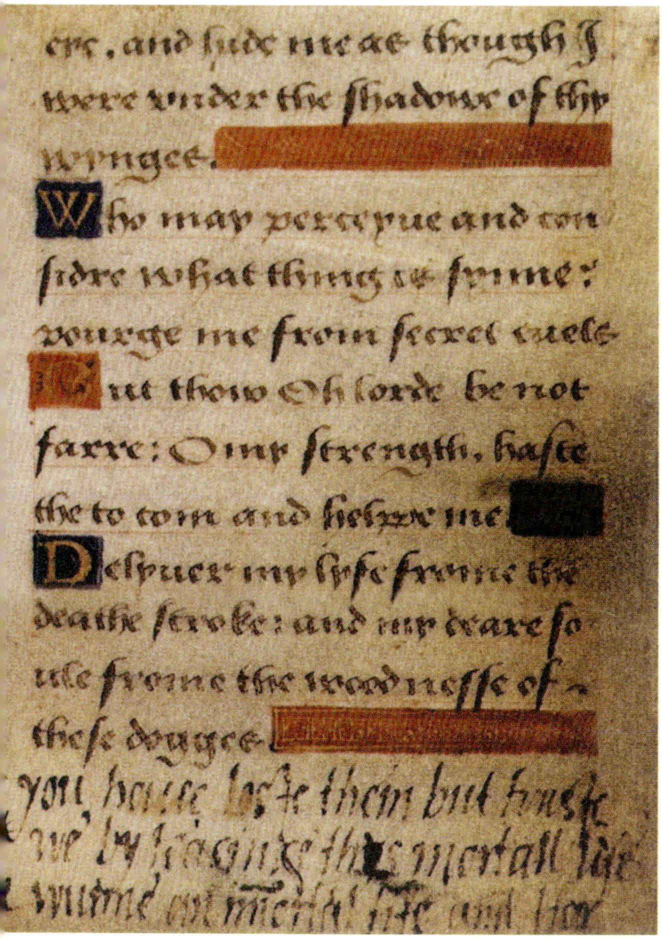
ers. and hide me as though I
were under the shadowe of thy
wynges.
Who may perceyue and con
sidre what thing is synne:
pourge me from secret euels.
But thow Oh lorde be not
farre: Our strength, haste
the to torn and helpe me.
Delyuer my lyfe frome the
deathe stroke: and my deare so
ule frome the woodnesse of
these dogges.

1554 年在伦敦塔中被处死的简·格雷的《祈祷书》，其中有她写给父亲和伦敦塔中尉的笔记，内容为她对死亡的思考

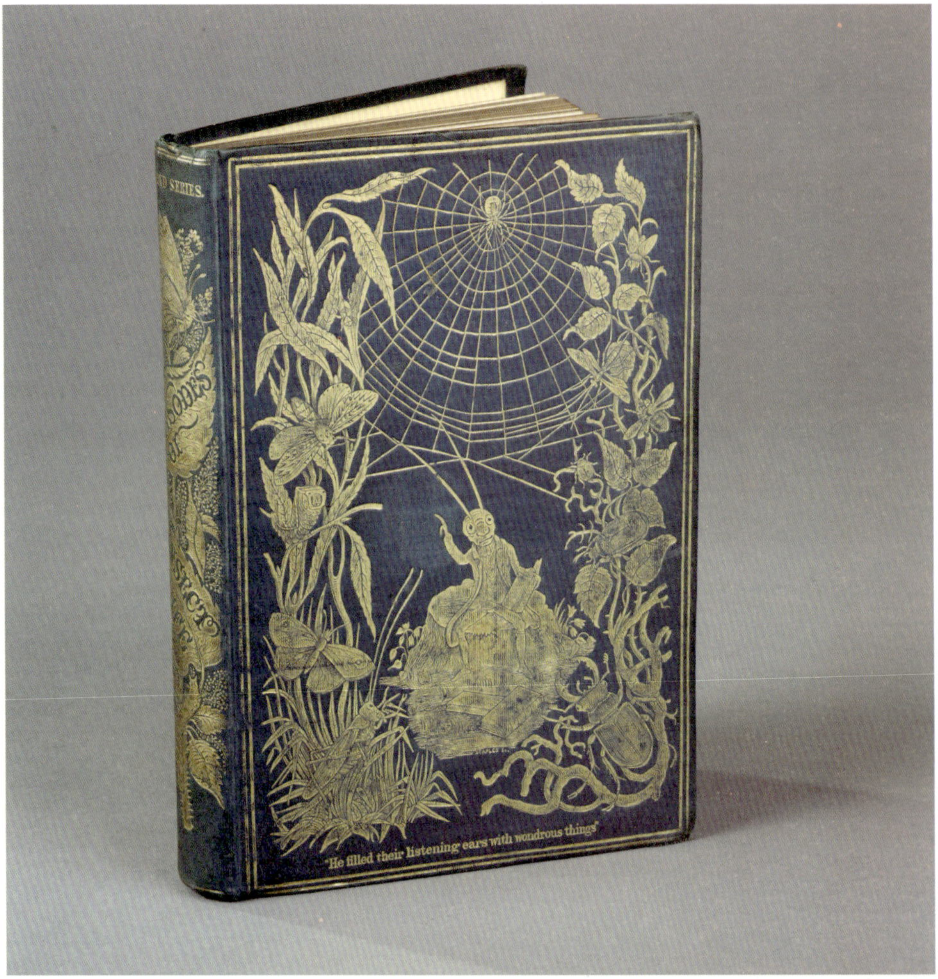

"He filled their listening ears with wondrous things"

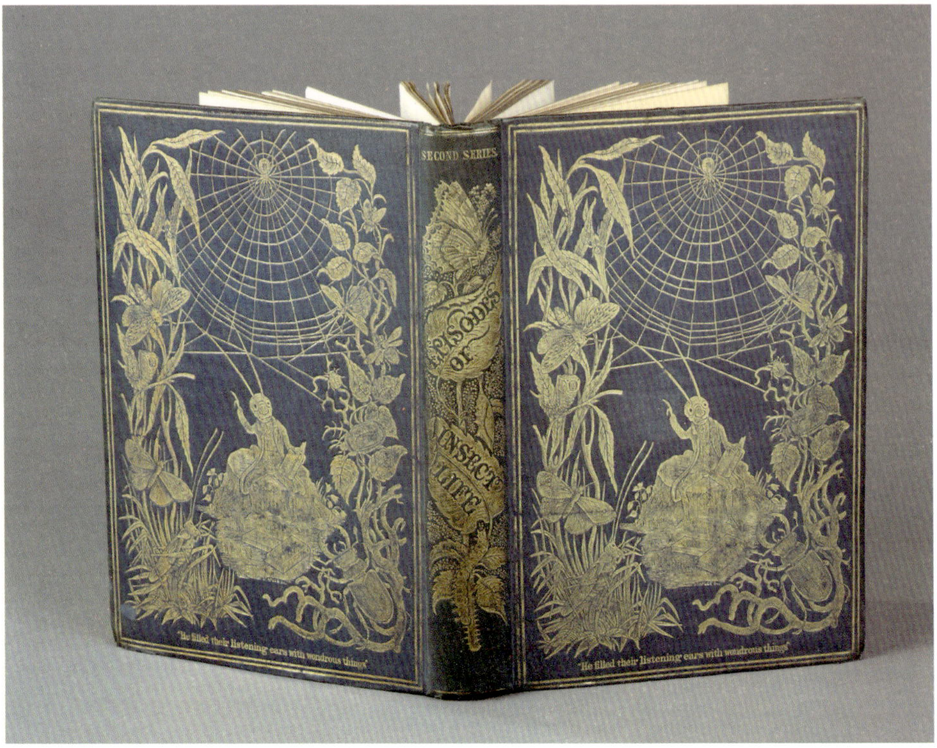

SECOND SERIES.
EPISODES OF INSECT LIFE
"He filled their listening ears with wondrous things"

5

CHAPTER FIVE
VARIETY THROUGH BINDING

第五章 因装帧而得不同

（左页图）
19 世纪中期书籍开始使用布面装帧，让维多利亚时代的设计师们有机会创造出色彩丰富、充满想象力的封面

书籍的封面设计及装订样式，是展示每本书独特个性及历史的另一处重要看点。和印刷一样，数百年来，书籍装帧也是一门手工工艺，这种情况一直延续到 19 世纪，因为需求的增长和技术的革新，整个出版业产生了巨大的变化。如今的书籍基本上都以统一装订的方式出版，按照出版商要求的规格进行大批量生产，对读者来说，除了区分精装和平装，很少或根本就没有其他的选择余地。这种统一装订的根源来自 19 世纪 30 年代，当时印刷技术上的一个突破是布面装帧的发明，可以直接用机械在上面进行装饰和印刷。在那之前，从中世纪开始，皮革一直是书籍封面装帧的主要材料。布面新技术加速了书籍封面从皮面装帧向更便宜的布面或纸面装帧的转化，而且也让同一版次的书籍拥有统一的封面成为可能。这一进步也带来了如今我们已经习以为常的带有图案设计的封面和护封。手工印刷的时代，书籍的封面也会有多种多样的装饰，但图案基本上都是抽象的，与书籍内容没有多大关系。这一情况在维多利亚时代开始改变，设计师们充分利用了布料封面所提供的新机会，并演变为一直持续到今天的封面设计传统。

在 19 世纪之前，书籍装帧和印刷一样，是由经过专门训练的工艺师来进行的，这些工艺师或是单独工作，或是与少数几人组成工作坊。书籍装帧师从印刷师那里拿到印好的书页，将它们折叠、缝制、

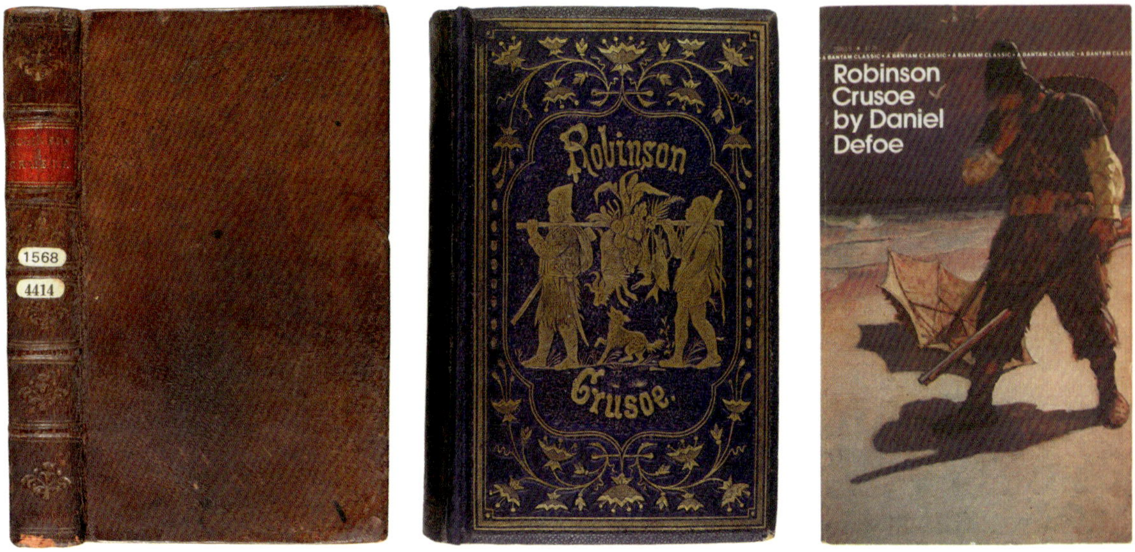

能够反映出文本内容的封面，是19世纪的产物。此三例为18、19和20世纪出版的《鲁宾逊漂流记》，均为原装帧

装订成书，书的封面具有保护作用，往往用皮革制成。所以，这些书籍中的每一本都是独特的手工制成品，和之前的手抄书一样，是独具个性的，特别是它们的装帧，与书页相比，更是独一无二的。即使同一位装帧师刻意制作两本式样风格相同的书，使用同样的材料和装饰工具，但因为每一本都是手工制作，两者之间会有不可避免的细微差异。

对书籍封面进行装饰非常重要。自从人们制作书籍以来，封面装帧就既有功能性，也有装饰性。装帧的技艺五花八门，几个世纪以来，最主要的方式是使用雕有图案的金属工具在皮革上压印花纹，这些花纹可能是素压花，也可能是烫金的。使用这些基本技术，历史上无数代的装帧师制作了从简单到豪华的精美书籍。每一代都有大师级的工匠，他们制作出美轮美奂的精品，被当时富有的藏书家们收藏，以其伟大的艺术成就被后代人崇拜欣赏。但每一本伟大的书籍，总会伴随

书籍装帧和印刷一样，过去都是手工技艺，每一步骤都是由工匠手工完成。首先要将印刷好的书页折叠，然后将它们缝制在一起，包括将它们用线绳固定在用作封面封底的硬板上，再用皮革包裹硬板，并在书脊的上下两端缝绑成护头，然后用加热的金属工具对封面封底进行装饰

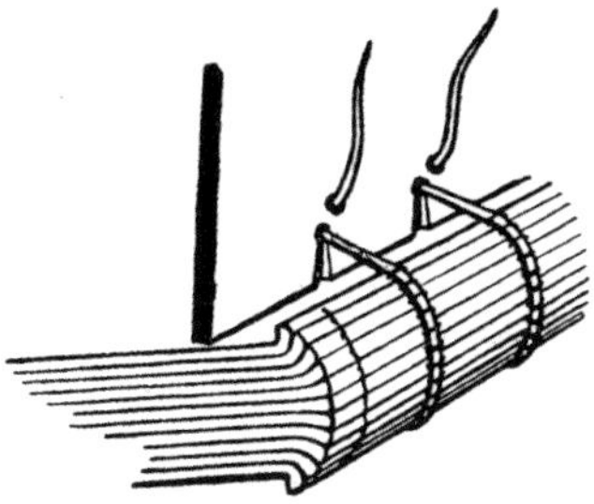

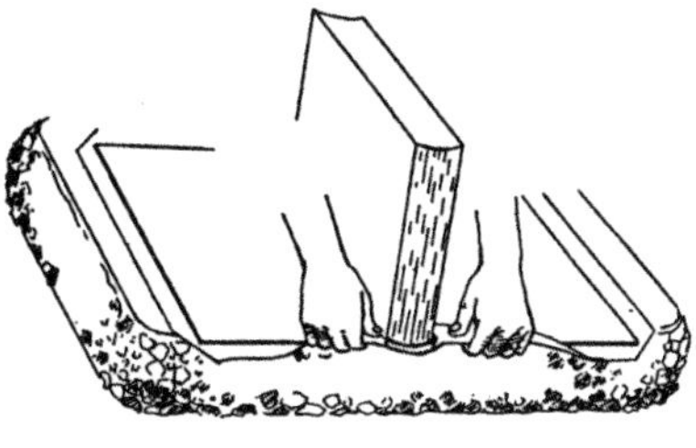

着许多不那么出色的书籍，它们共同构筑出历史。

不管某本书的装帧是奢华还是简单，每本都能讲述一个故事。装帧师会给顾客提供从简到奢的一系列方案，人们对装帧的选择展示他们的性格，也能表达他们对文本的理解。这些选择不仅在于装帧的外观，也在于装帧的内在。因为手工装帧时，要省钱的最好办法是在内部环节上偷工减料，例如缝订等内部结构方面。最后的成品如果价格便宜，可能就不会坚固耐用。早期的顾客给装帧师的指令很少有流传下来的，但从为数不多现存的例子来看，顾客更重视坚固的缝纫和高质量的手工，而不是漂亮的外表装饰。

花哨的书籍装帧显示出顾客能支付得起额外的费用，这些人可能

希望通过书籍来显摆自己的财富或地位，也可能他们送去装帧的是特别重要的书籍。简单的装帧也能揭示一些个人历史，例如当约翰·多恩还是一位贫困的穷诗人时，他的许多藏书都是用羊皮纸装订的，而不是厚一些的皮革，这种软装订在当时是一种便宜的选择。许多书籍在历史上可能不止被装订过一次，许多被后代人重新装订过，这些变化能够反映出人们对文本的态度。一本经过了几个世纪仍然干净如新的书，说明人们可能对它的内容没有多大的兴趣。如今，世界各大图书馆中都会藏有莎士比亚 1623 年的《第一对开本》，其中大部分都是 19 世纪最优质的装帧，反映出人们对此书的崇敬之情。也有为数不多的《第一对开本》保留了它们非常简单的原始装帧，其数量不超过

书籍有史以来，它们的外表就是人们可以装饰的空间，此为 16 世纪到 18 世纪一些高档的书籍装帧范例

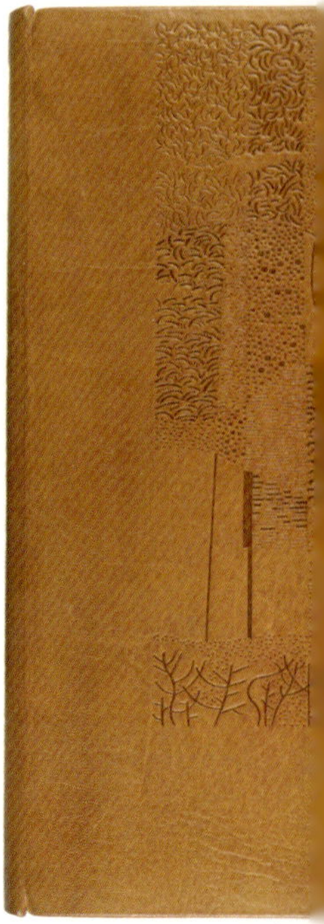

两百本。尽管我们现在认为文学比神学要重要得多，但 17 世纪的宗教祈祷文本的装帧远比文学作品要优异，这是与那个时代的价值观一致的。

书籍装帧不仅能传递一些可被后人解释的信息，而且也提供了何时何地制成此书的直接信息。许多世纪以来，皮革装帧所使用的基本材料和方法都没有太大改变，但是封面的装饰习惯却跟随着各代的时尚潮流不断地变化着，这一代和那一代很不一样。所以，乍看上去，一墙皮面书籍好像都差不多，其实不然。就像 16 世纪的建筑或银器与 18 世纪的大不相同，不同时代的书籍装帧也有着明显的特点。精美装帧的书籍如此，简单装帧的书籍也不例外。1600 年六便士装帧

本与 1700 年的，甚至 1650 年的都不一样。与印刷师不同，装帧师很少在他们的作品上签名，所以，通常我们无法识别单个工匠的作品。装帧师以及他们的客户大都会顺从整个时代的风格习惯，一般都不会独辟蹊径。后代研究者们可以根据某一时代和地区的特点，来鉴别某一装帧，这样我们能分辨出它们是英国、德国或法国的装帧，大约是在哪个时段，是在哪个地区制成。

书籍装帧师的客户可能是个人，也可能是书商。我们会偶尔看到一些独一无二的装帧，但更多时候，我们所看到的同一时代同一地区的装帧，都是比较相似的。尽管如此，因为整个制书业是由许多小作坊组成，所以，任何一本书的某一版本——已经印刷出来的那一千套

19 和 20 世纪，高质量的艺术化的书籍装帧传统一直延续，到了 20 世纪中期，在英国设计师装帧运动（Designer Bookbinders）的支持下，精美的书籍装帧更是蓬勃发展

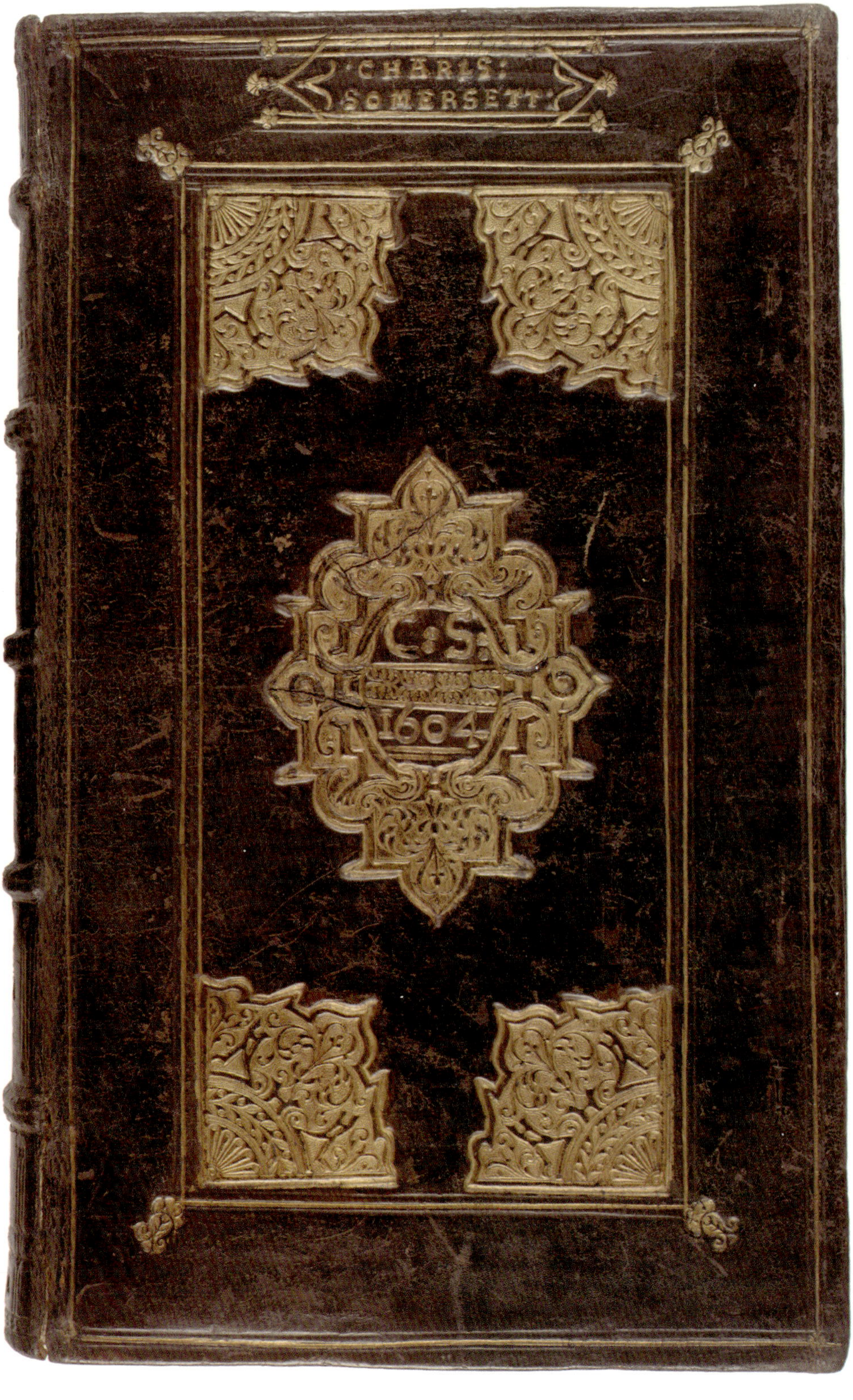
CHARLS:
SOMERSETT
C. S.
1604

富有的藏书家们可以将他们的藏书进行豪华装帧，不那么有钱的就得接受较为平淡的装帧风格。左为1604年为查尔斯·萨默塞特爵士（Sir Charles Somerset）装帧的书籍，右为诗人约翰·多恩在同一年代的藏书

莎士比亚的《第一对开本》，从那些保留了原装帧的书上我们能看出，此书最初的装帧非常简单平淡，此本为牛津大学博德利图书馆所藏1623年版本。到了19和20世纪，此书往往以非常豪华的风格被重新装帧，显示了后人对莎士比亚的作品更为尊重，也反映了后代藏书家的口味。此例（*右页图*）为19世纪仿17世纪末的装帧风格，现藏于美国华盛顿的福尔杰莎士比亚图书馆

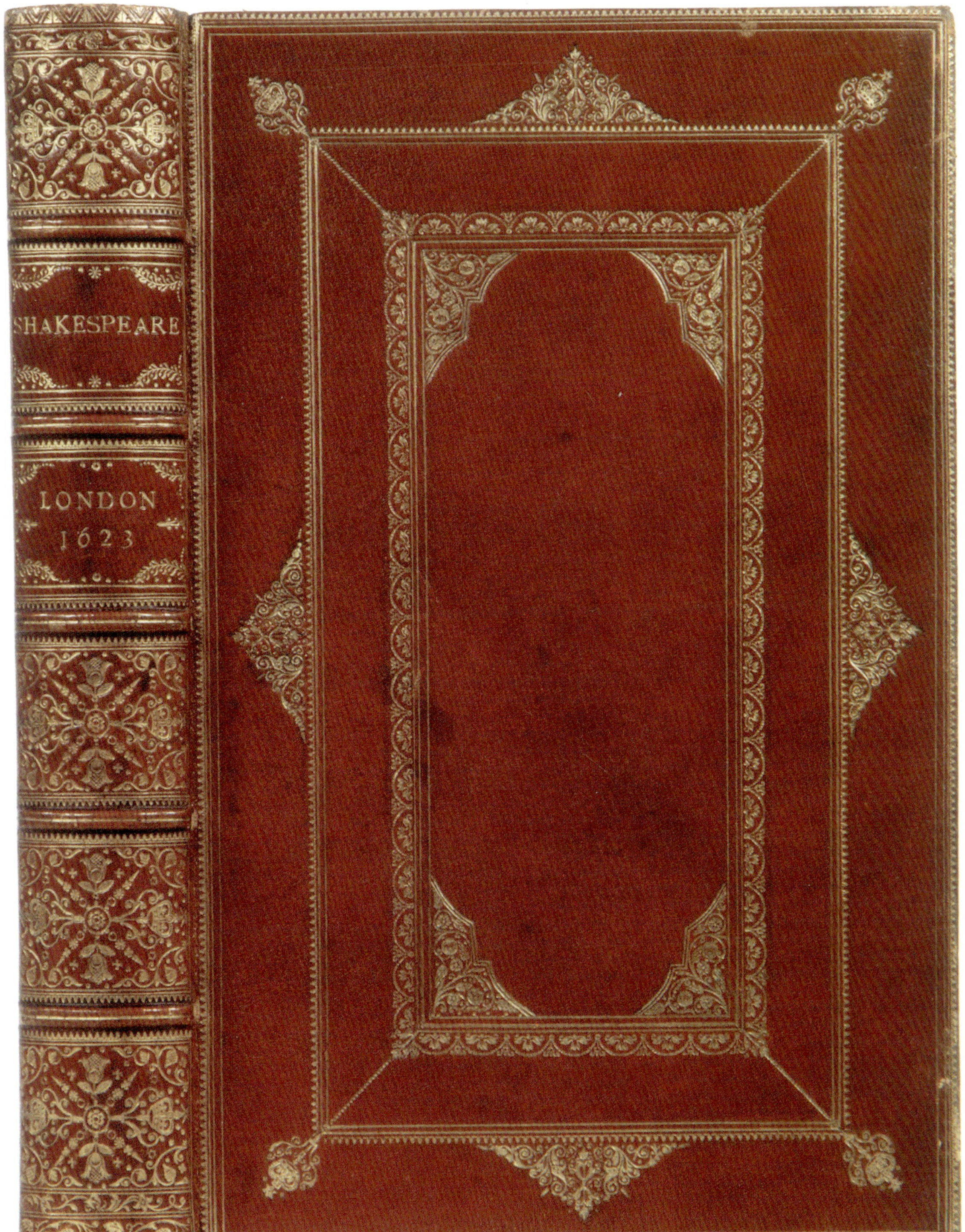
SHAKESPEARE
LONDON
1623

与如今的同一装订相比，过去的书籍装帧师们能为顾客提供多种装帧选择，这三本书都是 17 世纪早期由剑桥的书籍装帧师丹尼尔·博伊斯（Daniel Boyse）的工作坊装订的，虽然装订的时间大致相同，但风格和复杂程度区别很大

书页——最后可能会被交付给好几家装帧作坊去加工。再加上有些书在后代会被重新装订，所以，任何一本流传下来的同一版本的古籍都可能有许多种不同的装帧式样。如果你从多家图书馆或私人藏家那里收集某一种 16 世纪或 18 世纪书籍的二十本，将它们放在一起，你会看到这些书的装帧都不同，都拥有着独特的历史信息。20 世纪出版的书籍，我们看到的是统一装订，此本与彼本的区别可能只在磨损的程度以及是否仍有护封。但 19 世纪同一种书的二十本仍然会显示装帧的不同，一直到 19 世纪末，同一本书籍仍会有各类装帧，在质量、色彩和材料上都有不同等级的区别。

— 收集残片 —

此三本均为 17 世纪末的书籍，差不多在同一时间装订且出售。其装帧的不同，主要区别在于封面装饰的选择，价格也会有很大区别

历史上书籍装帧的过程会给后人留下意想不到的遗产，这就是装帧材料中所使用的废弃的旧物件。虽然如今对消费社会的劝诫越来越多，人们也知道回收的重要性，但我们早已习惯了足够的纸张及各类包装材料的供应，用过就扔是很平常的事。但对我们的先辈们来说，可用于装帧的纸张、纸板和羊皮纸都很有限，价格昂贵，不会有人将它们随手扔掉。特别是在 16 和 17 世纪，书籍的制作越来越多，材料供应仍很有限，从经济上来说，回收和再使用就很平常。书籍装帧师经常会利用废纸和旧羊皮纸来作为他们装帧的材料。

这些材料往往由印刷工坊提供，例如用过的校样、印坏的书页、多余的纸张等。有的装帧师甚至能在自己的作坊里找到材料，例如记

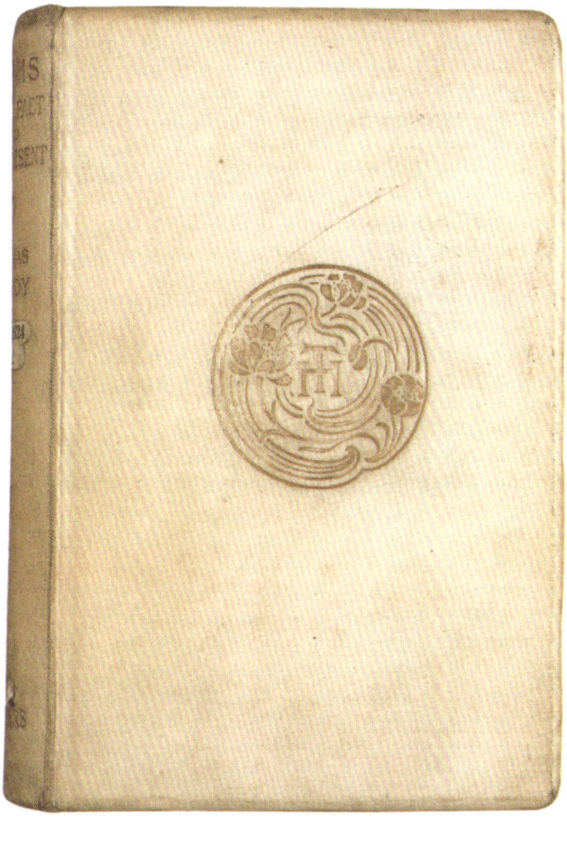

在布面装帧开始流行之后，19 世纪的许多新书仍会以多种装帧风格出版，这张 1881 年的新书广告就证明了这一点（**左页图**）。左为 1902 年出版的托马斯·哈代《新旧诗选》（*Poems of the Past and the Present*）初版本，当时同时发行的有绿色布面装帧，价格是 4 先令 6 便士，另一种是更为高级的乳白色布面装帧，价格为 7 先令 6 便士

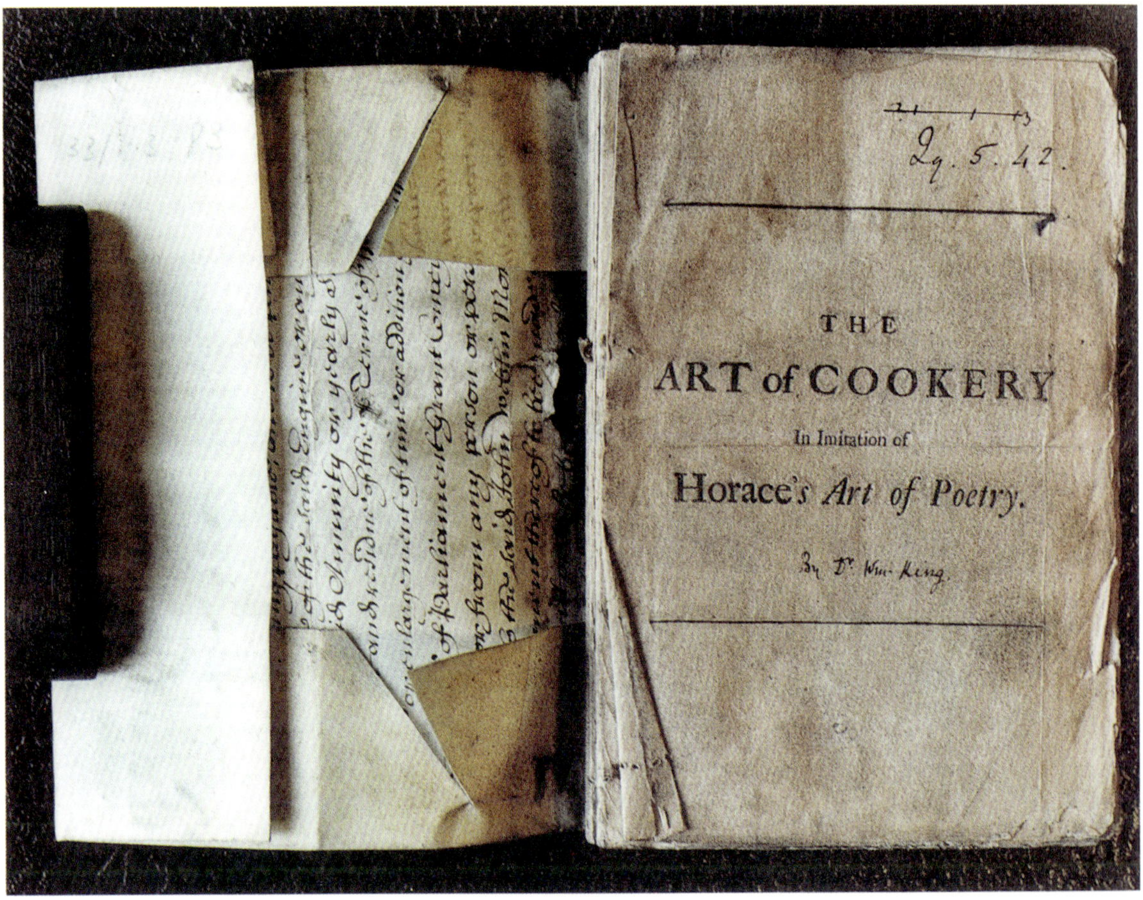

18世纪早期的一本小册子，包裹小册子的封面是用当时的一纸法律文书粗略剪出折叠而成

录作坊生意的账单等。有时，律师或其他文录员的办公室中，也有被舍弃的书或文件，可以被装帧师们重新利用。正如如今的医学或法律图书馆中，最新的文本和资料常常取代过时的内容。过去的书籍藏家也和图书馆一样，过时的文本会被丢弃。印刷的出现带来了对旧式手抄书的大量筛选，学者们对手抄书进行编辑整理，以新的印刷版的形式重新发行。16世纪英国政治和宗教的动荡，大大加快了这一进程。

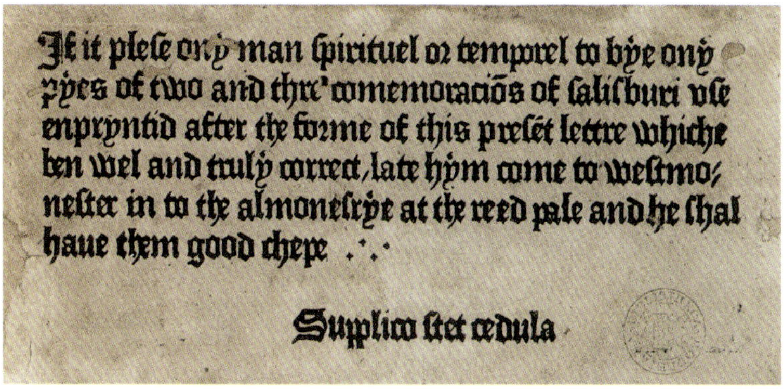
If it plese ony man spirituel or temporel to bye ony
pyes of two and thre comemoraciōs of salisburi vse
enpryntid after the forme of this presēt lettre whiche
ben wel and truly correct, late hym come to westmo-
nester in to the almonesrye at the reed pale and he shal
haue them good chepe .:.

Supplico stet cedula

英国第一位印刷师威廉·卡克斯顿1477年的广告页，宣布他最新印刷的一本教堂用书，这是已知最早的用英文印刷而成的传单。它之所以能幸存到今天，是因为有两份作为废料被书籍装帧师使用，这种保存不是刻意为之，完全出于偶然

英国与罗马教皇的分裂更导致了对与天主教教义及礼仪有关的无数书籍的刻意破坏。如牛津这样的著名学府，它古老的图书馆中藏有无数这类手抄或印刷的书籍，但这些书的内容不再被统治者接受，许多书籍都被废弃。当时的一位学者谈到牛津大学某学院堆满了散乱的书页，“它们被风吹得到处都是”。一些被撕毁的书页可能成为黄油包装纸、馅饼盒或被扎成稻草人，或有其他与书无关的用途。这些书籍中的大部分都完全被摧毁，不复存在，但有很小一部分被书籍装帧师救出，成了他们装订新一代书籍的材料。

旧书页可以被用作新书的扉页或是外层包装，更为零碎的也可以被用作书脊的衬里，或被切成小条用来增加书脊连接处的强度。它们也能被粘压在一起制成纸板，在上面包裹上皮革制成封面、封底。一张纸板可能有四十多层被废弃的书页，对书目学侦探来说，这可能会有许多潜在的令人兴奋的发现。在书籍装帧所用的材料中，我们能发现各类“废纸”：例如盎格鲁－撒克逊手稿的片段、早期的商业记录、稀有或独特的印刷品、与某些交易有关的法律文件等。英国第一位印刷师威廉·卡克斯顿（William Caxton）印制的许多作品直到今天才被发现，因为它们作为废料被后来的装帧师回收利用了。在一本

早期书籍的碎片被以各种方式再利用和回收。16世纪时，将中世纪手抄书切割为新书的扉页极为常见（下页图），也有将它们切割成长条用来加固封面封底与书脊连接处的强度，废弃的羊皮纸手稿有时被用来制成书籍的外包装

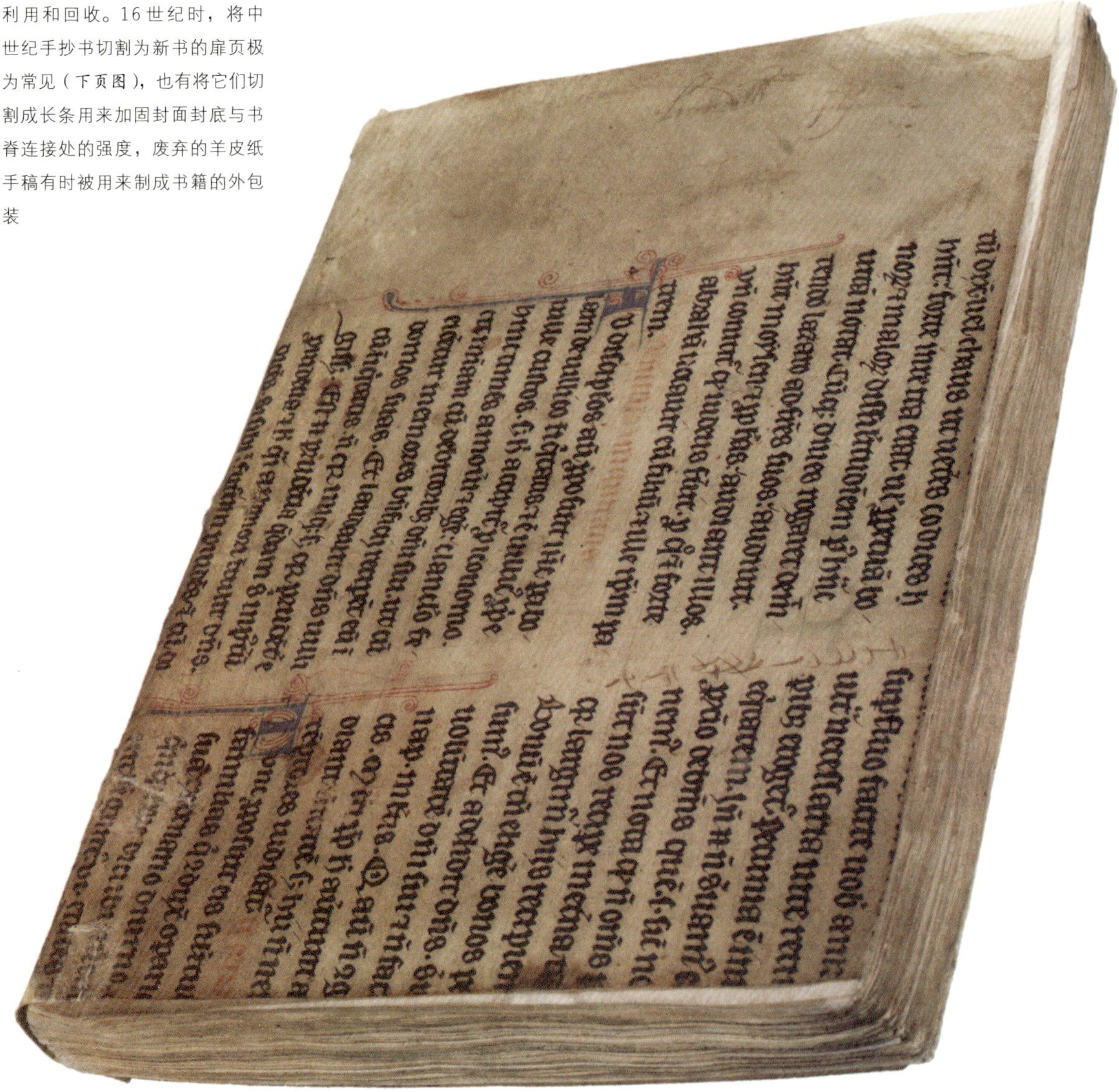

1630年左右的书籍装帧中，我们发现了17世纪早期一位书商的记录，记录中提到了莎士比亚的另一出剧作《爱的功劳》(*Love's Labours Won*)。早就有一些学者提出过莎翁曾写过对应《爱的徒劳》(*Love's Labours Lost*)的另一剧本，这个发现显然为这种观点提供了证据，虽然此剧文本一直未被找到。当然，并不是所有的残片都如此重要，但是打开一本16世纪的书籍，首先面对的可能是12或13世纪的作品，这种情况并不罕见。到了16世纪末，随着被舍弃的手抄书籍的供应减少，书籍装帧师越来越多利用印刷废物或废弃的印刷书籍。17世纪以后，人们很少再使用废弃材料作为扉页，但书脊内衬还经常使用印刷废品，这种情况一直延续到19世纪。

书脊经常使用废弃的印刷残片做衬里

Caseus datorem

Non nix, non argus. Methusala

Esau, ... Lazarus. Caseus est bonu

Optimus est caseus manibus quos dona

Caseus est nequam nisi dederit ora

Caseus insignis nō est dandus nisi dig

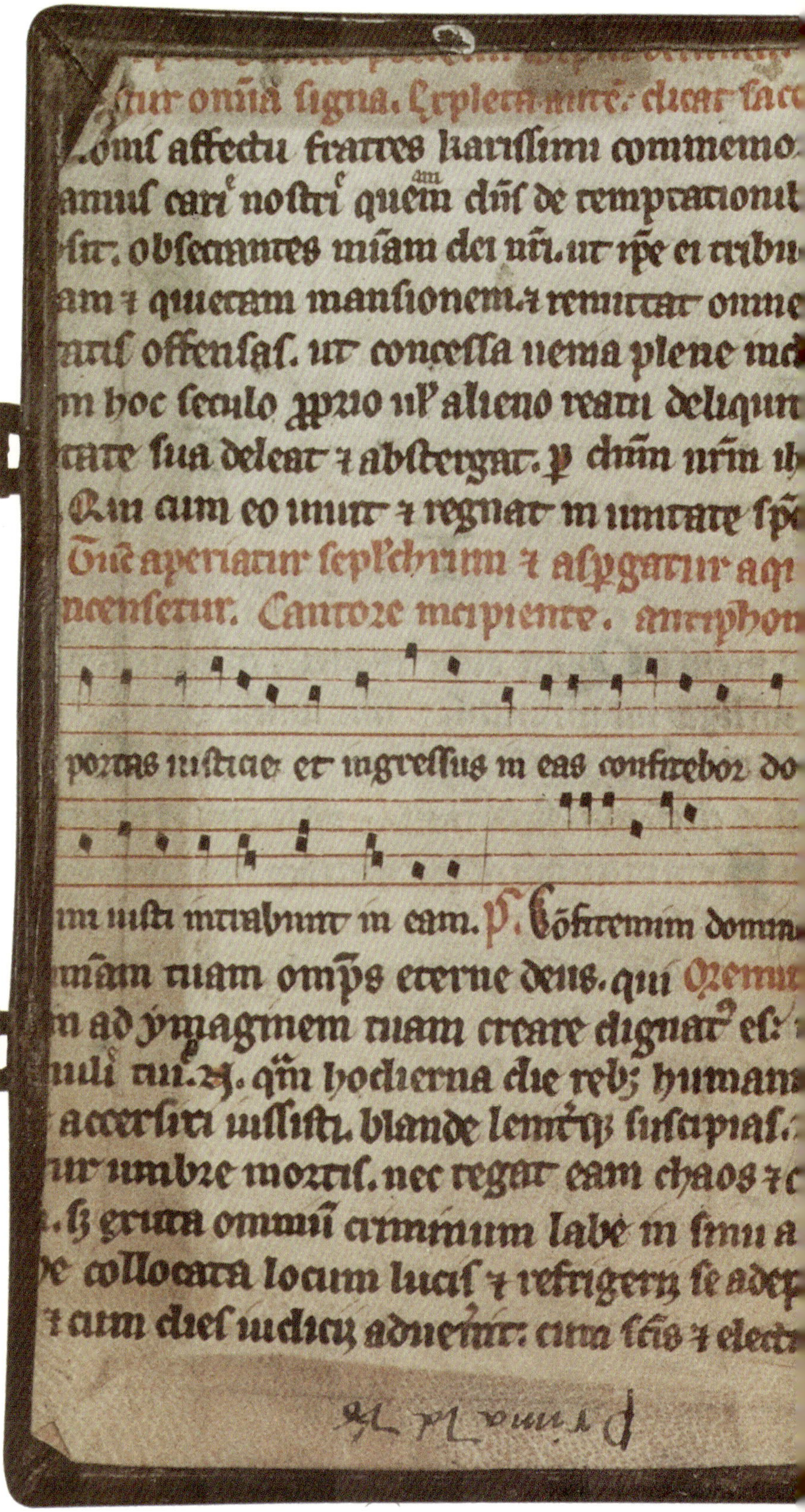
portas iusticie et ingressus in eas confitebor

6 CHAPTER SIX
THE COLLECTIVE VALUE OF LIBRARIES

第六章
图书馆的集体价值

书籍作为一种实体，人们对它的体验可以是个人的，也可以是集体的，所以，图书馆的意义就不仅仅是收藏文本资料。成功的图书馆，不论新旧，是将其提供图书资料的功能与良好的使用环境相结合，创造出一个让人满意的整体。虽然人们可以很容易地远程获取数字信息，但大学和政府仍在新建和扩建图书馆，这不仅是因为书籍的数量在增加，也因为人们喜欢把图书馆作为学习、工作和会面的场所。图书馆能让人们感受到与历史及知识积累的关联，许多人会记得第一次去大学图书馆或国家图书馆的经历，不仅因为这些图书馆的规模可能留给他们深刻的印象，也因为他们在图书馆中能感受到一种获取知识的特权。

除了储藏书籍资料的功能外，图书馆也能给人们美学上的享受。17 世纪晚期，英国巴洛克艺术家大卫·洛根（David Loggan）曾经制作过一幅牛津大学博德利图书馆的著名版画，此画曾被无数次复制，充分显示了图书馆的美学价值。1851 年，《插图版伦敦新闻》（*Illustrated London News*）上刊登了大英博物馆图书馆的图片，也是因为其景之美。如今，许多咖啡桌画册或日历上，会使用世界伟大图书馆的图片，就是这一传统的继续。风景如画历史悠久的图书馆经常也是游客必去之地，例如赫里福德大教堂的锁链图书馆（Chained Library at Hereford）或都柏林三一学院图书馆的长形阅览室，都是游客不断。

前面各章的侧重点在于从个性化的角度来审视书籍，关注它们如

（左页图）
国王图书馆，来自乔治三世的藏书，现藏于大英图书馆，这一图书馆于 1823 年被捐献给国家

（下页图）
大卫·洛根 1675 年制作的牛津大学博德利图书馆的版画

BLIOTHECÆ BODLEIANÆ OXONIÆ Prospectus interior ab Occidente
CODICES. MSS. DIVERSI GENERIS = CODICES. MSS. GRÆC. BIBLIOTHECÆ. BAROCCIANÆ.
BODLEIANA
IOHANNIS
SELDENI
F
F
E
G
E
E
G
iro admodum Reverendo vitæ integritate morum candore, spectatissimo; Scientiarum
cademiæ ornamento; pro Dna Margareta Comitissa Richmondiæ Theologiæ Professori
NÆ Typum, Cui (dum IPSE præfuit) AVCTARIVM SELDENI Pelion sc: Ossæ gigan
Dav. Loggan delin. et

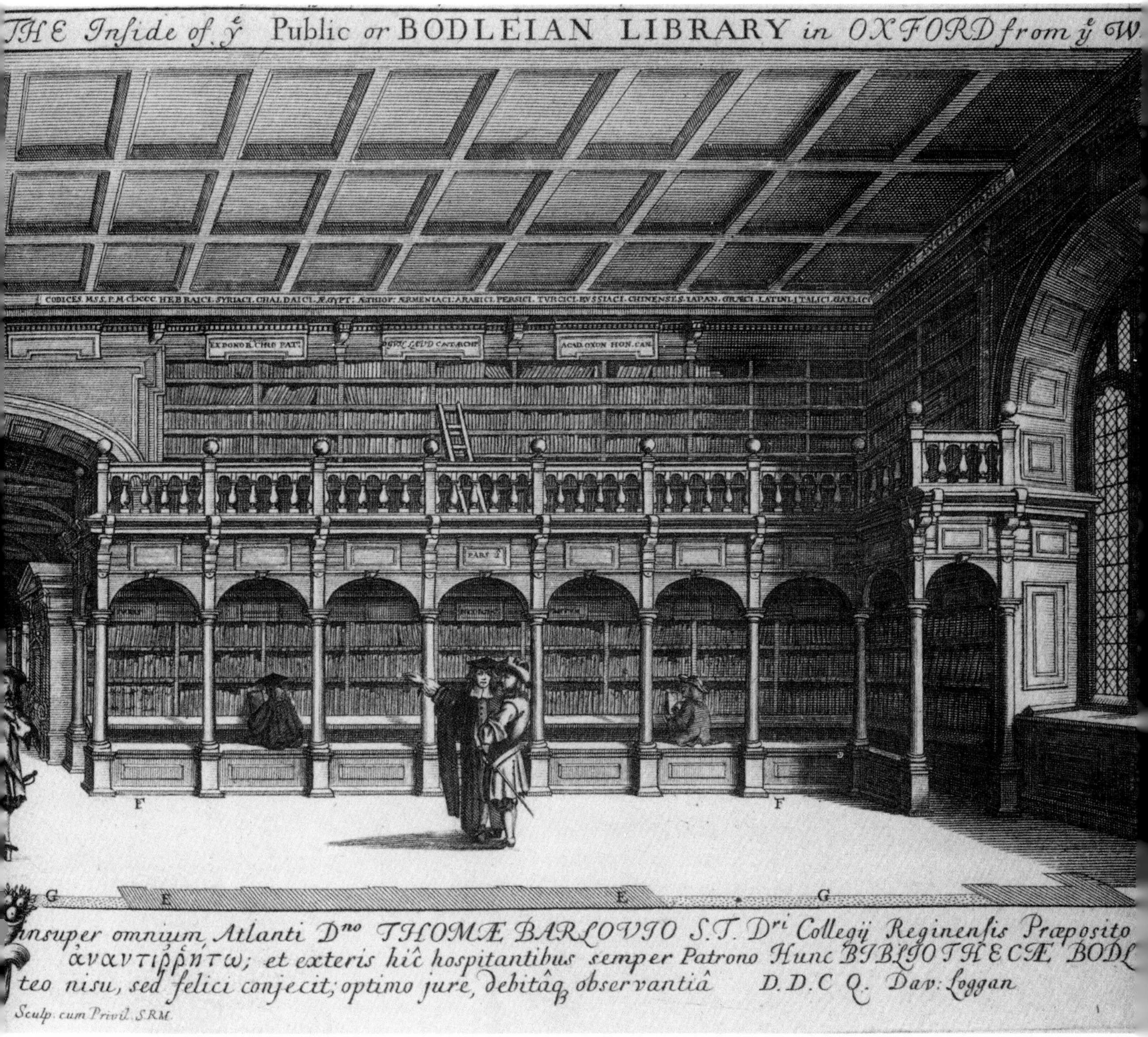
THE Inside of ye Public or BODLEIAN LIBRARY in OXFORD from ye W.
Insuper omnium Atlanti Dno THOMÆ BARLOVIO S.T. Dri Collegij Reginensis Præposito
ἀναντιῤῥήτῳ; et exteris hîc hospitantibus semper Patrono Hunc BIBLIOTHECÆ BODL
teo nisu, sed felici conjecit; optimo jure, debitâq observantiâ D.D.C.Q. Dav: Loggan
Sculp. cum Privil. S.R.M.

大英博物馆图书馆的拱门室，1851 年被刊登在周刊《插图版伦敦新闻》上

何以不同的方式来见证自己的历史，并陈述一些与读者有关的有趣信息。历史悠久的图书馆中充满了这样的书籍，但图书馆作为整体的价值远远超过其藏书的加总。因为图书馆本身显示了在不同的历史时间点上，读者群个人或集体的兴趣所在。了解某些私人或机构图书馆历史上的藏书内容，并将它们与同时代的其他图书馆进行比较，我们就能勾勒出几个世纪以来图书收藏的宏大画面。我们能够判断当时图书馆的平均规模是多大，藏书语言或主题的变化趋势，书籍的出版地区等。我们也能得知哪些书籍受欢迎，哪些书并不流行。那些流传到今

塞缪尔·佩皮斯的图书馆，在他去世后，捐赠给剑桥大学玛德琳学院。其中共有他的个人藏书约三千册，依然按照他生前的装帧、书柜及书架的陈列而收藏

天的书籍是参差不齐的，如今非常罕见的书籍，在当时可能是被广泛阅读的畅销书，而那些如今仍能见到许多复本的书籍，在当时可能阅读的人很少。研究一份 17 世纪末的书籍拍卖目录，我们能看到当时的苏格兰作家约翰·巴克莱（John Barclay）用拉丁文写成的浪漫小说《安格尼斯》（*Argenis*）很流行，常常出现在读者的书架上，远远胜过我们今天所认为的那些经典文学作品。人们因不同的原因而拥有书籍，阅读只是因素之一。有人借藏书来展示他们的财富和地位，有的是为了给子孙留下文化遗产。仔细研究先人的藏书，并且关注这些

杜伦的科辛图书馆，是科辛大主教在 1669 年创建的教区图书馆，专门收入他所捐赠的藏书。现在此馆书籍、书柜及陈列仍一如当年

收藏是如何生成的，会让我们更好地了解书籍在历史上扮演的角色。

英国作家和政治家塞缪尔·佩皮斯（Samuel Pepys，1633 — 1703）的私人图书馆，如今完好无损地保留在剑桥大学玛德琳学院（Magdalene College）中，所用的书柜及书架也是他当年的原物。这个图书馆能让我们全面了解他在 17 世纪晚期如何选择收藏了这三千多册书，我们能从知识和审美两个层面进行体验和解读。佩皮斯是一位活跃的藏书家，他对书籍的外观和内容同样感兴趣，所以，他的藏书的装帧都有赏心悦目的统一风格。他也经常在日记里记录购买或阅读书籍的情况，他写到的许多书都能在这个图书馆的书架上看到。

王政复辟之后的杜伦主教约翰·科辛（John Cosin，Bishop of Durham，1594 — 1672）创立了教区图书馆，位于杜伦大教堂和杜伦城堡之间，收有他的私人藏书五千五百册。直到今天，这些藏书仍被保存在这个专门设计建造的图书馆中。图书馆的建筑受到当时法国设计的影响（英国王政空位期间，科辛流亡巴黎），在英国，这是第一家书架倚墙而建并环绕四面的图书馆，之前的图书馆都继承中世纪晚期传统，书架与墙壁之间有一定的距离。图书馆原有的书柜至今完好无损，上面还有彩绘的圆形装饰画，画面反映出架上书籍的主要内容。这些画都是依据一些书籍插图而绘，这些书也依然在图书馆中，翻看书页，我们能看到有些插图边还有被溅上的颜料。这些藏书是科辛一生的积累：他就读于剑桥大学，后为剑桥教授，在英国内战前成为保皇派教士，1650 年后作为逃犯流亡欧洲大陆，王政复辟后返回英国成为杜伦大主教。他的藏书的外表特征和文本内容，都能反映出他一生的这些阶段。

维多利亚时代的政治家威廉·格莱斯顿（William Gladstone，1809 — 1898），曾四次担任英国首相，从他在伊顿公学上学时就开始藏书，一生中收藏无数。如今，他的三万两千册藏书都在威尔士北部哈登的圣德尼奥尔（St Deiniol's in Hawarden）图书馆中。这个图书馆也是特地建造的，格莱斯顿去世前将他的全部藏书捐赠给国家，他去世之后，公众筹资建成这个图书馆。格莱斯顿生前读书如饥似渴，还喜欢做眉批和题注。所以，他的藏书不仅显示了他的智识品位，也能让人看到他阅读时的思考和反馈。图书馆也提供住宿设施，在阅览室周围有居住和餐饮的空间。这个图书馆，为我们提供了 19 世纪与 20 世纪之交图书馆的发展、使用及其价值的有趣篇章。

当然，许多世纪以来，大多数的私人图书馆没能完整地保留下来，有时我们能依据历史文献重构图书馆的藏书内容。已经有人试图根据他们著作的内容来重构弥尔顿和莎士比亚的图书馆，但这是一种很不精确的科学。然而，历史上很多书商都有销售目录，一些藏书家也曾编过藏书目录，这些资料能够帮助我们了解当时私人藏书里的书籍。在 17 世纪，个人收藏几百本书籍并不罕见，到了 18 和 19 世纪，个人藏书数千本就很平常了。18 世纪的历史学家爱德华·吉本（Edward Gibbon）曾藏书二千多册，后人根据一系列资料将他的图书馆重构，这些资料包括他所编的图书目录（其中一张写在纸牌背面）、书商销

售目录和流落到其他图书馆中的卷册。英国贵族、作家、探险家沃尔特·雷利爵士（Sir Walter Ralegh）1618年曾因密谋反对查理一世被推上断头台，处决前他被关押在伦敦塔，当时伴随他在塔中的，还有他的私人图书馆，有五百多册藏书。虽然如今这些书籍很难追寻，但有一张书目清单却因被夹在笔记本中而幸存，清单还显示了他如何在书架上排列这些书籍，这本笔记本现藏于大英图书馆。这些书也曾是他撰写《世界历史》（*History of the World*）时的工作用书。《世界历史》出版于1614年，在以后的百年里又重印多次。外科医生查尔斯·伯纳德（Charles Bernard，1650—1711）的私人图书馆拥有三千多册藏书，在他去世后不久，他的家人将图书馆出售，印刷过一份按照主题列出的售书目录，我们由此得知他的藏书内容。数个世纪以来，许多机构图书馆收纳了无数私人图书馆的全部或部分藏书，例如，大英图书馆就是建立在许多重要的私人藏书基础上的，它们包括汉斯·斯隆爵士（Sir Hans Sloane）、乔治·托马森（George Thomason）、约瑟夫·班克斯（Joseph Banks）、克莱顿·克拉切罗德（Clayton Cracherode）等人的私人图书馆，还有罗伯特·科顿爵士（Sir Robert Cotton）和罗伯特·哈雷勋爵（Lord Robert Harley）的手抄书收藏。

大教堂图书馆、城镇或教区图书馆、历史悠久的大学和学院图书馆，它们的建立及藏书的收集，往往都是数代人的努力，它们揭示了受过教育的社会阶层在不同时代的偏爱和喜好，以及各类书籍在他们心目中的地位。保留至今的许多乡间庄园的图书馆也是如此，虽然这部分文化遗产很多都被打散销售而不复存在，但仍有一些重要收藏能让我们看到几个世纪来藏书家们的兴趣变化。一些富有的贵族图书馆拥有精美绝伦的藏书，例如德文郡公爵的查特沃斯庄园（Dukes of Devonshire at Chatsworth），或莱斯特伯爵的霍尔克姆庄园（Earls of Leicester at Holkham Hall）。也有一些不那么张扬的家庭图书馆，同样也让人痴迷，例如湖区温德米尔附近汤恩德（Townend）的一个私人图书馆，这个自耕农世家远离城市或高等学府，却连着几代人积累了一千五百多本藏书，并且保存了从当地拍卖行购买这些书籍的原始

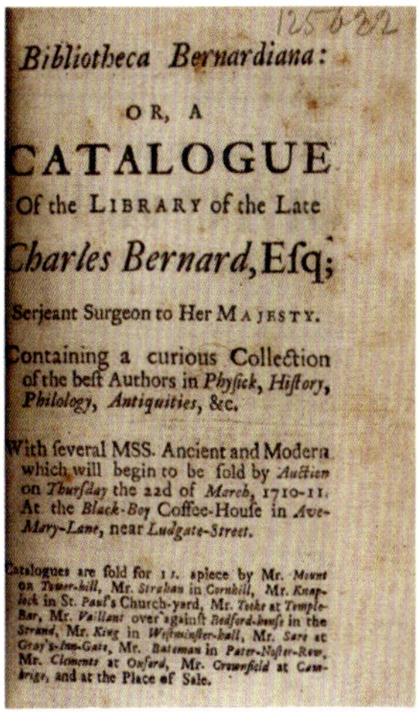
125622

Bibliotheca Bernardiana:

OR, A

CATALOGUE

Of the LIBRARY of the Late

Charles Bernard, Esq;

Serjeant Surgeon to Her MAJESTY.

Containing a curious Collection of the beſt Authors in *Phyſick*, *Hiſtory*, *Philology*, *Antiquities*, &c.

With ſeveral MSS. Ancient and Modern which will begin to be ſold by *Auction* on *Thurſday* the 22d of *March*, 1710-11. At the *Black-Boy* Coffee-Houſe in *Ave-Mary-Lane*, near *Ludgate-Street*.

Catalogues are ſold for 1 *s.* apiece by Mr. *Mount* on *Tower-hill*, Mr. *Strahan* in *Cornhill*, Mr. *Knaplock* in St. Paul's Church-yard, Mr. *Tooke* at *Temple-Bar*, Mr. *Vaillant* over againſt *Bedford-houſe* in the *Strand*, Mr. *King* in *Weſtminſter-hall*, Mr. *Sare* at *Gray's-Inn-Gate*, Mr. *Bateman* in *Pater-Noſter-Row*, Mr. *Clements* at *Oxford*, Mr. *Crownfield* at *Cambrige*, and at the Place of Sale.

早期的私人图书馆被拆散出售时的销售目录，有数千种流传至今，它们提供了当时私人藏书的宝贵资料

（左页图）
在威尔士北部哈登的圣德尼奥尔图书馆，建造于20世纪初，收藏有曾四次担任英国首相的威廉·格莱斯顿的藏书

记录，这些藏书揭示 17 和 18 世纪英国乡村书籍的供应与价格，以及人们阅读的情况。

1999 年，国家信托（National Trust）举办了其治下多家庄园图书馆的大型展览，展览介绍中写到了这些图书馆的重要性。文中说："这些藏书让我们看到庄园原主人的知识和文学兴趣，几乎和庄园宅邸一样生动。"介绍还提醒大家注意每本书的装帧、藏书票、眉批、题记等与众不同的个性，介绍总结说："书籍最好最重要的特性是它们可以被阅读，所以，这些乡间庄园藏书仍能与人们交流。"其实，我并不同意这一观点，因为这些庄园藏书的文本价值是有争议的。除了复印、数字化等现代技术对庄园藏书的冲击外，更重要的是，庄园藏书（也包括其他中小型历史图书馆的藏书）并不特别，它们中的绝大多数我们都能在大型研究机构的图书馆中找到，读者也更容易通过互联网目录检索到。所以，现在很少有读者会特地去这些庄园图书馆阅读书籍，因为他们更容易在大学或国家图书馆中，甚至在电脑屏幕上看到这些文本。然而，读者们仍然会去参观这些庄园图书馆，目的是为了学习并体验这些图书馆作为历史文物的独特品质，并在更广阔的历史背景下，整体地研究这些收藏。

位于湖区汤恩德的图书馆，由几代小农庄主建成，此地远离传统的知识及图书贸易中心，这个图书馆向我们展示了边远地区的人们是如何购买和使用书籍的

值得一提的是，大型研究机构图书馆中的藏书要被数代读者频繁使用，相比之下，那些在大教堂、教区、学院和庄园图书馆中的藏书，更有可能保留它们多层面的历史证据。对于大型研究机构图书馆来说，第一要旨是保证藏书能被人使用阅读，历代图书管理人员为了达到这一目的，经常会使用高效但无情的手段，虽然这些手段全无恶意。于是，书籍的原装帧被遗弃、扉页被取代、碎片被清理、眉批或题记被剪裁或清洗等，都是他们常用的手段。现在的古籍修复人员已经充分意识到保留古籍原始证据的重要性，但可惜对许多古书来说，为时已晚。完全没有遭受过重新装订、修复、清洁等处理的历史收藏实属罕见，可能只有一些较小的历史图书馆幸免于难。从大型研究机构图书馆的书库里取出一本 17 世纪的书籍，它很可能有 20 世纪的装帧，这也是取代了上一轮的 19 世纪装帧的，从这本书上，我们根本看不到任何历史线索和层面，所有的历史证据都已丢失。但乡村庄园图书馆所藏的同一本书，就可能仍有它的原装帧，让人体会到当年刚刚将它购买到手的那种感觉，也能见证之后的历代读者对它的使用和阅读。

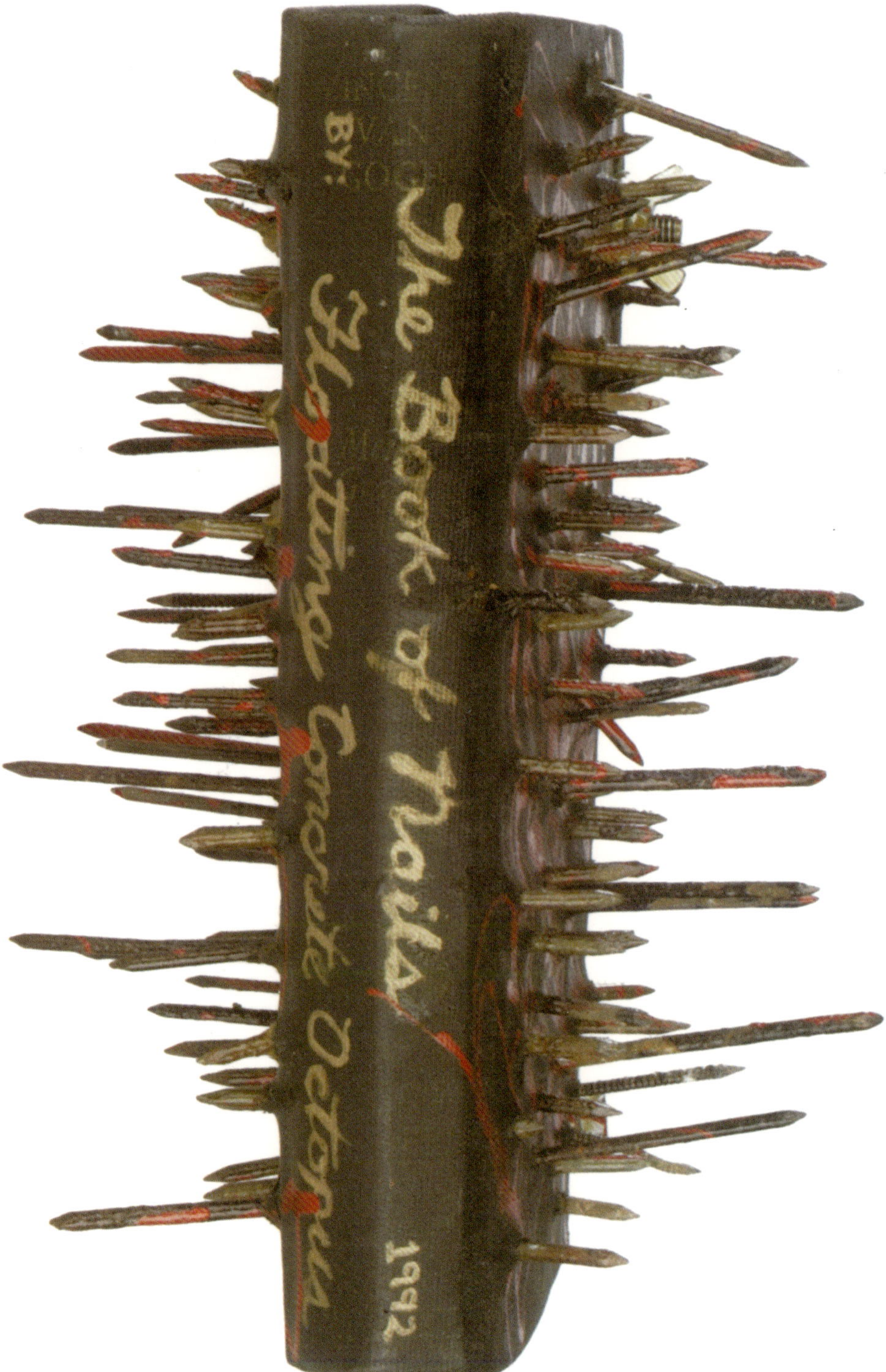
BY:
The Book of Nails
1992

CHAPTER SEVEN

VALUES FOR THE FUTURE

第七章
未来的价值

此书的基本主题是将书籍视为有趣的实物，它们可能是重要的历史见证，它们有着超越文本的意义。这些论点有其自身的价值，而且在发生巨大变化的当今书籍世界中，这一话题就格外重要，本书的第一章已经对此有所概括。新技术的快速发展让我们阅读文本的方式产生了巨大的改变。我们能预见到在未来社会，书籍将不再是传播思想和信息的主要媒介，在某些领域，这已经是现实。如果对这些新发展持否定态度，那不仅是如同鸵鸟般把头埋进沙子里，而且还有可能错过电子通信所带来的机会和益处。传统上由书籍承载的信息将会有新的传递和阅读方式，未来这种不可避免的变化也会影响我们的世界观和价值观，会影响到我们与书籍以及与图书馆的关系。未来我们将对如何保存现有的印刷文本做出选择，如果文本能由其他媒介进行承载的话，那么哪些印刷品值得保存，为什么？为什么某本书会值得被编入目录、存入库房、加入私人或机构的收藏之中？

图书馆的存在，不仅是为了给读者提供文本内容，也是为了能在将来照看这些内容。不同的图书馆会对不同的主题有所侧重，它们可能有自己特殊的使命。在世界各地，图书馆的藏书都是保存人类文学文化遗产的重要组成部分。自古以来，图书馆就是值得人们尊重的对象，这在法国版画家路易·杜·格涅耶（Louis du Guernier）1700 年前后创作的一幅版画上得到最好的表现。画面上，文学女神为了拯救

（左页图）
《钉子之书》（*The Book of Nails*），艺术家手制书，1992 年由艺术家群体“浮动混凝土章鱼”（Floating Concrete Octopus）制作。这是未来的图像吗？

（下页图）
1700 年前后法国艺术家路易·杜·格涅耶的版画，文学女神从时间之神的毁灭中拯救过去

L. du Guernier sculp.

（右页图）
20 世纪下半叶，公众抗议销毁纽约公共图书馆内所藏书籍及资料，他们将这种行为与越战期间的军事手段进行对比

“过去”，阻挡时间之神的摧毁，她的小天使将书架上的文件收起存放，为后代保存。一旦以电子方式传播新文本成为常规，数字化载体全面取代纸质印刷，那么，保护纸质文化遗产这个口号就很难喊响，书籍可能会被公认是陈旧的技术，它们的长远价值会受到质疑。不少人已经接受了这将是书籍和图书馆未来的悲观命运。

在这里，我们应该反思一下印刷发明之后的情况，那是上一次在技术上的重大突破，给文本的交流带来了本质的变化。16 世纪，这一新技术成熟并且被普遍接受后，无数的中世纪手抄书被销毁，因为当时大家认为手抄书从文本、哲学和实体上来说，都是多余的。16 世纪到 17 世纪的宗教改革时期，许多图书馆中的藏品都被筛选剔除，虽然处理掉旧书是常事，但此时是个高峰期。图书馆及私人藏书将不要的书籍清理丢弃，这没什么特别，好几个世纪以来，大家都是这么做的。大多数图书馆都有某种藏书管理政策，允许一些无用的书籍被剔除，例如那些过时的教科书及参考书，或是那些不再符合图书馆使命及目的的书籍。书籍在藏书家手中流转，也是好事，许多人对书的被收藏史很感兴趣。

清理图书馆的部分藏书，这种举动常常会引起热烈的争论。过去的一百多年中，学术图书馆和一些主要的公共图书馆都在积极扩展收藏，图书馆历史上的总体趋势是私人藏书向机构图书馆中的流动。所以，这种趋势出现逆转，势必会在人们头脑中敲响警钟。20 世纪 80 年代后期，曼彻斯特的约翰·赖兰兹图书馆（John Rylands Library）出售了一些比较值钱的古籍善本，以此为图书馆的活动筹集资金，这让英国媒体一阵骚动。类似的图书馆对馆藏的出售仍将继续引起媒体的关注。随着书籍越来越多被电子资源替代，公共和大学图书馆会清除一些比较普通的书籍，这也常常会招来媒体的报道和评论。

公众们反对的理由是什么？在 21 世纪初的英国，公共图书馆普遍衰落，国家拨给的预算削减，读者数量变少，服务的专业化水平降低。人们常常要议论图书馆用在购买新书上的钱越来越少，更多的经

"It became necessary to destroy the town in order to save it."

- attributed to an American officer firing on Ben Tre, Vietnam, February 8, 1968.

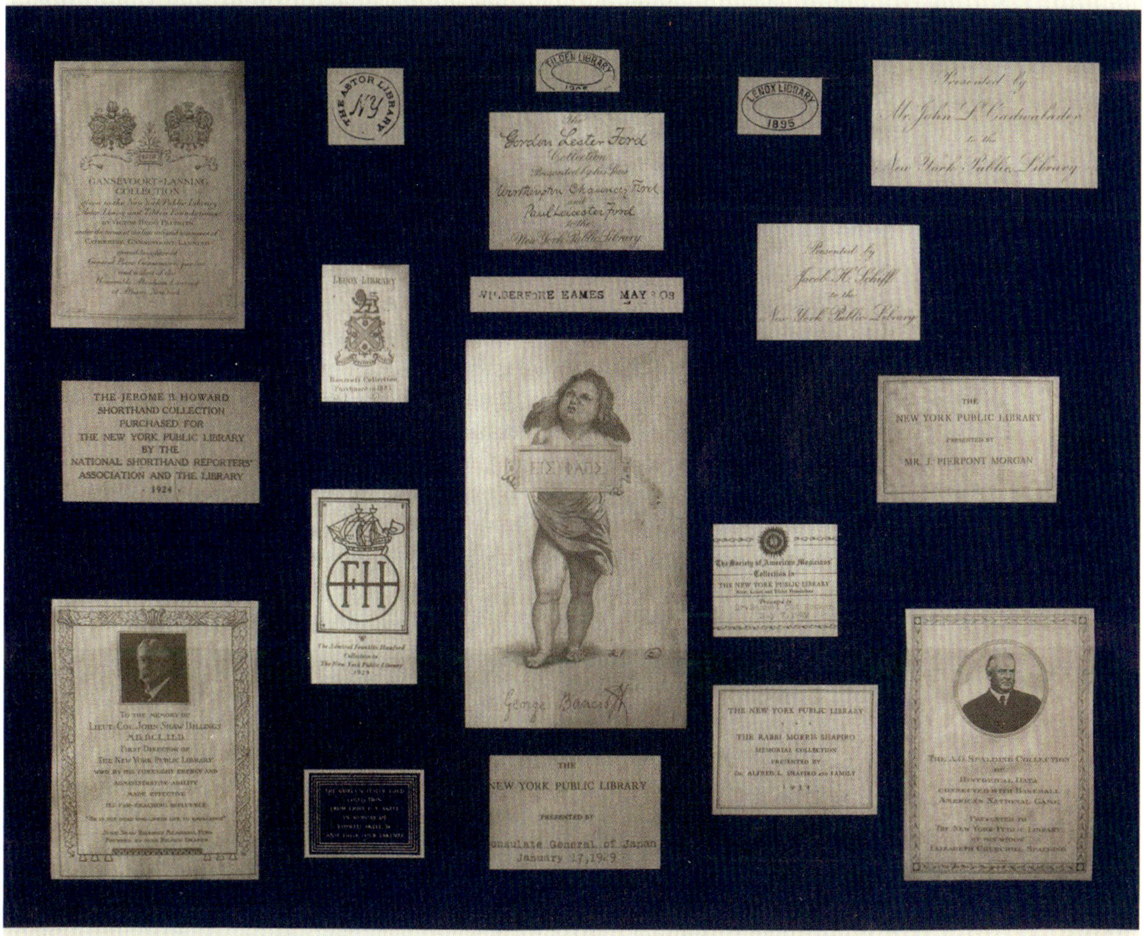

Beginning in 1978, the New York Public Library trashed these collections along with 100,000 other pamphlets. They are, lamentably, still saving their town.

A melancholy greeting for the holiday season, A.D. MCMXCVII, from Michael Zinman.

Libraries dum

A rush to liberate space for e-learning suites is blamed for disposal of printe material. **Rebecca Attwood** reports

Universities dispose of more than 1.8 million books and journals a year, according to official figures.

Statistics obtained by *The Times Higher* show that 36 institutions got rid of more books and printed volumes than they acquired. In 2005-06, ten universities disposed of more than 40,000 items. Dundee University disposed of 100,035 items and acquired 18,067 hard-copy texts in the year. Bangor University withdrew 55,500

ety of College, National, and University Libraries (Sconul).

With an increase in the use of online resources and with students demanding virtual learning environments and more study space, the number of books removed from university libraries is

Toby Bainton, secretary Sconul, said researchers rega printed resources as less u than electronic ones. "The ave number of e-books available library has risen by more tha per cent since last year and r than half of serials acquired

费被用在投资新技术、新媒体和以其他方式来使用图书馆空间上。于是，两种不同的意见拉开战线：一方主张应该彻底改造图书馆的用途，以适应新的社会潮流；另一方认为图书馆的衰落是因为它们偏离了图书馆的基本价值，没能购买更多的新书。这些问题在比尔·韦斯特（Bill West）1991 年出版的《英格兰半文盲阶层之奇异崛起》（*The Strange Rise of Semi-literate England*）中就被提出，他质问公共图书馆为什么要清除藏书，这些书都是前人收购或捐赠的，而现在的管理人员和读者们却对这些藏书表示厌烦，真是不可思议。他的批评主要集中在保存优秀书籍的重要性上，在他看来，这些书籍的文本价值应该得到更好的尊重，它们应该被人阅读。

图书馆传统主义者们所面对的危险，是他们拒绝承认世界一直在发生的巨大变化，或是希望这些变化根本没有发生。读者对公共图书

2m volumes

nior lecturer in philosophy at ·deen University. "They sug- that a lot of items are being wn away for lack of space. aries should not have to dis- of items for that reason."

; reported last week, acade- at Exeter University reacted ·usly to the disposal of 12,000 .s in the past year. "Why not burn down the library," said Exeter academic.

lly Hunt, general secretary of Jniversity and College Union

rush to embrace new technology has not always worked out the way people hoped it might."

Overall, the figures submitted by higher education institutions show that acquisitions outstrip the number of items defined by Sconul as being "sold, destroyed, given away or written off". Some 2.8 million printed volumes were added to libraries in 2005-06.

Nick Smith, director of Aston University's library and informa- tion services, which had disposed

posal policy enabled them "to in- crease the amount of study space and the number of much-needed PCs and laptop facilities".

Deborah Shorley, director of library services at Imperial Col- lege, said the university withdrew items that were no longer rele- vant. "Superseded editions, infre- quently used books and books in poor physical condition are also removed from stock," she said.

Dundee queried the figures, saying it discarded 59,000 books

大学中越来越多使用电子资源进行教学和研究，肯定会给图书馆施加压力，要图书馆让出书库这一宝贵的空间

馆使用的减少，大多数情况下，并不是因为图书馆中没有他们需要的书，而是因为人们收入提高，娱乐方式的多样化，亚马逊等公司成功地开发了全新的购书渠道。图书馆过去的一大特殊功能是提供信息，现在，这些信息可以通过谷歌或维基百科免费得到。比尔·韦斯特等人的错误也表现在“千禧年图书馆信托”（Millennium Library Trust）项目上，这一计划在 2000 — 2007 年间，花费九百万英镑将经典文学作品送给学校，但是许多学校却根本就不愿意接受这些赠书，很多都被退回。这个项目的目的，是为了鼓励孩子们阅读，这当然值得赞扬，但是，如果这笔经费能够花在提供给孩子们他们想要的东西上，那可能会更有效果。

2001 年，尼科尔森·贝克（Nicholson Baker）的新书《两次折叠：图书馆和对纸质印刷品的攻击》（*Double Fold: Libraries and the*

Assault on Paper）掀起一阵激烈的争论。在这本书中，贝克抨击了美国和英国的一些研究机构图书馆用微缩胶片取代报纸之后，便将大量原件销毁的举措。贝克的观点是片面而极端的，他把那些管理着有限资源的图书馆工作人员斥责为“只顾成本的傻瓜”，压根没有试图理解他们的困境。他发现图书馆中的很多旧报纸不复存在，取而代之的是微缩胶片，就认为这是图书馆的集体失败。贝克还认为：“一个伟大的研究机构图书馆，它的收藏都必须一式二份，甚至一式三份，这样做的原因有很多，最根本的是因为图书会磨损、遗失、遭窃或错置。”如果有一天，文本主要以电子方式存储和传播，而且大家对电子媒体的持久性更有信心，那么他的论点将变得无关紧要。有些人的论点比贝克有说服力，他们认为如果要通过报纸来了解人类交流的历史，就要牵扯到报纸实体以及上面的文字，在这种情况下，微缩胶片和电子文本是无法取代的。

2009 年，哈佛大学的图书馆馆长罗伯特·达顿（Robert Darnton）出版了《书之辩》（*The case for books*），收入了他的一系列关于数字时代书籍前景的文章。其中有一篇是关于图书馆的未来，他认为，谷歌发起的数字化项目，可能会创造一个全球超级图书馆，这能与启蒙时代的理想主义者们最宏大的梦想相提并论。他并不担心这样的图书馆最后的样式，而是担心它的所属地和控制权。他非常正确地指出，把控制世界信息的权力从公众图书馆转交给商业化的机构，这是个巨大的变化，所带来的后果是值得我们思考和警惕的。达顿感到遗憾的是，整个数字化的进程原本是可以采取更符合公众利益的方式的，之所以没能这样做，是因为整整一代图书管理员的集体失败，他们没能认识到并且相信这种未来。图书管理员可以找出一系列政治和经济上的原因为自己辩解，但这场比赛的最终的结果仍然是谷歌 1，图书馆 0。

除非有某种造成国际计算机网络混乱的自然或人为的灾难，或是所需的电力不足，从纸质向电子出版物的过渡不可避免，对已有藏书的大规模数字化也势在必行，随着时间的推移，书籍的价值也会受到越来越多的质疑。2010 年，大英图书馆公布了未来的收藏政策，也就是“首选格式为数字资料，积极地从纸质印刷向数字化过渡”。在这个快速变化的世界中，应该用什么标准来衡量一本书是否值得保存？某一本书具有其他任何替代物都无法复制的特征，这无疑是一个至关重要的考虑因素。与档案资料不同，印刷书籍的本质就不是独一无二的，古腾堡发明最主要的核心是相同书本的大量复制。我希望这本书中的陈述，证明了事情并不那么简单，书籍可以通过各种方式拥有独一无二的特征，这可能是因为它们的制作方式，也可能是它们所积累的历史证据。在评估一本书的价值时，我们不应该仅仅关注它的文本，也应该关注它能为研究者们提供的其他东西。

提高大家对文本之外的书籍的重要性的认识，不仅仅是为了启发当代人以一种更广的视角来看待书籍，也是为了鼓励和发展一种文化价值，以防止我们做出对未来不负责任的决定。当书籍成为历史时，让我们意识到它们并不是“古旧”与“过时”的代名词，而是一种在文化遗产结构中具有独特意义的历史文物。这本书的目的就是要鼓励大家进行思考，拓宽大家的视野，提高对书籍多层面的认识。各位读者，请把你们的想法写在这本书（当然这本书得是你的）的扉页和空白处，以你们的眉批和题记，把这本书变得独一无二。

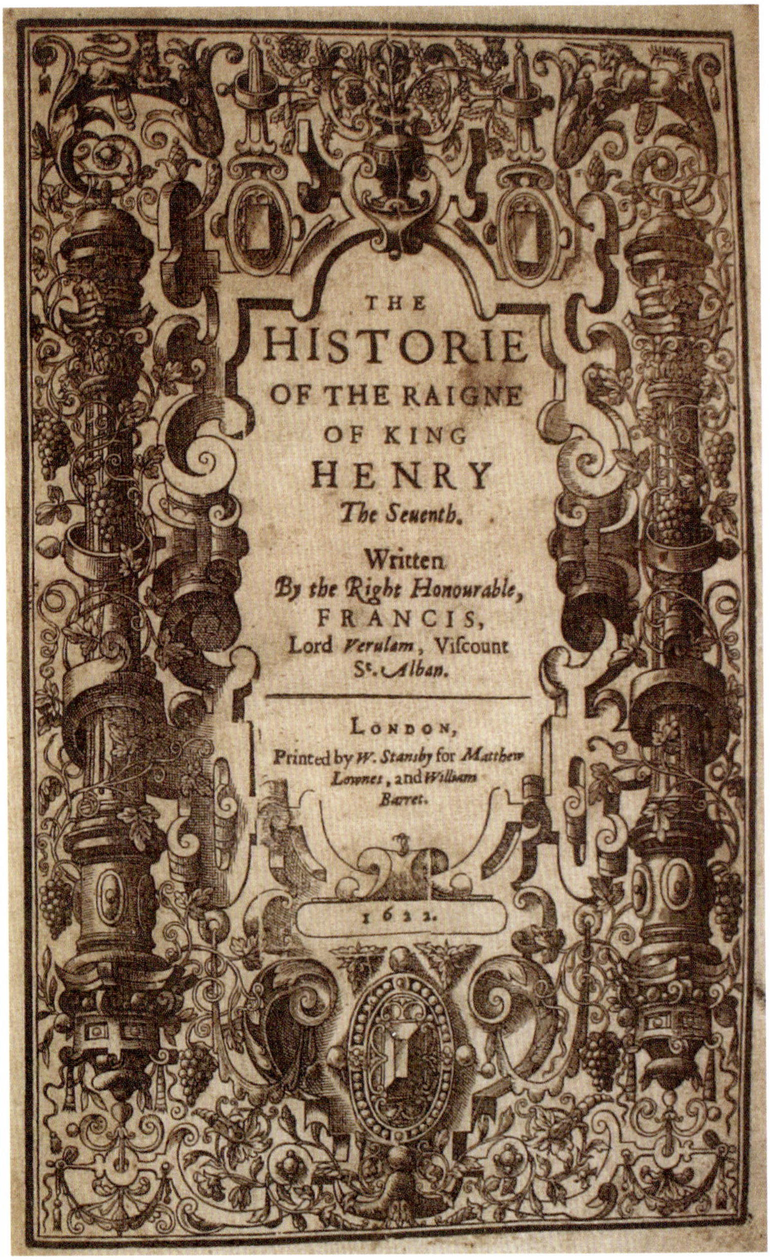
THE
HISTORIE
OF THE RAIGNE
OF KING
HENRY
The Seuenth.
Written
By the Right Honourable,
FRANCIS,
Lord Verulam, Viscount
St. Alban.

LONDON,
Printed by W. Stansby for Matthew
Lownes, and William
Barret.
1622.

弗朗西斯·培根最为人所知的是他的哲学和科学著作，他为17世纪下半叶英国科学旺盛期奠定了基础。他也曾有过一段重要的但大起大落的政治生涯，1621年在专利权的发放问题上他被指受贿而遭弹劾，政治生涯从此结束。他的著作《亨利七世治国史》（*Historie of the Raigne of King Henry VII*）是晚年被强制退休后的第一部作品，他写作此书的部分原因是希望能与詹姆斯一世和睦相处。此书在当时很受欢迎，后来被认为是17世纪初英国史学著作的典范

CHAPTER EIGHT
VARIETY BETWEEN COPIES: A CASE STUDY

第八章
案例分析：不同版本的多样性

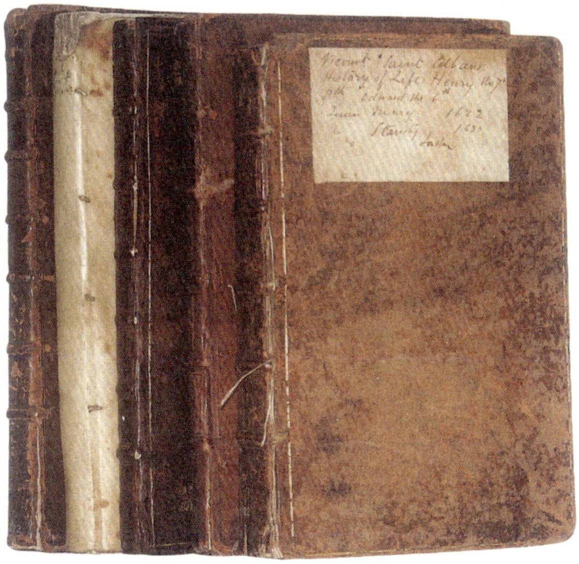

此书的大部分内容致力于阐明书籍中所拥有的超越文本以上的各种各样的历史证据，特别是历代读者如何看待和使用单本书籍。在此，我将以同一本书的五个单本为例来进行说明，此书是英国学者、政治家弗朗西斯·培根（Francis Bacon，1561 — 1626）在1622年出版的关于亨利七世治国的史论，这些单本，都具有历史的个性和不同的特征。

第一本：当时的小牛皮装帧，除了边框上本色的压线之外，没有其他装饰，小牛皮下为硬纸板。这是当时的标准装帧样式，朴素、结实、持久，没有不必要的装饰

第二本：当时的软面羊皮纸装帧，没有装饰，与在硬纸板上裹上皮革的装帧相比，这是更便宜的选择。如果以现代装帧的样式来类推，这是 17 世纪初的平装本

第三本：也是当
的小牛皮装帧，
面的中心和边界上
有金饰的图案，属
高端的产品。此书
第一位拥有者可能
是在标题页上题字
那位，显然他希望
己的书籍与第一本
比，在装帧上更美观
更昂贵

第四本：小牛皮装帧，本色压印图案装饰，这种装帧大约是17世纪末或18世纪初的风格。当时的主人选择了对此书重新装订，书内的证据也证明了此书最初没有固定的装帧（见下一页）

第五本：18世纪中后期的羊皮硬板装帧（比小牛皮的装帧要便宜）。它与另一本书装订在一起，那是1630年出版的弗朗西斯·戈德温（Francis Godwin）的《英格兰编年史》（*Annales of England*）。此书是培根著作的合理补充，因为它覆盖了从亨利八世到玛丽女王统治时期的英国历史。封面上贴有纸质标签，是18世纪时的手书，注明了此书的内容

第五本虽然是18世纪的装帧，但我们能从此书中看到更早的装帧残片，有些边缘处的手书被剪裁掉了，18世纪的装帧师们经常对书边进行裁剪，这是当时的标准做法

第三本的装帧使用了当时一些废弃的羊皮纸手稿碎片，用以加固书脊的连接处，在扉页和文本页之间，我们能够看到一些残段

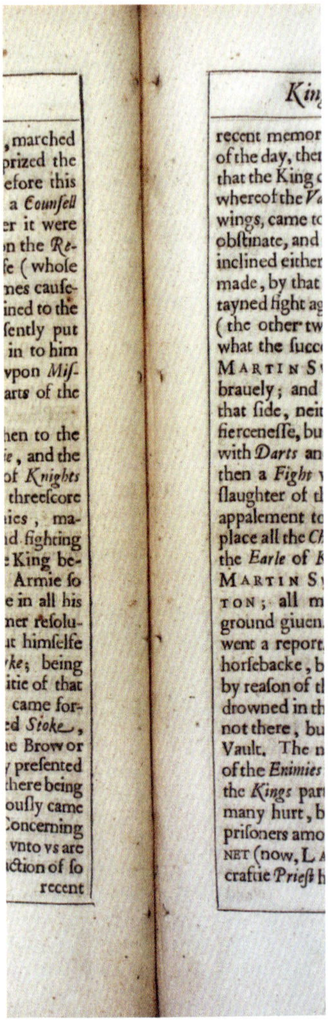

第四本不是原装帧，它的内留白为我们提供了一些此书原装的证据。靠近书脊处，我们能看到一些等距离的小孔，表明这些书页最初是被临时装订在一起的，可能用纸或牛皮做封面，然后用大针扎孔后缝订，而不是正规的装帧

第三本的封面环衬上贴有伯肯黑德爵士（Viscount Birkenhead，本名Frederick Smith，1872 — 1930）的藏书票，他曾于1919 — 1922年间任英国政府的最高法官，1924 — 1928年间任印度大臣。在扉页上，有此书17世纪的主人理查德·富兰克林（Richard Franklin）的签名，还有他当时购买此书所付的价格：4先令。封底的环衬上，有玛丽亚的签名和1636年的日期，估计她是富兰克林的妻子

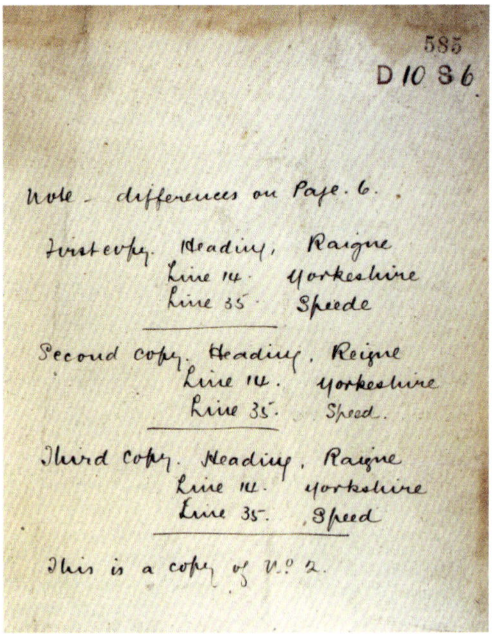

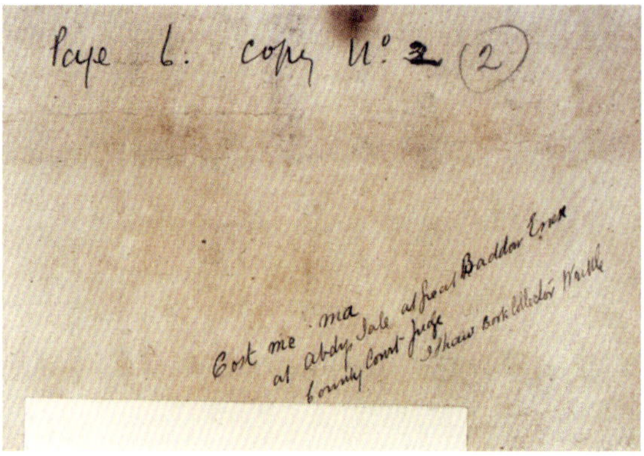

第五本也曾经是德宁－劳伦斯爵士的藏书，此书扉页上有一段大约写于1900年的文字，我们能推测他之前的藏家。这题记是J. 肖恩（J. Shaw）所写："埃塞克斯郡大巴多镇的阿布迪藏书拍卖会上购得，瑞特尔镇的藏书家肖恩。"阿布迪是剑桥大学民法学教授约翰·托马斯·阿布迪（John Thomas Abdy，1822—1899）。购买此书的价格，肖恩可能想保密，就用了一个密码"ma"代替

第一本曾为埃德温·德宁－劳伦斯爵士（Sir Edwin Durning-Lawrence，1837—1914）收藏，他是国会议员，积极提倡并试图证明培根创作莎士比亚剧作这一说法。此书扉页上有他独特的藏书上架顺序号，也有他手书的笔记，记录了他所藏此书的所有版本，并注明了每个版本的区别

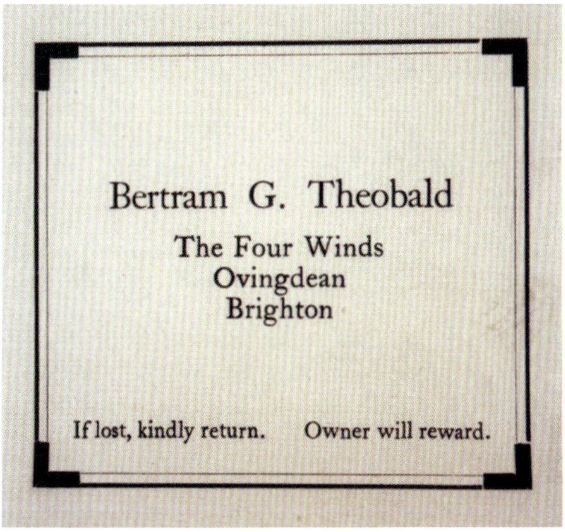

第四本的封面环衬上贴有一张藏书票，表明它曾是伯特伦·西奥博尔德的私藏（Bertram Theobald，1871 — 1940），此公也积极支持培根写作莎士比亚剧作这一说法（关于莎士比亚的作品是否由培根写成，在 19 世纪与20世纪之交有过很多争论）。此书的更早一些的藏家们不知其名，但其中一位 17 世纪末的藏家显然对此书的年龄很感兴趣，在标题页的下端，有他 1696 年做的一个推算，认为此书出版已 64 年

第三本上的题字，可见图书史家们遇到的沮丧和困难。一位 17 世纪的藏家在扉页上写下了他姓名的首字母和得书日期，“WR1676”，但我们根本查不出来他究竟叫什么。标题页的上部有另一位藏家的题字，还有一句座右铭，但这两行后来被涂抹掉了，座右铭依稀看出可能为“顺其自然”，但名字完全看不清楚

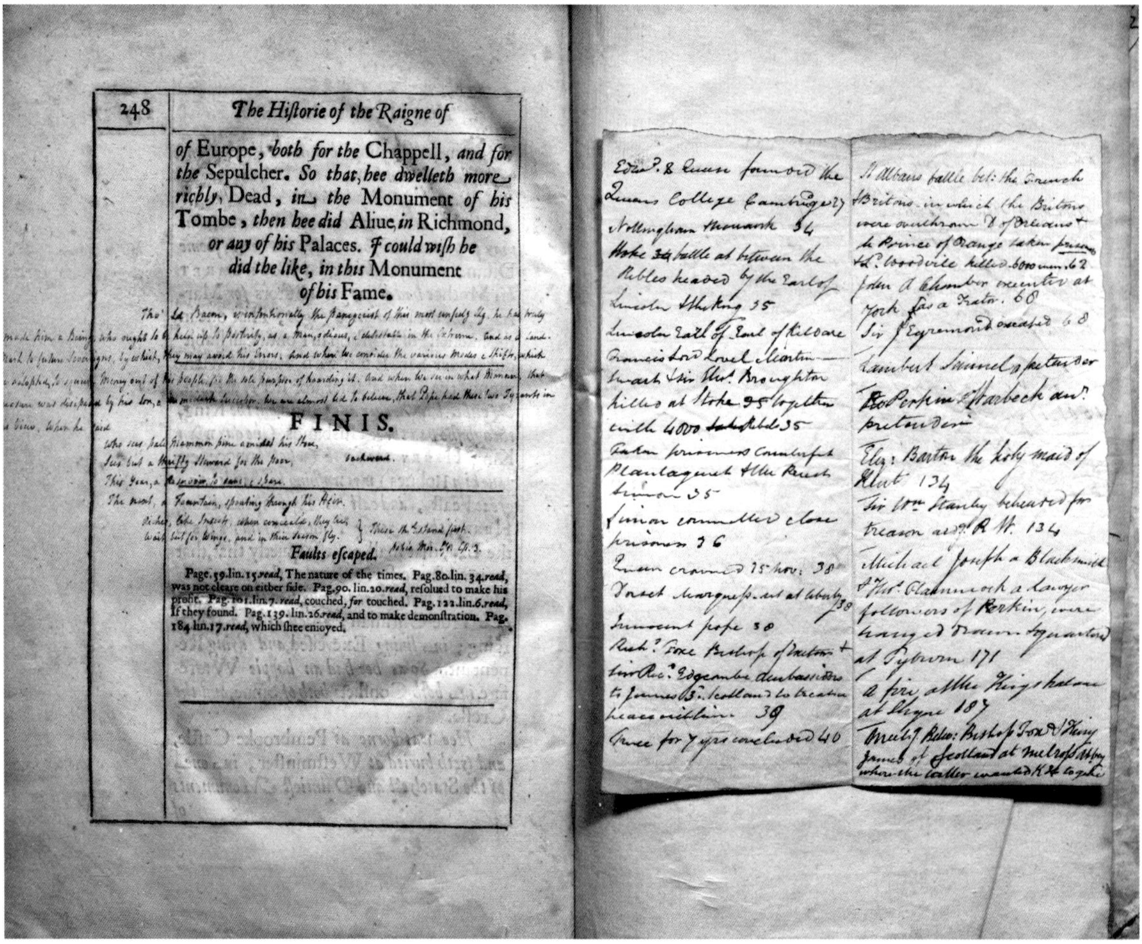

第一本上有19世纪手书的题记，还有夹在书中的被折叠的一页纸，纸上是藏书者对培根传记的总结，以及他对亨利七世的看法："虽然培根爵士试图为这位最无情的国王唱赞歌，但实际上，后代的人还是能读到，这位国王极端可恶，值得憎恨……"

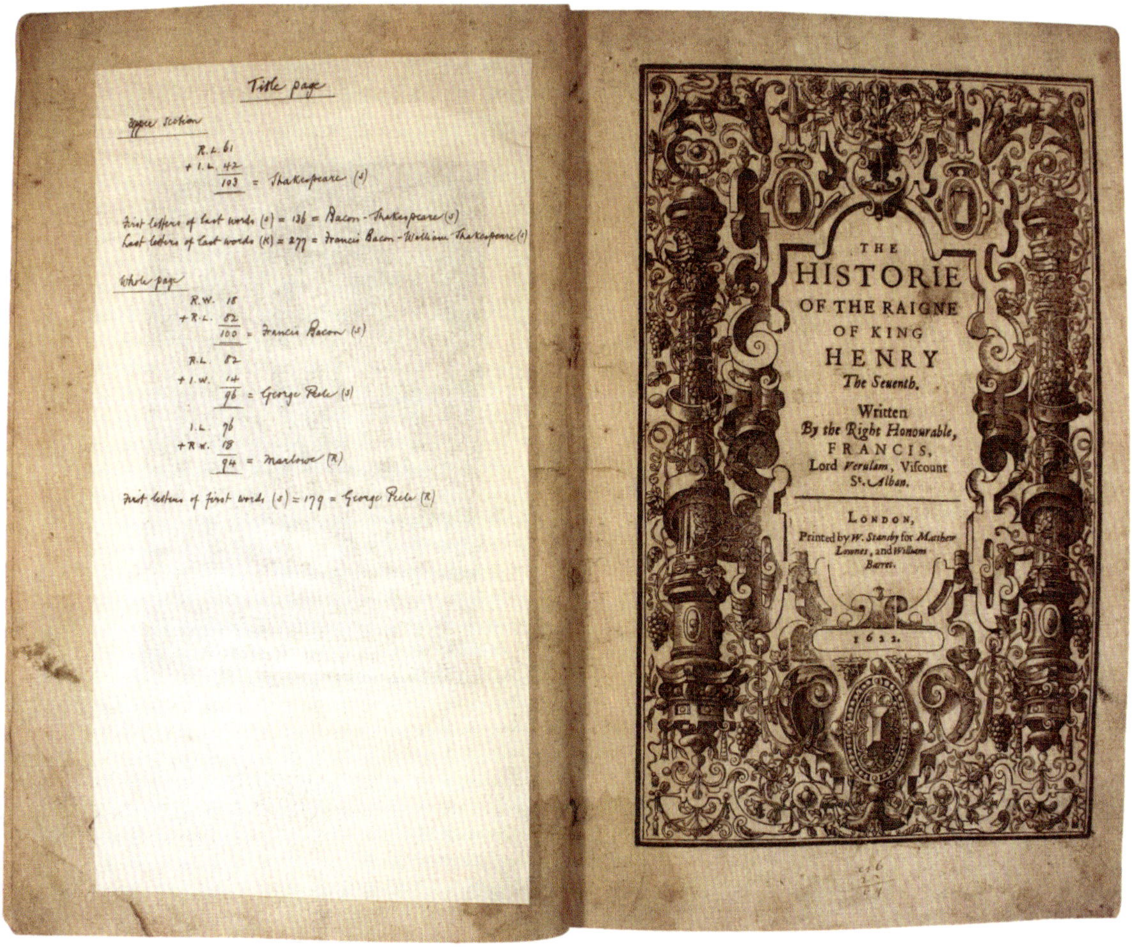

第四本显示了另一种不同方式的后代藏家对文本的兴趣，此书中有许多伯特伦·西奥博尔德手书的笔记，它们被粘贴在书页上，上面记录了许多基于字母和数字的解码工作，试图解释暗含的信息，据此证明培根就是莎士比亚剧本的作者

培根这本书的出版历史很复杂，它有两个版本，排版和文本都有所不同。两个版本都出版于1622年，并且拥有相同的标题页。每本书的内容可能混合了两个版次所印刷出的书页。我在这里举例所用的五本书，从技术上来说都属于同一版本，但是如果我们仔细对比，还是会发现一些差异。大家可以比较标题上的“Raigne / Reigne”的不同拼写和第14行里的“Yorkshire / Yorkeshire”的不同拼写，这两页分别取自第一本和第二本

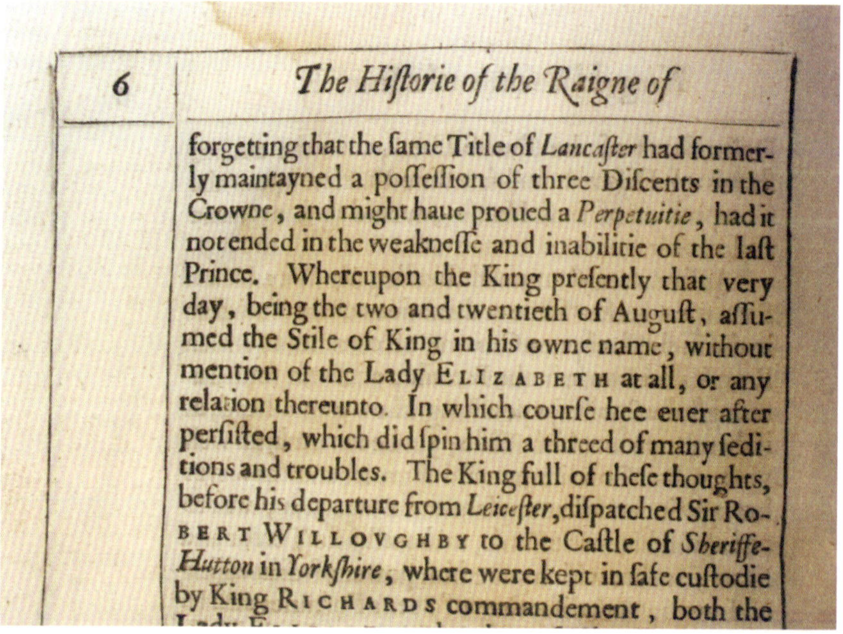

6 *The Hiſtorie of the Raigne of*

forgetting that the ſame Title of *Lancaſter* had formerly maintayned a poſſeſſion of three Diſcents in the Crowne, and might haue proued a *Perpetuitie*, had it not ended in the weakneſſe and inabilitie of the laſt Prince. Whereupon the King preſently that very day, being the two and twentieth of Auguſt, aſſumed the Stile of King in his owne name, without mention of the Lady ELIZABETH at all, or any relation thereunto. In which courſe hee euer after perſiſted, which did ſpin him a threed of many ſeditions and troubles. The King full of theſe thoughts, before his departure from *Leiceſter*, diſpatched Sir ROBERT WILLOVGHBY to the Caſtle of *Sheriffe-Hutton* in *Yorkſhire*, where were kept in ſafe cuſtodie by King RICHARDS commandement, both the

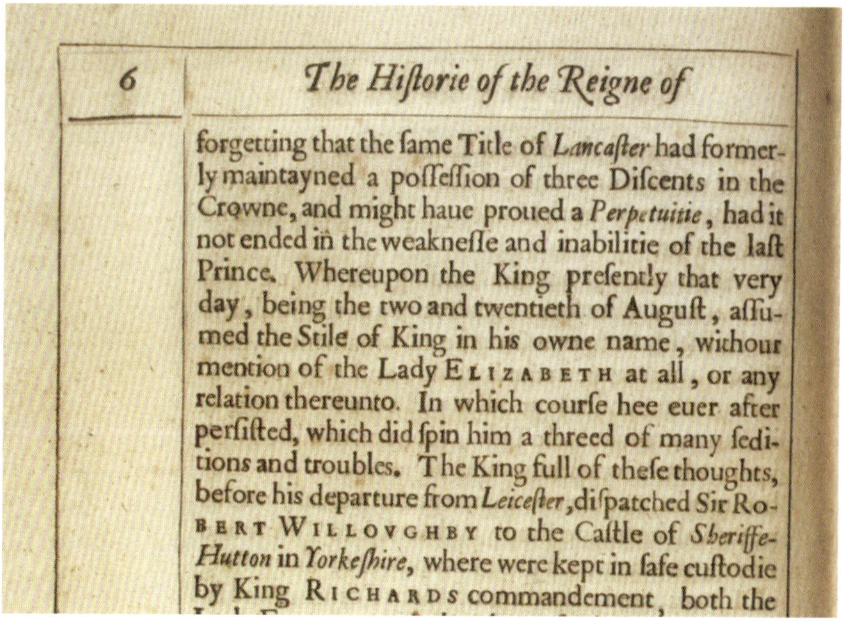

6 *The Hiſtorie of the Reigne of*

forgetting that the ſame Title of *Lancaſter* had formerly maintayned a poſſeſſion of three Diſcents in the Crowne, and might haue proued a *Perpetuitie*, had it not ended in the weakneſſe and inabilitie of the laſt Prince. Whereupon the King preſently that very day, being the two and twentieth of Auguſt, aſſumed the Stile of King in his owne name, without mention of the Lady ELIZABETH at all, or any relation thereunto. In which courſe hee euer after perſiſted, which did ſpin him a threed of many ſeditions and troubles. The King full of theſe thoughts, before his departure from *Leiceſter*, diſpatched Sir ROBERT WILLOVGHBY to the Caſtle of *Sheriffe-Hutton* in *Yorkeſhire*, where were kept in ſafe cuſtodie by King RICHARDS commandement, both the

延伸阅读

F U R T H E R — R E A D I N G

以下为延伸阅读书目，按主题排列。

[书籍及图书馆的未来]

S. 伯基茨：《古腾堡的挽歌：电子时代的阅读命运》，波士顿：费伯与费伯出版社，1994 年。
S. Birkets: *The Gutenberg elegies: the fate of reading in an electronic age*. Boston (Faber and Faber)，1994.

比尔·科普 & 安格斯·菲利普斯（主编）：《数码时代书籍的未来》，牛津：柴多斯出版社，2006 年。
Bill Cope and Angus Phillips (eds): *The future of the book in the digital age*. Oxford (Chandos Publishing), 2006.

罗伯特·达顿：《书之辩：过去，现在和未来》，纽约：公共事务出版社，2009 年。
Robert Darnton: *The case for books: past, present, and future*. New York (Public Affairs), 2009 .

J. 戈麦斯:《印刷之死：数码时代的书籍》，伦敦：麦克米伦出版社，2007 年。
J. Gomez: *Print is dead: books in our digital age*. London (Macmillan), 2007.

罗伯特·洛根 & 马歇尔·麦克卢汉:《图书馆的未来：从电子媒体到数字媒体》，纽约：皮特朗恩出版社，2015 年。
Robert K. Logan and Marshall McLuhan: *The future of the library: from electric media to digital media*. New York (Peter Lang), 2015.

G. 萨普:《图书馆未来之简史：资料目录》，马里兰州兰哈姆：稻草人出版社，2002 年。
G. Sapp: *A brief history of the future of libraries: an annotated bibliography*. Lanham (Scarecrow Press), 2002.

R. 温道夫（主编）:《二十一世纪的珍本书及手稿图书馆》，马萨诸塞州剑桥：哈佛大学出版社，1993 年。
R. Wendorf (ed.): *Rare book and manuscript libraries in the twenty-first century*. Cambridge, Mass. (Harvard University Library), 1993.

J. 耶洛利斯·道格拉斯:《书籍末日或书籍之永恒？阅读互动叙述文本》，安娜堡：密歇根大学出版社，2000 年。
J. Yellowlees Douglas: *The end of books – or books without end? Reading interactive narratives*. Ann Arbor (University of Michigan Press), 2000.

[书目学和书籍历史研究]

约瑟夫·A. 戴恩:《何为书？早期印刷书籍研究》，印第安纳州诺特尔达姆：圣母大学出版社，2012 年。
Joseph A. Dane: *What is a book? The study of early printed books*. Notre Dame (University of Notre Dame Press), 2012.

S. 艾略特 & J. 罗斯（主编）:《书籍历史指南》，牛津：布莱克威尔出版社，2007 年。
S. Eliot and J. Rose (eds): *A companion to the history of the book*. Oxford (Blackwell), 2007.

D. 芬克尔斯坦 & A. 麦克利里（主编）:《书籍历史选读》，伦敦：洛特利奇出版社，2002年。
D. Finkelstein & A.McCleery (eds.): *The book history reader.* London (Routledge), 2002.

L. 豪萨姆:《旧书新史：书籍印刷文化研究指南》，多伦多：多伦多大学出版社，2006年。
L. Howsam: *Old books and new histories: an orientation to studies in book and print culture*. Toronto (University of Toronto Press), 2006.

D. F. 麦肯齐:《文本目录社会学研究》，剑桥：剑桥大学出版社，1999年。
D. F. McKenzie: *Bibliography and the sociology of texts*. Cambridge (Cambridge University Press), 1999.

D. 麦基特里克:《印刷、手稿及其顺序：1450 — 1830》，剑桥：剑桥大学出版社，2003年。
D. McKitterick: *Print, manuscript and the search for order 1450-1830*. Cambridge (Cambridge University Press), 2003.

詹姆斯·雷文:《什么是书籍史？》，剑桥：政体出版社，2018年。
James Raven: *What is the history of the book?* Cambridge (Polity Press), 2018.

M. F. 苏亚雷斯，S.J. & H. R. 沃德尼森（主编）:《牛津书籍指南》，牛津：牛津大学出版社，2010年。
M. F. Suarez, S. J., and H. R. Woudnuysen (eds): *The Oxford companion to the books*. Oxford (Oxford University Press), 2010.

[书籍设计、字体及其历史]

菲尔·贝恩斯:《企鹅丛书封面设计，1935 — 2005》，伦敦：艾伦莱恩出版社，2005年。
Phil Baines: *Penguin by design: a cover story 1935-2005*. London (Allen Lane), 2005.

艾伦·巴特然:《书籍设计五百年》，伦敦：大英图书馆出版社，2001 年。
Alan Bartram: *Five hundred years of book design*. London (The British Library), 2001.

杰弗里·道丁:《印刷字体历史简介》，伦敦：维斯出版社，1961 年，大英图书馆出版社，1998 年再版。
Geoffrey Dowding: *Introduction to the history of printing types*. London (Wace), 1961, reprinted London (The British Library), 1998.

N. 德鲁:《以貌取书：现代美国书籍封面设计》，纽约：普林斯顿建筑出版社，2005 年。
N. Drew: *By its cover: modern American book cover design*. New York (Princeton Architectural Press), 2005.

理查德·亨德尔:《书籍设计》，纽黑文与伦敦：耶鲁大学出版社，1998 年。
Richard Hendel: *On book design*. New Haven and London (Yale University Press), 1998.

S. 洛克斯利:《字体秘传》，伦敦与纽约：I. B. 托里斯出版社，2005 年。
S. Loxley: *Type: the secret history of letters*. London and New York (I. B. Tauris), 2005.

D. 马丁:《书籍设计概论》，伦敦：蓝图出版社，1989 年。
D. Martin: *An outline of book design*. London (Blueprint), 1989.

艾伦·鲍尔斯:《封面：书籍护封和封面设计》，伦敦：米奇比兹利出版社，2001 年。
Alan Powers: *Front cover: great book jackets and cover design*. London (Mitchell Beazley), 2001.

H. 威廉姆森:《书籍设计技法》第三版，纽黑文与伦敦：耶鲁大学出版社，1983 年。
H. Williamson: *Methods of book design*. 3rd edn. New Haven and London (Yale University Press), 1983.

[作为艺术品的书籍、插图和书籍的艺术]

《1455 — 1955 年印刷书籍艺术：纽约比尔波特摩根图书馆所藏印刷精品》，纽约：比尔波特摩根图书馆，1973 年。
Art of the printed book 1455-1955: masterpieces of typography ... from the collections of the Pierpont Morgan Library New York. New York (Pierpont Morgan Library), 1973.

J. 贝特利（主编）:《书籍艺术：从中世纪手抄书到漫画小说》，伦敦：维多利亚和艾尔伯特博物馆出版社，2001 年。
J. Bettley (ed): *The art of the book: from medieval manuscript to graphic novel*. London (V&A Publications), 2001.

D. 布兰德:《书籍插图史话》，伦敦：费伯与费伯出版社，1958 年。
D. Bland: *A history of book illustration*. London (Faber and Faber), 1958.

S. 布里:《艺术家手制书：作为艺术品的书，1963 — 1995 年》，布鲁克费尔德：思哥拉出版社，1995 年。
S. Bury: *Artists' books: the book as a work of art, 1963-1995*. Brookfield (Scolar Press), 1995.

C. 德・哈梅尔:《泥金手抄书史话》，伦敦：费顿出版社，1986 年。
C. de Hamel: *A history of illuminated manuscripts*. London (Phaidon Press), 1986.

D. 迪林格:《泥金书籍：历史及制作》，伦敦：费伯与费伯出版社，1958 年。
D. Diringer: *The illuminated book: its history and production*. London (Faber and Faber), 1958.

J. 哈森:《西方传统插图书籍史》，伦敦：泰晤士与赫德逊出版社，1981 年。
J. Harthan: *The history of the illustrated book: the western tradition*. London (Thames and Hudson), 1981.

C. 霍格本 & R. 沃森（主编）:《从莫奈到霍克尼：现代书籍插图艺术》，伦敦：维多利亚和艾尔伯特博物馆，1985 年。

C. Hogben & R. Watson (eds.): *From Manet to Hockney: modern artists' illustrated books*. London (V&A Museum), 1985.

Y. 考沙克 & R. 鲁本:《超越文本：罗伯特 · J. 鲁本所藏艺术家手制书》，纽约：格洛里俱乐部，2010 年。
Y. Korshak and R. Ruben: *Beyond the text: artists' books from the collection of Robert J. Ruben*. New York (Grolier Club), 2010.

S. 莫里森:《四个世纪的精美印刷》，伦敦：恩内斯特本恩出版社，1924 年及后续版本。
S. Morison: *Four centuries of fine printing*. London (Ernest Benn), 1924, and later editions.

K. 沃瑟曼:《作为艺术品的书：国家妇女艺术博物馆所藏艺术家手制书》，纽约：普林斯顿建筑出版社，2007 年。
K. Wasserman: *The book as art: artists' books from the National Museum of Women in the Arts*. New York (Princeton Architectural Press), 2007.

[印刷历史]

P. 加斯凯尔:《目录学简介》，牛津：克莱雷顿出版社，1972 年。
P. Gaskell: *A new introduction to bibliography*. Oxford (Clarendon Press), 1972.

C. 克莱尔:《英国印刷史》，伦敦：卡塞尔出版社，1965 年。
C. Clair: *A history of printing in Britain*. London (Cassell), 1965.

S. 斯坦伯格:《印刷五百年》，伦敦：费伯与费伯出版社，1955 年。
S. Steinberg: *Five hundred years of printing*. London (Faber and Faber), 1955.

M. 特怀曼:《印刷 1770 — 1970 年》，伦敦：大英图书馆出版社，1998 年。
M. Twyman: *Printing 1770-1970*. London (The British Library), 1998.

[藏书家印记、批注、收藏者及阅读历史]

J. 安德森 & E. 索尔（主编）:《早期现代英国书籍与读者的材料研究》，费城：宾夕法尼亚大学出版社，2002 年。
J. Andersen and E. Sauer (eds): *Books and readers in early modern England: material studies*. Philadelphia (University of Pennsylvania Press), 2002.

S. A. 拜伦:《披露读者》，西雅图与伦敦：华盛顿大学出版社，2001 年。
S. A. Baron: *The reader revealed*. Seattle and London (University of Washington Press), 2001.

E. 达菲:《时段的标记：英国人与祈祷书，1240 — 1570 年》，纽黑文与伦敦：耶鲁大学出版社，2006 年。
E. Duffy: *Marking the hours: English people and their prayers, 1240-1570*. New Haven and London (Yale University Press), 2006.

S. 费希尔:《阅读之历史》，伦敦：瑞可辛出版社，2003 年。
S. Fischer: *A history of reading*. London (Reaktion Books), 2003.

O. 金格里奇:《哥白尼〈天体运行论〉版本普查及注释》，荷兰莱顿：布瑞尔出版社，2002 年。
O. Gingerich: *An Annotated Census of Copernicus' De revolutionibus (Nuremberg, 1543 and Basel, 1566)*. Leiden (Brill), 2002.

H. 杰克逊:《批注者：读者在书中的写作》，纽黑文与伦敦：耶鲁大学出版社，2001 年。
H. Jackson: *Marginalia: readers writing in books*. New Haven and London (Yale University Press), 2001.

罗宾・梅耶等（主编）:《藏书者、批注者及阅读的痕迹》，纽卡斯尔与伦敦：欧科诺尔出版社及大英图书馆出版社，2005 年。
Robin Myers *et al (eds.), Owners, annotators and the signs of reading*. New Castle and London (Oak Knoll Press and the British Library), 2005.

史蒂文·奥格尔：《书中之读者》，牛津：牛津大学出版社，2015年。
Stephen Orgel: *The reader in the book*. Oxford (Oxford University Press), 2015.

D. 皮尔森：《书籍历史中的来源研究指南》，伦敦：大英图书馆出版社，1994年。
D. Pearson: *Provenance research in book history: a handbook*. London (The British Library), 1994.

K. 夏普：《阅读革命：早期现代英格兰的阅读政治》，纽黑文与伦敦：耶鲁大学出版社，2000年。
K. Sharpe: *Reading revolutions: the politics of reading in early modern England*. New Haven and London (Yale University Press), 2000.

W. H. 舍曼：《用过之书：文艺复兴时代英格兰的读者印迹》，费城：宾夕法尼亚大学出版社，2008年。
W.H. Sherman: *Used books: marking readers in renaissance England*. Philadelphia (University of Pennsylvania Press), 2008.

R. 斯托达德：《书中的印记》，马萨诸塞州剑桥：霍顿图书馆出版社，1985年。
R. Stoddard: *Marks in books*. Cambridge, Massachusetts (The Houghton Library), 1985.

[书籍装帧]

M. 富特：《作为历史镜像的书籍装帧》，伦敦：大英图书馆出版社，1998年。
M. Foot: *The history of bookbinding as a mirror of society*. London (The British Library), 1998.

R. 刘易斯：《20世纪精美书籍装帧》，纽顿艾伯特：大卫与查尔斯出版社，1984年。
R. Lewis: *Fine bookbinding in the twentieth century*. Newton Abbot (David & Charles), 1984.

P. 马克斯：《大英图书馆书籍装帧指南：历史及技巧》，伦敦：大英图书馆出版社，1998年。

P. Marks: *The British Library guide to bookbinding: history and techniques*. London (The British Library), 1998.

H. 尼克松 & M. 富特:《英格兰装饰书籍装帧史》，牛津：克莱雷顿出版社，1992 年。
H. Nixon & M. Foot: *The history of decorated bookbinding in England*. Oxford (Clarendon Press), 1992.

D. 皮尔森:《英国书籍装帧风格，1450 — 1800 年》，伦敦：大英图书馆出版社，2005 年。
D. Pearson: *English bookbinding styles, 1450-1800*. London (The British Library), 2005.

[书籍装帧中的残片]

L. 布朗里格 & M. 史密斯（主编）:《中世纪书籍残片的解释与收集》，加州洛思阿图斯与伦敦：红鸥出版社，2000 年。
L. Brownrigg & M. Smith (eds.): *Interpreting and collecting fragments of medieval books*. Los Altos Hills and London (The Red Gull Press), 2000.

[图书馆的历史及美学]

N. 巴克:《国家信托庄园图书馆宝藏》，纽约：皇家橡树基金会与格洛里俱乐部，1999 年。
N. Barker: *Treasures from the libraries of National Trust country houses*. New York (The Royal Oak Foundation and the Grolier Club), 1999.

J. 博索尔 & G. 德・罗比尔 :《世界最美图书馆大全》，伦敦：泰晤士与赫德逊出版社，2003 年。
J. Bosser and G. de Laubier, *The most beautiful libraries of the world*. London (Thames and Hudson), 2003.

詹姆斯・坎贝尔 & 威尔・普赖斯:《世界图书馆史》，伦敦：泰晤士与赫德逊出版社，

2015 年。
James Campbell and Will Pryce: *The library, a world history*. London (Thames and Hudson), 2015.

P. 霍尔（主编）:《剑桥英国及爱尔兰图书馆史》三卷本，剑桥：剑桥大学出版社，2006 年。
P. Hoare (ed): *The Cambridge history of libraries in Britain and Ireland*. 3v. Cambridge (Cambridge University Press), 2006.

C. 霍弗:《图书馆》，伦敦：泰晤士与赫德逊出版社，2005 年。
C. Höfer: *Libraries*. London (Thames and Hudson), 2005.

D. H. 斯塔姆（主编）:《图书馆史国际词典》两卷本，芝加哥与伦敦：菲兹洛尔迪尔宝恩出版社，2001 年。
D. H. Stam (ed): *International dictionary of library histories*. 2v. Chicago and London (Fitzroy Dearborn), 2001.

[书籍的销毁及遗弃]

N. 贝克:《两次折叠：图书馆和对纸质印刷品的攻击》，纽约：兰登书屋，2001 年。
N. Baker: *Double Fold: Libraries and the assault on paper*. New York (Random House), 2001.

K. W. 汉弗莱斯:《16 世纪英格兰遗失之书籍》,《书籍》杂志第 36 期（1986 年），第 249 — 258 页。
K. W. Humphreys, 'The loss of books in sixteenth-century England', *Libri* 36 (1986), pp.249-258.

R. 克努特:《谋杀书籍：20 世纪政府支持下的对书籍及图书馆的破坏》，韦斯特伯特：普莱杰出版社，2003 年。
R. Knuth: *Libricide: the regime-sponsored destruction of books and libraries in the twentieth century*. Westport (Praeger), 2003.

D. 麦基特里克:《我们要保留旧报纸吗？》，伦敦：人文学科交流办公室，2002 年。
D. McKitterick: *Do we want to keep our newspapers?* London (Office for Humanities Communication), 2002.

L. X. 普拉斯特恩:《焚书：有史以来对图书馆的摧毁》，伦敦：泰晤士与赫德逊出版社，2007 年。
L. X. Polastron: *Books on fire: The destruction of libraries throughout history.* London (Thames and Hudson), 2007.

J. 雷文（主编）:《遗失的图书馆：自古以来对藏书的破坏》，贝森斯多克：帕尔格拉夫麦克米伦出版社，2004 年。
J. Raven (ed): *Lost libraries: the destruction of great book collections since antiquity.* Basingstoke (Palgrave Macmillan), 2004.

W. 韦斯特:《英格兰半文盲阶层之奇异崛起：图书馆之毁灭》，伦敦：达克沃兹出版社，1991 年。
W. West: *The strange rise of semi-literate England: the dissolution of the libraries.* London (Duckworth), 1991.

大卫·皮尔森谈西方书籍

恺蒂 采写

问：您的著作中，大部分学术性很强，但有一本很通俗化，图片多于文字，那就是《大英图书馆书籍史话》，请您谈谈这本书的主题是什么？

答：这本书有两个主题。首先，它是关于作为一件实物、作为艺术品的书本身。书不仅是文字的载体，不仅能表达作者的思想和故事，书本身就是历史。书拥有超出它所承载的文字之上的东西。一本书如何印刷、如何装帧，曾经被谁拥有过，谁在里面涂写过、眉批过，是否被人损坏过，这些都是关于这本书的文化和历史的记录，也反映着人类文明的发展史。书作为一件实物拥有它独立的价值。

我想探讨的第二个主题是在电子文本的时代中，实体书究竟是否还有意义。我非常支持人们阅读电子书，或是网上阅读，我要研究的是，书作为文字载体的传统功能是否正在消失？书是不是有其他存在的原因和价值？电子阅读是不是给书提供了从传统身份中解放出来的机会？

问：能请您介绍一下这本书的内容吗？

答：这本书虽然是关于西方历史中的书籍，但它不是一本线性的书史。我在这本书中谈到书籍的许多方面，就像七巧板一样，它们一起组成关于西方书籍的完整图像。

第一部分我写到历史中的书籍，书是人类文明史的一部分，也是我们日常生活中的常见物品。因为书是文化的载体，所以，摧毁书也就是摧毁文化。自古以来，世界各地的许多当权者都有焚书的举动，德国纳粹也烧毁了很多书。第二部分是关于书籍如何超越它们所承载的文本，例如人们常常会利用书的形象让自己变得更庄严，我也谈到书的排版、设计、字体、封面、插图、装饰，书与它所要传递的文本内容的关系，如何才能最有效果。作为艺术品的书籍也被归类在这一章里，这包括 20 世纪上半叶由艺术家设计或插图的书，也包括这三十多年来才开始流行的艺术家手制书。

下面几个章节我更关注的是能让书籍个性化的东西。印刷术的发明，让书籍被大批量生产，所以，许多人会觉得这本书和那本书没有什么区别，我这里要探求的，就是书籍在同一性中的个性。书籍的纸质、开本、版式、装帧等元素，都能让同一作者同一标题的书拥有不同的个性。当然书籍的拥有者们、藏书家们更给书带来了多样性，他们的签名、藏书票、眉批、注释甚至是涂鸦不仅给某本书带来独一无二的个性，从中也反映出历史。还有一章专门谈到书籍装帧，装帧的素朴或奢华能反映出拥有者的财富和趣味。更有趣的是，在纸张稀有的年代里，许多书籍装帧的内衬使用旧书废纸，在无意之间倒可能保留下珍贵的史料。我也谈到了图书馆的价值以及它们对文化历史收藏的贡献，这是我的本行。书的最后一部分是一个案例研究，我用了弗朗西斯·培根 1622 年出版的《亨利七世治国史》的五个不同版本，分析了它们的历史的个性和不同的特征。

这本书浅显易懂，我的目的是让一般公众了解实体书籍的特性和历史。这本书的插图也极多，大都来自大英图书馆、英国国立艺术图书馆、伦敦大学图书馆，还有英美欧陆的一些其他公共机构图书馆。在我所有的书中，这本书最受普通读者的欢迎。2008 年出了第一版后，2011 和 2012 年都进行了再版。现在也出了日文版。

问：能否请您简单谈谈西方书籍装帧的发展过程？

答：古埃及的书籍大多抄写在莎草纸上，中国最早的书籍有简牍和帛书，包括后来雕版印刷的《金刚经》，它们大都以手卷的形式存在。而西方书籍的装帧与东方书籍来自不同的传统，它们来源于近东及中东地区的公元 2 世纪到 4 世纪的古抄本书籍，也就是将书页折叠起来，缝制成册。我们称这种书籍形式为册子本（Codex）。

所以，从那时开始，西方书籍就呈现出我们现在所熟悉的样式。到了 8 和 9 世纪时，书籍的装订开始分流，伊斯兰和中东地区的书籍仍然用滑针的方式进行装订，欧洲则开始将书页首先固定在几条横线上，形成书脊，然后再把横线穿插固定到两块硬板上，这两块板就是封底和封面。西方书籍延续着这样的装订传统，在 19 世纪之前，书籍的装帧都是手工完成的。做封面和封底的硬板上会贴上不同的皮料或布料，并进行装饰，压花烫金，但西书装订的基本方式都大同小异。

19 世纪中期，因为整个欧洲的工业化进程，书籍装帧也开始机械化，出版商使用机器生产出统一规格的装订材料和模版。到了 19 世纪末，作为对这种机械化倾向的反抗，威廉·莫里斯等开始推动艺术工艺运动，将书籍的手工印刷、制作、装订和装帧重新发现并重新发明为一种艺术工艺形式，也有许多私人印书坊和装帧公司成立，例如多弗印书装帧坊（Doves Press and Bindery）、埃塞克斯印书坊（Essex House Press）、桑格斯基－萨克利夫装帧坊（Sangorski & Sutcliffe）等，都是在莫里斯的凯尔姆斯科特印书坊之后成立的，这种风潮一直持续到20世纪，例如金鸡印书坊（Golden Cockerel Press）等。

当时这种复苏在欧洲各地都有，当然，这些被重新定义的手工书籍印刷制作和装帧在整个书籍出版中的作用和地位，与工业化之前非常不同。工业化之前，人们没有选择，工业化之后，人们可以选择将自己的书以精美的手工印刷或装帧的形式呈现出来。手工印刷和装帧都变成了一种艺术、一种奢侈。

问：现在英国两家手工书籍装帧师协会，它们之间是什么关系？

答：对，英国的手工书籍装帧师们大多属于两个不同的协会，一个是设计师书籍装帧师协会（Designer Bookbinders），这个协会成立于五十年前，是一个全球性的协会，北美、欧洲大陆和英国都有。这个协会的成员都是更为资深的专业的书籍装帧师们，都是这一领域里的专家。要成为这个协会的资深会员，你还得通过一定的考试。所以，真正能被称为设计师装帧师的，在英国可能只有几十人。有一些是特别著名的，例如布鲁克曼（James Brockman）、金恩（Flora Ginn），当然，其中的泰斗是今年九十岁的米德尔顿（Bernard Middleton），国立艺术图书馆就收藏有这个协会的资深会员们在20世纪60、70、80年代装帧的许多书籍。90年代的图书馆馆长致力于收藏艺术家手制书，就停止了收藏这些手工装帧的书籍。

在英国，还有另一个组织叫书籍装帧师协会（Society of

Bookbinders），这个协会从专业和艺术水准上来说，都比不上设计师书籍装帧师协会。成员有书籍装帧师，也有许多书籍装帧的业余爱好者们，进协会的门槛不是很高。

这两个协会每年都会举办国际书籍装帧的比赛。设计师书籍装帧协会的比赛一般是和牛津大学的博德利图书馆合作，例如，今年的比赛的主题是“英雄之书”，参赛的作品会在英国进行巡展。书籍装帧师协会的比赛虽然也叫国际比赛，但水准和奖金都比不上前者，而且作品也只会在评奖过程中进行陈列而已。

问：如今在英国，能以手工装订来维持生活吗？

答：从 20 世纪初开始，真正手工装帧的公司，就不是很多了，桑格斯基－萨克利夫装帧坊是遥遥领先的。后来这家公司被谢泼德装帧公司（Shepherd Bindery）收购，如此规模的，非常少。许多书籍装帧师都是个体户，他们主要以修复古籍来维持生活。单靠手工装订书籍谋生，那会非常困难。当然，有一些收藏家会收藏高级奢华的手工装帧的书籍，但并不多。若论价钱，独一无二的设计师装帧师的手工作品可以卖到四千到八千英镑。

当然，也有收藏家希望将他们的图书馆进行统一装帧，或者有的大公司会送给员工退休礼物，或者将公司年报等用皮面豪华装帧一部分，或者某个大富翁过生日或结婚纪念日时要送每位客人一本皮面书作为礼物，这样，他们就可能去谢泼德装帧公司订货。

问：我看到设计师装帧师协会的比赛，往往也是和对开本协会（Folio Society）合作。对开本协会也会出版一些已经没有版权的仿古书，他们是不是也对英国的书艺出版颇有贡献？

答：对，上面两个协会的比赛都是从对开本协会的出版物中选择可以进行重新装订的书籍。对开本协会成立于第二次世界大战时，他们声称其目的是出版可供收藏的书籍，宣传说他们的出版物从封面到设计到装帧到插图都很精美，也常说他们的书是独一无二的。许多人喜欢对开本协会的出版物，但我个人并不喜欢。

问：英国是否有仿真复制古籍的出版商呢？

答：兰登书屋下有“人人系列”，他们会出版一系列的经典作品，这些作品是大批量印刷出版的，但从视觉美感、设计、字体、装帧等，都是下了一番功夫的。他们给人的感觉很传统，有些守旧。很明显，这些书有一定的市场。

也有一些人在复刻中世纪手稿，例如西班牙的出版社莫勒瑞（M. Moleiro Editor）就是很有名的一个。瑞士也有。他们复刻精美的中世纪的彩绘插图抄本，或是中世纪的祈祷书，装帧也是按照中世纪的原作仿制，有的还镶着宝石等。这样的仿真出版物非常昂贵，有一小批收藏家会定制这类仿真品。但这样的出版物在市场上转手流通的并不多。

问：英国关于古籍的收藏及研究的协会又有哪些呢？

答：对书感兴趣的人有许多种。有人是把书当作一种物件来欣赏，有人对书的内容更感兴趣，有的只对善本书感兴趣，有的喜欢初版本，有的则看中书的历史内容。对古籍、善本书籍感兴趣并进行研究的，英国有不少学术机构，例如目录学家协会（The Bibliographical Society），成立于 1892 年。剑桥、牛津等地也有自己的目录学协会。牛津大学博德利图书馆中有“书籍研究中心”（The Centre for the

Study of Books），你可以去那里参观、学习，去听讲座，参加活动。

而对藏书家来说，有的人收藏古籍，有的人收藏现代经典的初版本，这些藏书家们也有协会，例如“私人图书馆协会”（The Private Library Association）。另外，还有一个非常高级非常排外的协会，叫罗克斯伯俱乐部（Roxburghe club），这个俱乐部成立于1812年，它也是世界上最老的藏书家协会，成员限定在四十位，他们大都是英国的贵族，都有自己庞大的图书馆。这个俱乐部也出版书，每个成员都必须自费出版一本书，为了让其他成员们欣赏，内容风格都可以自己决定。俱乐部也出版一般公众可以购买的书，他们的书都必须用统一的罗克斯伯装帧风格来装订。

书商们有“古籍书商协会”（Antiquarian Booksellers Association，ABA）、“外省书商协会”（Provincial Booksellers Fairs Association，PBFA)，它们是古籍书商最大的两个组织，每年都要在英国各地举办好几次古籍书展。

问：有人说书籍装帧是艺术中的“灰姑娘”，一本书的装帧和内容，究竟哪个更重要？

答：书籍的内容和装帧是否同等重要，这一直有争议。历史上，大部分的观点是认为内容比装帧更重要，装帧是二等公民。有许多人会看不起那些花大价钱把书装帧得很漂亮的人。17世纪时，法国的一位著名的图书馆学家、学者加布里尔·诺德（Gabriel Naudé）曾写过一本关于如何建立私人图书馆的书，1662年，这本书由约翰·伊夫林（John Evelyn）翻译成英文。书中说：只有傻瓜才会根据它的外表来判断一本书。

但他这个意见一直无人听从，还是有许多人花大价钱要把他们的藏书弄得更漂亮些。

现在，不仅是藏书家，从学术的角度来说，也有越来越多的人把书当作一件独立的实体来看，认为装帧、设计等也非常重要。书不仅仅是文字的载体，书本身也是独立的艺术品，属于印刷名物。许多传统的历史目录学家过去一直不在乎书籍的装帧，现在这种情况也有改变。同样一本书，拥有精美的皮面装帧的永远会卖出更高的价格，对许多普通书来说，精美的装帧能大大增加它的价值。当然，如果你有一本牛顿的《自然定律》或莎士比亚的《第一对开本》，那不管它们的装帧如何，都没有关系。

（此文原发表于《上海书评》2017年10月1日，此处稍作修改。）

译后记

POSTSCRIPT

二十多年前，我与大卫曾在维多利亚和艾尔伯特博物馆的国立艺术图书馆共事，他是我的顶头上司，收藏部主任。当时，我们刚进博物馆的几位都对他颇为尊重，因为他年长我们十来岁，剑桥大学博士，典型的学者，已有专著出版。

1996年，世界图联大会在北京举行，图书馆的老馆长彦、大卫和我一起出席。当时我还准备了一个演讲，关于中国艺术书籍及资料在英国的情况，是根据我在伦敦城市大学的硕士论文改写的。初稿请大卫过目，他用细钢笔在上面做了不少修改，字迹秀丽，就像老师批改学生的作业一样，就差没打分了。

当时正好陆灏也在北京，开会之余，我们俩带老馆长和大卫一起去看老北京的四合院，还逛了琉璃厂，老馆长生动活泼，拿着相机东拍西拍，还拽着街上的大爷大婶合影，大卫则拘谨很多，安静地看着周围的一切，他说他出门从来不带照相机，所有的东西都看在眼中，记在脑子里。大卫在“前言”中提到他曾在琉璃厂买了个瓷罐，还拿到了很好的价格，这件事我一点印象都没有，可见他记忆力之好。但此罐如果真如大卫所说是件宝贝，得到他家朋友们的频繁赞赏，那更可能是陆灏的眼光和讨价还价的本事。

从北京回到伦敦后不久，我就去西敏大学就职，大卫也去了维康信托。一晃二十多年，其间我们没再联系过。去年，草鹭俱乐部约我写一些关于西方书籍的文章，为了不出硬伤，我得复习功课，就在网上找到大卫，向他请教一些基本知识。多年没见面，我想象他应该学术味更浓，可能是正宗老学究了，但没想到他也离开了传统的图书馆领域，在伦敦市法团当了多年高管。他还笑着说，他不仅在工作上世俗化了，在写作上，他也跳出了学术著作的小圈子，他最受欢迎的书，是大英图书馆出版的一本关于西方书籍历史的通俗读物。他顺手从书架上取下这本 *Books as History*，我一看，哇，图多字少，简直如同绘本。他说此书已经出了日文版，我就想，这本入门读物，也是应该介绍给中国读者的。

也是因为这本书字数不多，所以，我就自告奋勇当了翻译。应该说明一下的是，这本书的题目直译应为《书为历史：超越文本的书》，但总觉得它有些拗口。所以，在与译林出版社编辑、大卫及大英图书馆出版社商量后，大家同意以《大英图书馆书籍史话》为本书中文版书名。

此外，大卫也为书后附录的延伸阅读增加了新的条目，所以，这本书虽然是入门读物，但对这个领域有兴趣的读者，可以顺藤摸瓜，进入一个更为学术的广阔天地。

恺蒂

2018 年 6 月 21 日于伦敦

图书在版编目（CIP）数据

大英图书馆书籍史话：超越文本的书 /（英）大卫·皮尔森（David Pearson）著；恺蒂译．—南京：译林出版社，2019.1

书名原文：Books as History

ISBN 978-7-5447-7538-0

Ⅰ. ①大… Ⅱ. ①大…②恺… Ⅲ. ①随笔－作品集－英国 Ⅳ. ① I561.65

中国版本图书馆 CIP 数据核字（2018）第 231677 号

大英图书馆书籍史话：超越文本的书

［英］大卫·皮尔森（David Pearson）/ 著　恺蒂 / 译

责任编辑　张远帆
特约策划　草鹭文化
装帧设计　朱赢椿　皇甫珊珊
校　　对　张　萍
责任印制　颜　亮

出版发行　译林出版社
地　　址　南京市湖南路 1 号 A 楼
邮　　箱　yilin@yilin.com
网　　址　www.yilin.com
市场热线　025-86633278
印　　刷　恒美印务（广州）有限公司
开　　本　787 毫米 ×960 毫米　1/16
印　　张　14
版　　次　2019 年 1 月第 1 版　2019 年 1 月第 1 次印刷
书　　号　ISBN 978-7-5447-7538-0
定　　价　128.00 元

ISBN 978-7-5447-7538-0

9 787544 775380 >

定价：128.00 元